James P. Simmons

Peace on Earth

James P. Simmons

Peace on Earth

ISBN/EAN: 9783337225643

Printed in Europe, USA, Canada, Australia, Japan

Cover: Foto ©Lupo / pixelio.de

More available books at **www.hansebooks.com**

PEACE ON EARTH.

"Shall not the Judge of all the earth do right?" — *Genesis* xviii. 25.

"They shall beat their swords into ploughshares, and their spears into pruning-hooks, nation shall not lift up sword against nation, neither shall they learn war any more." — *Isaiah* ii. 4.

"Glory to God in the highest, on earth peace," &c. — *Song of the Angels.*

PEACE ON EARTH.

IN WHICH IS PRESENTED

THE BRIEF AND PLAIN SYSTEM OF RELIGION WHICH IS REVEALED
IN THE BIBLE, WHEN CONSTRUED AS APPLYING TO
PRE-EXISTENT SPIRITS,—FALLEN ANGELS;

AND

SHOWING THE PERSONAL AND DISTINCT ENTITY OF THE FATHER
AND THE SON, AND THE IMPERSONALITY OF
THE HOLY GHOST;

That this view Settles all Questions

WHICH RELATE TO THE NATURE AND EXTENT OF THE ATONEMENT,
ELECTION, FREE WILL, PERSEVERANCE, FUTURE REWARDS
AND PUNISHMENTS, ETC.; AND OPENS A WAY TO

*A PRACTICAL UNION AND CO-OPERATION OF ALL WHO
ACCEPT JESUS AS THE CHRIST.*

By JAMES P. SI[...]

AUTHOR OF "WAR IN HEAVEN," "OR[...]

BOSTON:
A. WILLIAMS AND COMP[ANY]
ATLANTA: PHILLIPS & CREW.
1878.

PREFACE.

"PEACE ON EARTH" is a necessary sequel to "War in Heaven." In that work (and in a more recent one, "Origin of Man") the writer has argued that there is a God, who created all things; that man is immortal; that we existed before the creation of this world, and are of the fallen angels; that a future state of retribution awaits us, &c.

In the following pages, other questions which arise out of that state of facts will be considered. And inasmuch as the evidence (much less the argument) by which that theory of our being is sustained cannot be reproduced here, all that is affirmed there must be admitted as true here, for the purposes of further consideration, and as constituting the premises from which the following conclusions are drawn. And as the proofs by which the *premises* are sustained are drawn from the sacred Scriptures *alone*, as viewed in the light of natural facts, laws, and reason, — so let the *conclusions* which follow be submitted to the same unerring tests; but to no other.

The practical value of that hypothesis, to the advocate of the cause of Christ, lies in the fact that *it is the true one;* and hence it is the only theory of our origin that consists with the revealed Word of God: and, most assuredly, there is no other which can be maintained by evidence found in that Word. And, furthermore, we as Christians cannot successfully meet the objections of modern scientists to our system of religion on any other ground.

It must be a painful necessity on the part of highly-educated and well-paid ministers of the gospel, when unable (from their present standpoint) to meet the arguments of the adversary either with reason or authority, to invoke the bigotry of an intelligent congregation to their aid, by exhorting them (as they often do) that they must believe what the Bible teaches (and, of course, as they construe it), although it may appear to be unreasonable in some particulars, *because it is God's Word!*

Has God said things that are unreasonable? Minister of Christ, weigh well such insinuations before repeating them! For it is true, and offered here as an irrefragable aphorism, that every narration, affirmation, and proposition which is unreasonable is false; and, therefore, whatsoever *appears* to be unreasonable *appears to be false*, and cannot be accepted for truth by any reasoning man. If envy is ever commendable, such teachers of religion should envy the happy state and condition of

> "The unletter'd Christian, who believes in gross,
> Plods on to heaven, and ne'er is at a loss."

It was a leading purpose with the writer, in the publication of "War in Heaven," to bring the religious world back if possible to the old belief that the souls of men were in being before the world was made, and to show our identity with the fallen angels, and that this world was made as it now is expressly for our race while on a probation which God had determined to give us. And it is the chief design of this writing to indicate the effect which that view of our nature and origin must have upon some of the most important questions of faith, about which Christians differ in opinion between themselves.

It is also designed to call the attention of both Catholic and Protestant Christians to a grave error into which both have fallen, in regard to the pious intentions of each other; to point out the cause of that error, and to urge upon each the propriety of reviewing the ground on which their unfavorable views, each of the other, are based, and of cultivating a better feeling for one another; and, at the same time, to insist that all Christians should fraternize and co-operate as one body against their common foe.

But comparatively few people of our age have acquainted themselves with questions which relate to the origin and nature of the human soul. It is thought best, therefore, to prepare those who have not read " War in Heaven," nor otherwise examined that subject, for a better understanding of the Scriptures referred to and arguments offered, in reference to the matters of difference between Christians hereinafter noticed. And for that purpose a few of the many texts of Scripture which bear upon that subject will be quoted or cited in this, and such brief remarks made on them as it is deemed advisable to submit here as preliminary to the consideration of the weighty matters discussed in this work.

Norcross, Ga.

CONTENTS.

CHAPTER I.
                                                            PAGE

Introductory. — In all Pursuits, start right. — Christian Teachers all agree in four cardinal Points. — From these, divergent Ways are taken, and different Theories found. — The first Question arising from admitted Facts. — Other Inquiries growing out of that. — Three Opinions as to our Origin. — On one or another of which all Christian Creeds are founded. — Pre-existence of the Soul the old belief. — The View presented by "War in Heaven." — That War progressing here 13

CHAPTER II.

This life a Warfare. — War begun in Heaven, progressing here. — The opposing Forces. — Read without prejudice. — Rev. xii. construed. — Dr. Clark on that chapter. — Notes of American Tract Society on the same. — Dr. Gill as to identity of Michael and Christ. — What the Son came to do. — His plan for doing it. — This War to end in the triumphant establishment of "PEACE ON EARTH" 18

CHAPTER III.

The same Subject continued. — Claims of Fallen Angels and of Men to God's mercy contrasted. — Effect of the Fall in Eden. — Eternal punishment. — Was not the sin of Adam and Eve pardoned? — Inconsistency of the popular theory of the Fall and Redemption of Man. — Perfect, in the other view. — Conclusion . 30

CHAPTER IV.

A brief Statement of the leading Facts revealed, and which constitute the Bases of the Christian Religion. — First Proposition considered. — A Creator; not chance. — A personal God. — Why Jehovah should assume a personal Form. — Opinions of Heathen. — Of the masses of Christians. — Locality of God 39

CHAPTER V.

The same Subject continued. — Scriptural Proofs. — Was it the Soul or the Body of Adam that was made in the Image of God? — Moses talked with God about his Body. — New Testament Authorities. — Spiritual and natural Bodies. — Conclusion 47

CHAPTER VI.

The Glory of God. — Happiness of his Creatures. — All were made as best for themselves. — God has a Home, a Throne, a Mercy-seat. — His All-seeing Eye penetrates the Universe. — He sees us, observes our ways, and by them tries us, proves us. — Closing Remarks 60

CHAPTER VII.

Fifth Division. — Jesus Christ a Spirit. — Distinct from all others. — And the Beloved Son of the Father. — The term Eternal defined. — John i. 1, 2, construed. — Proof of individuality of Son. — Apparent Biblical discrepancies reconciled 67

CHAPTER VIII.

The same Subject continued. — Prophecies of the Son consulted. — How they are construed in the New Testament. — Application. — Conclusion 80

CHAPTER IX.

Of the Holy Ghost. — His Office. — Is he a Person, or a Power of God? — Doctrine of a Trinity of Persons in one considered. — Its Origin. — History of. — Evil effects of. — Inconsistent, Unreasonable, Unscriptural 89

CHAPTER X.

The same Subject continued. — Doctrine of Three Persons in One unscriptural. — Trinity, Triune, &c., not Bible language. — The word "Godhead" noticed. — 1 John v. 7, 8 examined. — Many other Texts cited. — The Holy Ghost a Power exercised both by the Father and the Son. — The Holy Ghost has no Name; has never been seen, &c.   102

CHAPTER XI.

Concerning Gods, Devils, and Angels. — "There be Gods many and Lords many." — "God of Gods." — Prophets, Apostles, and Judges called Gods. — "Sons of God." — All to become Gods or Devils. — All to be called Angels. — The lost Song   121

CHAPTER XII.

The Atonement. — Scriptures relating thereto clear, when viewed as applying to Fallen Angels. — Antinomianism a device of the Devil. — A change of opinion produced, how. — Texts relied upon to sustain Predestination noticed. — Other Scriptures contrasted with them. — A certain Class elected. — Another Class rejected. — All to be judged by our Works   126

CHAPTER XIII.

The same Subject continued. — How to reconcile all Scriptures touching Election. — For whom Christ died. — A Class and not Individuals elected. — Texts relied upon by Antinomians noticed. — Who are the Elect. — The Central Bible-Truth. — "Top-not come down." — The case of Jacob and Esau. — St. Paul and Pharaoh. — Temporary blindness. — The Potter and his Clay. — Origin of Election-dogma. — Injurious effects thereof, &c.. . .   140

CHAPTER XIV.

Perseverance of the Saints. — Apostasy. — A free Fight. — The Unpardonable Sin. — Of Heathen. — Infants, how saved . . .   165

CHAPTER XV.

Christian Union and Co-operation. — "A new commandment I give unto you, That ye love one another; as I have loved you, that ye also love one another" (John xiii. 34). — Introduction   179

CHAPTER XVI.

Of Christian Love. — All Christians should co-operate against the common Foe. — Cause of alienation between Catholic and Protestant Christians. — How it can be removed. — Is such Union desirable? — Good people deceived. — Should not be more than two Christian Churches. — Heavenly Treasures, &c. 184

CHAPTER XVII.

The same Subject continued. — Judge not, lest ye be judged. — Duties of the educated Laity. — Appeal to Lawyers. — Their advantages over the Ministry in construing the Scriptures. — Gold is King. — Small Errors lead to great Evils. — Nature of the Union advocated. — Conclusion 207

PEACE ON EARTH.

CHAPTER I.

Introductory. — In all Pursuits, start right. — Christian Teachers all agree in four cardinal Points. — From these, divergent Ways are taken, and different Theories found. — The first Question arising from admitted Facts. — Other Inquiries growing out of that. — Three opinions as to our Origin. — On one or another of which all Christian Creeds are founded. — Pre-existence of the Soul the old belief. — The View presented by "War in Heaven." — That War progressing here.

THAT the reader may be the better prepared to understand and therefore duly appreciate the arguments which follow on each proposition submitted, it is thought best to state briefly here the different popular theories of our being on which modern theologians have founded their various creeds of religion; so that, seeing the starting point of each, it may readily be discovered how and why they have arrived at conclusions so variant. If we attempt to go to a certain place, to do a particular job of work, or solve a given problem, and *start wrong*, we will never succeed until our incipient error is detected, and we *start right*. Is not this true? Then, should we start right, and afterward take a wrong road or a wrong measure, or adopt a wrong rule, will not the result be the same? It is, therefore, not only important that we start right in all our undertakings, but to success it is necessary that we keep so all the time.

Christian teachers all start right. They all agree: (1) That there is a God, who created all things; (2) That we *all have sinned* against our Creator; (3) That the *soul of man* is immortal, and there will be a general resurrection of the dead, and a final judgment; (4) And that Jesus Christ has become the mediator between God and man.

These may well be considered the chief corner-stones on which Christ's temple was built and now stands, and in the fitness of each and every one of which all who trust in him for salvation are agreed; but, whenever we leave these cardinal points of Christian faith, and start out theorizing over the broad field for thought which revelation spreads out before us, we soon take divergent paths, and the further we go along these crooked ways the wider grows the space which lies between us. And it is moreover true, as to all who start off in a wrong direction, that the longer they travel in that way the further they get from the truth.

We all admit that an all-wise, omnipotent, and very merciful God created man. Would it not be well to pause here a moment for sober, serious thought? But little reflection must satisfy every well-trained mind that the first question which here presents itself to the earnest seeker after truth is, "What is man?" To all who believe the Bible, the answer is, "A living soul." From this answer other grave inquiries arise, as, Why — *for what purpose* — did God create us? *When* were we made? *How* were we, *as immortal spirits*, first brought into being? And upon his answers to these questions the whole system of every consistent theologian must rest; for no intelligent Christian can fail to observe that old sinners, such as we are (if our origin is to be found in that war which was waged in heaven and resulted in the expulsion of Satan and his hosts out of and from that holy and happy place, and in our confinement "in chains under darkness" in this sin-smitten world), deserve a different treatment from such as would be due to newly-created beings, who come into this world fresh from the hand of an omnipotent, pure, holy, and merciful God, and who are free from all stain of sin, except such as would be imputed to them by such Creator in consequence of the fall in Eden. Is not this true? Then, is it not a matter of the first importance to a proper interpretation of God's word concerning us, that we first determine whether we have lived before, — or are we new creatures?

We should, therefore, after having formed answers to all these questions, such as appear satisfactory to ourselves when considered alone, compare them each with the others and see that they are all consistent with one another and with all the attributes of our Creator; and so try to get a general view of the whole matter (and which is so mysterious to us now) that is consistent with itself and with human reason at least. And, lastly, when you have found a theory which can stand these tests, you should compare it carefully with God's word, and, if it is well sustained by *the touch-stone of truth*, you may safely exclaim, with Archimedes, "Eureka!" (I have found it out.)

There has been in all ages of the world, and still is, a class of people who deny the existence of a personal God and the immortality of the soul; and there is now another class who also insist that all things which exist are and were produced by natural laws, yet who hold, not only that the soul is immortal, but that a happy eternity awaits all men. Passing both of these theories by for the present, it is designed in this place to state substantially the three different popular views in relation to our origin which have been and are now entertained by those who accept the Bible as true.

The first is: "That, at the beginning of the world, God created the souls of all men, which, however, are not united to the body till the individuals for whom they are destined are begotten or born into the world."

The next is: "That the soul is created at the moment when the body is produced for its habitation."

And the last is: "That the soul and body are alike and together propagated by the parents, neither having had any previous existence."

The writer has already reviewed all the above theories and the arguments offered by the respective advocates of the last two at some length, and has examined them in the light of revelation and of natural reason, and has compared them also (and in the same light) with that which is, as he feels well satisfied, the true and the only hypothesis as to the origin of our race which finds any support in the Bible; and which is, in brief, "That the souls of all men existed before the creation of this world; that they are of the fallen angels who were engaged in rebellion under Satan in heaven, and were by Michael and his hosts 'cast out into the earth,' and that when the body destined for each is prepared, the spirit is sent to occupy it merely as a tenement."

That this theory of our being may be more clearly understood by such as have devoted but little time or care to the investigation of such things, it is deemed best to restate it, and in an enlarged form, by saying: That this world, as now constituted and inhabited, is the gift of God to his rebellious creatures, and that the necessity for it, with all things as we see them around — and feel them within us — grew out of that war which was waged in heaven between Michael and Satan and their respective angels, and which resulted in the expulsion of the latter and his followers from heaven, and in his and their confinement here (see Rev. xii. 7–11). That after those who were engaged in that rebellion under Satan had been "cast out into the earth," for their sins committed under the delusive influence of the Devil, they became penitent, — sorry beyond all comparison for what they had done. Their agonizing cries for mercy and pardon excited the deepest sympathies on the part of both the Father and "his Christ," and who was then and previously known as "Michael," "The Archangel," &c.

And thereupon a covenant was made between the Father and Son, in and by which it was agreed that the Son should follow after the lost angels, and offer them pardon and restoration to the Divine favor, on specified terms. That, pursuant to which covenant, Jesus Christ descended from heaven and (in virtue of the power and in the presence of the Father) prepared this world for a place in which to try and to prove those penitent spirits, and *formed* the body of Adam, "and breathed into his nostrils the breath of life," "and (with which breath) man became (possessed of) a living soul."

> And which *soul* was one of Satan's vile host —
> An angel of light — led into the fight,
> Beguiled into sin by the god of night;
> Who seeing their plight — o'erwhelmed at the sight —
> Cried, O Michael, save! Jehovah, forgive!
> Dear Christ! intercede, that we may yet live!

That Christ made the body of Eve also, and as described in Genesis, "and breathed into (her) nostrils the breath of life" in like manner; and with that breath another lost spirit, of the same family, entered her body, as a prison-house, and for the purposes of probation.

"That the bodies, not the souls, the physical and not the spiritual part of subsequent generations, were created in Adam."

"That the account given in the Bible of the temptation and fall of man in Eden, although literally true, is also a clear, symbolical, and allegorical representation of his real temptation and fall by and with Satan in heaven."

"That this arrangement will be continued until all who were embraced in that divine, antemundane covenant have, or shall have had, a probationary term here; then will come the final judgment, when all will be restored to their primeval favor with God, or doomed to that final punishment which is due for individual sin by each committed." [1]

The view first given above, as to the pre-existence of the soul, was the common belief with the Jewish Rabbins, heathen philosophers, and everybody else, infidels only excepted — as far at least as the writer has been able to learn — who lived before or at the time of the crucifixion of Jesus Christ. And, as the reader must have observed, the idea that we are of the fallen angels is but an enlargement and application of that old theory, by showing to what class or family of spirits we belong. And which important fact had never been fully revealed to the world until the vision of St. John in Patmos.

And lastly: "That the war which began between Michael and Satan in heaven has been transferred to this world and is now progressing here; and that it will terminate when Christ shall have accomplished his purpose, to 'destroy the works of the Devil.'"

[1] War in Heaven, p. 37.

CHAPTER II.

This life a Warfare. — War begun in Heaven, progressing here. — The opposing Forces. — Read without prejudice. — Rev. xii. construed. — Dr. Clark on that chapter. — Notes of American Tract Society on the same. — Dr. Gill as to identity of Michael and Christ. — What the Son came to do. — His plan for doing it. — This War to end in the triumphant establishment of "PEACE ON EARTH."

IN the closing chapter of "War in Heaven," it is remarked: "That the war which Satan so ingloriously waged in heaven above has been transferred to earth, and is now being prosecuted by Christ below. The captains are the same, but the opposing hosts are not. When peace was restored in heaven, Christ, sympathizing with those who had been deceived and betrayed into sin and rebellion by Satan, followed us here; and having himself expiated our crimes, and purchased pardon for all our iniquities, now invites all who repent of their sins and ingratitude to God their Maker, and desire restoration of their allegiance to him, to come and receive full and free pardon for the past, and enlist under the banner of the Cross, and fight with him and his the more glorious battles of righteousness, truth, and love."

And further: "That this warfare will continue until all shall have an opportunity to repent and turn again to the love of God; when Christ will return in person, as the Judge of quick and dead, and stern avenger of the unrepented wrongs to God the Father and his unsuspecting creatures." [1]

The writer now proceeds to prove the above proposition; beginning this argument just where that was closed. And therefore (for the purposes of further exegesis) all that is affirmed there must be considered as true here. For it is indispensably necessary, to a profitable reading of this work, that those who have never investigated the subject, but have

---

[1] War in Heaven, p. 296.

grown up and lived on under the impression that we are new creatures, should read the Scriptures cited as applicable to pre-existent spirits; as without at least such hypothetical admission, their value will be lost to the reader.

We are never enlightened by reading or hearing an argument, when we are all the time trying to answer and reply, in our own minds, to the writer or speaker. We can always shut out *Truth* from the understanding, *or put her out.*

> "Convince a man against his will,
> He's of the same opinion still."

It is worse than a loss of time merely, to hear or read under strong opposing bias, except when engaged in debate. For, in so reading or hearing, you put yourself in the attitude of a disputant; and although you may produce evidence and give reasons that your opponent cannot successfully reply to, and which may be satisfactory to all others present, yet you cannot satisfy him that you are right and he is wrong in regular debate, or otherwise, "against his will." But more of this anon.

Now, admitting that there was some sort of "war" in heaven — was that *war* transferred to this world? and is it still progressing here? Although such war, or its consequences rather, are referred to, incidentally if no more, in perhaps as many places as any other fact which is recorded in the Bible, the most direct and full account we have of it is found in the twelfth chapter of Revelation. In verses nine to eleven of that chapter we are informed that Satan and those who were engaged under him in that war "were cast out into the earth," and that "they overcame *him* by the blood of the Lamb," &c.

On this passage I will only remark here, that, construed in its most natural, literal, and (doubtless its) true sense, *it means just what it says;* as do all the other Sacred Scriptures, when so construed and read in the light of other revealed laws and facts. And to give his language that sort of construction, we must understand St. John as saying about this: That they who were cast out of heaven, and down to this world, with Satan, were, in virtue of the atonement made by Jesus Christ, enabled to overcome him (Satan); and to find deliverance from all the sad calamities which engulfed them in consequence of their own folly and wickedness, in suffering themselves to be led by the wiles of the Devil so far away from the peaceful paths of duty and love as to engage under him in that rebellion and war in heaven against "the law of the Lord."

That this Scripture has been very differently construed is frankly admitted; but that it has been, and is, construed erroneously is as positively affirmed. Does the reader want some evidence to sustain language so strong? Here it is: Dr. Adam Clark, in his preface to the valuable notes he made on Revelation, says: "Among the interpreters of the Apocalypse, both in ancient and modern times, we find a vast diversity of opinions; but they may be reduced to four principal hypotheses or modes of interpretation: —

"1. The Apocalypse contains a prophetical description of the destruction of Jerusalem, of the Jewish war, and the civil wars of the Romans.

"2. It contains predictions of the persecutions of the Christians under the heathen emperors of Rome, and of the happy days of the Church under Christian emperors from Constantine downward.

"3. It contains prophecies concerning the tyrannical and oppressive conduct of the Roman pontiffs, the true Anti-Christ, and foretells the final destruction of popery.

"4. It is a prophetic declaration of the schisms and heresies of Martin Luther, those called Reformers and their successors, and the final destruction of the Protestant religion."

From the above analysis of Dr. Clark, it is observable that, notwithstanding the "vast diversity of opinions" which have in every age obtained as to the solution of some questions which have arisen between commentators of the same age, those of each period have uniformly so interpreted the Apocalyptic prophecies as to direct them against those who were, at the time, considered their most dangerous enemies.

"Thus, in the age immediately succeeding that of St.

John, Christians generally, whether originally Jews or Gentiles, looked upon the infidel Jews as their common and most to be dreaded enemies; and they construed them as applying to the Jews and Jerusalem. The heathen emperors of Rome became the next persecutors of the Church, and they were accepted as the parties intended.

"The Roman pontiffs next became the terror of dissenting Christians, and they found a ready solution of the whole mystery in applying it to them and the Catholic Church generally. And, in turn, the Catholics appear quite as well satisfied that Luther and his Protestant followers are the great Anti-Christ predicted. And so stands the controversy between these two great and opposing families of Christians at the present time,"—

"Each claiming truth and
Truth disclaiming both."[1]

Here we have proof conclusive: (1) That four different constructions, each of which is wholly inconsistent with all the others, have been put upon this Revelation. (2) That the two first mentioned were generally accepted as correct during the ages of the Church in which each was entertained. (3) And that the two modern interpretations of it are not only in direct opposition to each other, but when taken together supply the evidence required to sustain our proposition beyond all doubt. For it is impossible that the Pope and his adherents on one side, and the whole Protestant Church on the other, is and are the great adversary of Christ and his kingdom referred to there, as each party insists is true of the other.

In an edition of the Bible with notes, published by the American Tract Society (1862), and on Rev. xii., the following is the introductory note: "With the seventh trumpet the mystery of God was to be finished, chap. x. 7. This has already sounded, and the kingdoms of this world are become the kingdoms of our Lord and of his Christ, chap. xi. 15. We cannot therefore, with any degree of probability, suppose that the long series of persecutions and trials predicted

[1] See "War in Heaven," chap. vii.

in this and the following chapters belongs to the seventh trumpet, both the numbers contained in the prophecies, and their general character, identifying them with those previously recorded. Accordingly there is a general agreement among expositors that the vision here goes back to the primitive days of Christianity, *and gives a new series of revelations containing a more interior and spiritual view of the history of the Church*, that of the preceding series having been more outward and providential."

This is given as the general view of that chapter as held by Protestants, and from which we learn first: That a "long series of persecutions and trials of the Church is there *predicted*" (prophesied of as to come thereafter); and secondly, that "There is a general agreement among expositors that the vision here *goes back* to the primitive ages of Christianity, and gives a new series of revelations" (past events made known). That, as far as it goes, is indubitably a correct view of the Apocalypse. Facts which relate to the past, and things yet to come, are both revealed there. Now, what that new series of revealed facts is, becomes an interesting subject for inquiry.

On the eleventh verse (which is this: " And they overcame him by the blood of the Lamb, and by the word of their testimony; and they loved not their lives unto the death ") the following note is made: " *By the blood of the Lamb — by the word of their testimony ;* not by carnal weapons, but by faith in the efficacy of Christ's atonement and their faithful testimony to his truth. *Loved not their lives unto the death ;* would not renounce the truth to save their lives."

By this it appears that the part of the verse quoted is understood by such " general agreement " as applying to those who have been or will be redeemed by Jesus Christ in this world. Now, if those of whom it is said, " *And they overcame him*," &c., are not of the same who are said, in the ninth verse, to have been " cast out with him," who are they? And if Satan is not the party intended by the words, " And they overcame him," in the eleventh verse, who is that party?

Then, if we construe this revelation as meaning that Satan and his angels were cast out into this world, and that they (or a part of them) have or will overcome him by the blood of Jesus Christ, we must believe also that the war which was begun in heaven is still progressing here.

The opposing chiefs in that celestial war, and in the one in which St. Paul said, "I have fought a good fight," &c., are the same — Michael and Satan.

In his commentaries on Jude 9, Dr. Gill says: "*Yet Michael the archangel.* By whom is meant, not a created angel, but an increated one, the Lord Jesus Christ, as appears from his name *Michael*, which signifies *who is as God;* — and who is as God or like unto him, but the Son of God, who is equal with God? — and from his character as the *archangel*, or *prince of angels*, for Christ is the head of all principality and power; and from what is elsewhere said of *Michael*, as that he is *the great Prince*, and on the side of the people of God, and to have angels under him and at his command. (Dan. x. 21 and xii. 1; Rev. xii. 7.)"

So Philo, the Jew, calls the most ancient Word "first-born of God, the *archangel.*"

On Rev. xii. 7, the same distinguished author, after repeating very much the same as to Michael that he had said on Jude 9, and after reviewing several Rabbinical writers on that subject, proceeds thus: "Lord Napier thinks that the Holy Ghost is designed, who is equally and truly God, as the Father and the Son, and who in the hearts of the saints opposes Satan and his temptations; but *it seems best* to interpret it of Jesus Christ, who is equal with God, is one with the Father, and in whom the fullness of the Godhead dwells bodily; *he is the archangel, the first of the chief princes*, the head of all principality and power, who is on the side of the Lord's people, pleads their cause, defends their persons, and saves them."

Dr. Gill is quoted here to prove that he, and others quoted by him, believed that Michael and Jesus Christ are the same. And for that purpose I have *italicized* some of his words as above. But, as it will appear hereinafter, I do not agree with him, nor with Trinitarians generally, in regard to the personality of the Holy Ghost, nor as to the personal identity of the Father and Son. And by reference to his commentaries on that text (Jude 9), and on Rev. xii. 7, and to the authorities cited by him, any remaining doubt as to the spiritual identity of Michael and Christ will be removed.[1]

Matthew Henry, in his Commentaries on Genesis, says that "the original word which is translated 'Lord' and printed in small capital letters in our Bible is *Jehovah*, and that 'Jehovah' is the great and incommunicable name of God, which denotes his having his being of himself." He also says that the word "Elohim" means "a God of power," and "Jehovah Elohim" means "a God of power and perfection."

We should therefore understand the term "angel of the Lord," wherever so found, as meaning the *angel of Jehovah*, or of God the Father; that is, Jesus Christ. If the translators of our Bible had preserved the distinction between the words *Jehovah* and *Elohim* by transferring the first, as it is here and as they often did, into our copy, and by translating the latter "God" as they did in most cases if not in every instance, it would perhaps have been better, as leaving it easier for us to determine whether the Father or Son was intended. To read the term "angel of the Lord" angel of Jehovah, as it would then have stood, and to admit that Jesus Christ is indicated both by the name *Michael* and the term *angel of Jehovah*, it will be found that what is said of the Being referred to under both appellations consists with the idea that the same is intended, and agrees perfectly with what is said of the Messiah, however denominated elsewhere in both the Old and New Testament Scriptures.

By reference to Rev. xix., it will be seen that he who sat on the white horse and was called the "Word of God" was Christ himself beyond doubt; and of him it is said, "And he was clothed with a vesture dipped in blood, and his name is called the Word of God. And the armies which were in

---

[1] See further on that subject Dr. A. Clark's Commentaries on Jude 9, and Religious Encyclopedia, title "Angel of the Lord."

heaven followed him upon white horses, clothed in fine linen, white and clean."

Thus, in the twelfth chapter of Revelation, we find the leader of the hosts of heaven is called " Michael," and in the nineteenth chapter he is called the " Word of God." What better evidence as to the identity of the two could be desired? And it is assumed that no sane man will deny that the term " Lamb," as used in Rev. xii., means Christ also. In fact, we find our blessed Redeemer designated in that one chapter by the four appellations " Michael," " Christ," " The Lamb," and " The Man Child."

In forming an opinion on this subject, however, we are not left without other revealed evidence in abundance. It is not only true that the *captains* are the same, but the armies are both constituted of the same "angels" who fought above, although they are not all enlisted here on the same side as there. The present army of the Lord is composed of two divisions; one of which is made up of converts from Satan's ranks, and they are commonly called " Soldiers of the Cross," " Soldiers of Jesus Christ," &c. (2 Tim. ii. 3, 4); and the other division consists of the same "angels" who fought under Christ's victorious banner in heaven, and they are now called variously " God's host " (Gen. xxxii. 1, 2), " Angels of God " (Gen. xxviii. 12 and John i. 51), and " Ministering spirits " (Heb. i. 13, 14).

The army of Satan now consists of the same rebel sinners who fought under him in heaven, and were cast out with him into this world, except those who have repented and been converted here; and his troops are now called " Evil Spirits " (1 Sam. xvi. 23), " Devils," &c. (James ii. 19, and Jude 6).

The purpose for which Christ would come into the world (as well as the manner and time of his coming), was clearly foretold by the prophets of old. But only one of them will be referred to here however, because he is so full on this subject that it cannot be necessary to cite others. Isaiah says, " So shall the Lord of hosts *come down* and fight for Mount Zion, and for the hill thereof " (Isa. xxxi. 4); " Behold, a king shall reign in righteousness, and princes shall rule in judgment (Isa. xxxii. 1); "For the Lord is our judge, the Lord is our law-giver, the Lord is our king; he will save us" (Isa. xxxiii. 22).

Let us next turn to Revelation, and see what is there said of the advent of the Saviour. "And I saw, and behold a white horse: and he that sat on him had a bow; and a crown was given unto him; and he went forth conquering, and to conquer" (Rev. vi. 2). Again, "And I saw heaven opened, and behold a white horse; and he that sat upon him was called Faithful and True, and in righteousness he doth judge and make war. His eyes were as a flame of fire, and on his head were many crowns; and he had a name written, that no man knew but he himself. And he was clothed with a vesture dipped in blood; and his name is called The Word of God: and the armies which were in heaven followed him upon white horses, clothed in fine linen, white and clean" (Rev. xix. 11–14). Read also in this connection the forty-second chapter of Isaiah. Now, do not these passages from Revelation refer to the same glorious events which had been so predicted by Isaiah?

And, lastly, we will examine a few texts of New Testament Scriptures, and find what is said there as to the object of Christ's mission to this world, and the means by which he purposed to accomplish it. He said: "The Son of man is come to seek and to save that which was lost" (Luke xix. 10). As an evidence that this remark of the Saviour is properly interpreted here, see the thirty-fourth chapter of Ezekiel, where it is said, among other things, in prophetic language of him: "I will seek that which *was lost,* and bring again that which *was driven away,*" &c. St. John says of him: "For this purpose the Son of God was manifested, that he might destroy the works of the Devil." (1 John iii. 8; see also Heb. ii. 14.)

On such evidence we must believe that Christ came to seek and to save lost sinners; and to do that he must *destroy* (neutralize) the evil influences of Satan. Then how did he propose to do that? Let him answer again for himself: "Think not that I am come to send peace on earth; I came not to send peace, but a sword. For I am come to set a man at variance against his father, and the daughter against her mother, and the daughter-in-law against her mother-in-law: and a man's foes shall be they of his own household. He that loveth father or mother more than me is not worthy of me: and he that loveth son or daughter more than me is not worthy of me. And he that taketh not his cross, and followeth after me, is not worthy of me. He that findeth his life shall lose it; and he that loseth his life for my sake shall find it." (Matt. x. 34-39; see also Luke xii. 49-53.)

Do not the Scriptures above cited look decidedly belligerent? They are, however, very few of many found in the Bible which reveal the sad truth that the Christian life in this wicked world is at best but a continuous warfare; and the best assurance we have of a triumphant result, as individuals, is found in the gracious promise of our victorious chief, that "He that endureth to the end shall be saved." (Matt. x. 22.)

Upon this promise a number of grave questions arise, and should be pondered well by all who attach any considerable importance to the future life. Of such are the following: Will I endure to the end? does my success depend in any way, or in any degree, on my own efforts? if so, how, and to what extent? and, "what *must I do* to be saved?" We must fight under Christ if we would reign with him. St. Paul charged Timothy to "war a good warfare," and warned him also that he must endure hardness "as a good soldier of Jesus Christ," and that "No man that warreth entangleth himself with the affairs of this life; that he may please him who hath chosen him to be a soldier." (2 Tim. ii. 3, 4.)

The great apostle to the gentiles, when he felt that his sands of life had well nigh run, and that the time for his departure was at hand, said, in pious exultation, to his son Timothy: "I have fought a good fight, I have finished my course, I have kept the faith; henceforth there is laid up for me a crown of righteousness, which the Lord, the righteous Judge, shall give me at that day." (2 Tim. iv. 7, 8.)

Believing that no earnest seeker for truth will fail, on examination of the authorities already cited, to see that the war which originated in heaven is now progressing on earth, I will not therefore stop to comment on them, but will proceed to show what the final result, according to prophecy, will be.

Of the coming and character of Christ's kingdom, Isaiah says: " And they shall beat their swords into plough-shares and their spears into pruning-hooks; nation shall not lift up sword against nation, neither shall they learn war any more " (Isa. ii. 4; see the same prophecy in Micah iv. 3). And, on that subject, Daniel says: " And at that time shall Michael stand up, the great prince which standeth for the children of thy people; and there shall be a time of trouble such as never was since there was a nation, even to that same time; and at that time thy people shall be delivered, every one that shall be found written in the book." (Dan. xii. 1.)

Christ, who is called " Michael " — " the great prince " — by Daniel, is also called " Prince of peace " (Isa. ix. 6), " God of peace " (Rom. xvi. 20). And the multitude of the heavenly host, which was with the angel who announced the advent of the Saviour to the shepherds, praised God saying: " Glory to God in the highest, on earth peace," &c. (Luke ii. 14.)

In relation to the texts last quoted it may be well enough to remark, that from the prophecies of Isaiah, Micah, and Daniel it is manifest that some war should cease, and that the people of Jesus Christ, after a time of unprecedented trouble, shall be *delivered* from their troubles, and that the nations of this world shall not " learn war any more." We must therefore believe that peace will be restored here. And inasmuch as Christ made the world and put our race upon it, inaugurated the war which now rages among us, commands one of the opposing armies, and is designated by such titles as " Prince of peace," " God of peace," " King of peace," &c., — it is but fair to suppose that he is, and will be, entitled to full credit for having established peace on earth.

The authorities cited in this chapter, as it is insisted, prove the following facts: (1) That there was a war of some sort in heaven. (2) That Jesus Christ and Satan led the opposing armies in that war. (3) That Satan and his followers " prevailed not " there, and were cast out of heaven and down to this world. (4) That there is a warfare in progress here, and that Christ and his celestial angels are engaged in this fight on one side, and Satan and his angels are engaged and fighting on the other side. Such being the facts, is it more reasonable to believe that this is the same war and among the same parties, or that it is a new war and between different parties?

CHAPTER III.

The same Subject continued. — Claims of Fallen Angels and of Men to God's mercy contrasted. — Effect of the Fall in Eden. — Eternal punishment. — Was not the sin of Adam and Eve pardoned? — Inconsistency of the popular theory of the Fall and Redemption of Man. — Perfect, in the other view. — Conclusion.

REMEMBER, the proposition now before us is, in substance, that the war in heaven, of which we are informed in Revelation, has been transferred to this world and is now progressing here; and that this war will continue until Christ shall have destroyed " the works of the Devil," and fully established his peaceful kingdom on earth.

Now, reader, you must determine for yourself, and in your own way, whether the war now progressing in this world is the same which was begun in heaven, or whether we are a new and entirely different race of sinners; and whether or not all of Satan's deluded followers in that war above were driven away into an eternal hell, and denied any sort of chance whatever to implore their Heavenly Father for his pardoning grace, or even to be heard in extenuation of their own crimes or in mitigation of their punishment.

Every man is, or should be, the architect of his own faith. God will, if desired, help us in this grave work; but he will not control our judgment against the will.

If God so deals with his once holy angels of heaven, although thereafter seduced by Satan into forbidden paths, what may such sinners, as we of this world are known to be, expect at his hands?

They are the creatures of his power, and so are we. They were made just as he wanted them to be, and so were we. Is not this true? They sinned and fell under the curse of the law, and so have we. Then for what good reason can we, as a family or class, expect more grace than was, or will be, extended to them? Have we any evidence in the Bible that God has dealt, or will deal, less mercifully with them than he will with us? If there is, what is that evidence, and where is it to be found?

In the absence of any Scriptural authority (and there is none such) for saying that God manifests such partiality between his children, in the government of his rational and accountable creatures, what sufficient reason can be given why he should act partially in our favor and against them? Are we by nature better than they were? Whether we and they are of the same family or not, we all have one Creator, one God, one Father, — have we not?

All Christians admit, as it is believed, that the angels who fell, under the lead of Satan, were originally as pure and holy, free and happy, as the steadfast angels now are. And it is the most popular theory, *with us Protestants*, to-day, that God condemned them (the fallen angels) to everlasting punishment, in the deep and dark abyss, at once; and that he has not, and does not feel, the least commiseration for them, but is deaf to all their piteous moans and cries and lamentations! And that he created this world — put the progenitors of a new and innumerable race of eternal spirits in that ill-fated garden, and fully within the power, and subject to the controlling influence, of the same archfiend who had already debauched and brought to sudden destruction (as it is said) his thousands, millions — yes, to us unknown billions — of God's own dear children, right around and before his throne in heaven!

And it is moreover believed, held, and taught, by the same conceited (though sincere) teachers, that we derive our being, soul and body together, from our parents; that we inherit the sinful nature which accrued to Adam and Eve after, and in consequence of, their fall in Eden; and that but for the timely intervention, suffering, death, and resurrection of Jesus Christ our whole race would have gone to hell, and there, with Satan and his (other?) angels, to burn for ever, as a result of and for that one (comparatively) *little* sin in Eden!

And yet many of them, in concluding such harangues,

proclaim with floods of grateful and sympathetic tears the unbounded love of God for his sinful creatures! Where is their consistency? Or what fiend would punish his own creatures (if he had any) more cruelly than they represent our merciful God as punishing his misguided children?

The preceding remarks are made as applicable to Protestants only, because it is their view of our origin which is given as a basis on which to found them. But the theory that the soul of each is a new creature of God, brought into being when the body is born and ready for occupation, but which had no previous existence, — as held by the Mother Church, — gives our Catholic brethren no advantage in this respect. For, as it will be observed by every one who is capable of connecting two ideas together, this objection applies with equal force to one of these systems of religion as it does to the other.

My dear Christian brethren, who minister in sacred things, permit one who is but an unprofitable lay member of the Church to submit a case for your consideration severally, and which I think is a fair one by which to test your common creed. Suppose that you are right as to our nature and origin (we agree as to the destiny of the finally impenitent), and that our blessed Redeemer had stood aloof, and left the whole Adamic family to their own fate, under the curse of his sin; that you had died in infancy, never having violated any law whatever yourself, and that God had consigned you to that dread abode, there to wail and writhe in torment for ever, — and all that for a sin that you did not commit, could not prevent, and the act of another done some six thousand years before you had any real existence, — would you, in that case, have felt yourself under any very great obligation to your Creator, Lawgiver, and Judge, *for his tender mercies to you*? Would you?

And should it turn out, contrary to all your fond expectations, that you are not one of the elect, but that you have failed to keep your body under and bring it into subjection; and "that by any means," when you "have preached to others," you yourself should become "a castaway," — would you not think such punishment *too severe* for a merciful Creator to inflict *on you*, for no more than that sin and the part you have acted *in this life?* Is it not unreasonable to believe that a God of great compassion and tender mercy toward all his rational creatures would punish the worst sinner that ever lived, *eternally*, for the sins of this life only? Just think of *eternity*, and compare it to the life of Methuselah! The term of his life is to *eternity* less than one second is to ten thousand years! Law-givers and courts of this world all agree that punishment for crime should bear some due proportion to the offense committed; but in the case supposed there is none.

If any doubt is entertained as to that case, take this one. Suppose a kind-hearted, blithesome school miss, of fifteen summers; one who was baptized into the Church when an infant, was blest with a pious mother who taught her to say her prayers night and morning as soon as she could lisp the name of Jesus; one who has attended Sunday-school and day-school also regularly all her life; one who is well educated and intelligent for one of her age, and who may never have *done an act* in violation of the decalogue in all her life, yet one who has not been "*born again*," should die in that condition, — would a merciful God punish her eternally with "*the Devil and his angels*" for her sins of this life? She would die under the curse, would she not? And according to the Orthodox creed she is lost — damned to all eternity! And for what? In the case supposed, it would appear to have been done for no sufficient reason, if not for the *pleasure (?)* of seeing such an innocent, lovely creature tormented for ever with devils and damned spirits! Is not the very thought of having charged our Maker and kind Benefactor with such horrid cruelty inexpressibly abhorrent to every true friend of God and of his Christ?

Upon the hypothesis that we are of Satan's rebellious host, and that the Mosaic account of the temptation and fall in Eden (although literally true) is a figurative representation of our real temptation, sin, and fall in heaven, — all such difficulties vanish away, as the darkness of night before the morning sun. For if we come into this life the trained servants of Satan, we must so remain, and abide with him and his for ever, if not pardoned, regenerated, or born again.

As long as the leading advocates of the Christian religion so construe their own text-book, is it strange that Spiritualists use such language as the following, in reference to the God of Moses, and whom we adore? "We do not say this ignorant bigot, calling himself God, is not Jehovah: that, for aught we know, may have been his name; but we do say that this whiffling, jealous Deity has not sense enough to govern the world."[1] They consider him (the God of Moses) the very wicked spirit of *a dead Jew!* and in every respect as being greatly inferior to Moses himself.

And if we admit that ours is a new race of beings "*created in Adam*," soul and body together, and that we have so descended from him, and that the purposes for which this world was made and man placed here were as is generally understood and taught by leading theologians, and believed by Christians generally of this age, — it should not be a subject of wonderment that men and women too, of clear, discriminating minds, and who have been educated in the best schools of Europe or America, and learned to think for themselves, should become skeptical or even infidel, rather than embrace our theory of religion.

In that view of our origin, and of the Divine purposes in our creation, and that all this was the workmanship of an omnipotent and merciful God, who foreknew all things and just as they would transpire when he made the world and put our common progenitors upon it, — how can we understand why it was that God permitted Satan to enter Eden, and there to accomplish his fiendish purposes? Having all power, our Maker could have prevented the Devil from entering that garden at all, could he not? And could he not have controlled the will of Adam and Eve so perfectly, that the enemy could not have induced them to violate the Divine command? He certainly could have so governed his own creatures, but he did not. Why did he not? He foreknew precisely what Satan would do, if not restrained; and he likewise knew the

[1] Hull: Origin of Man, p. 9.

weakness of his own (new?) creatures, if left without his support: yet he did not restrain the one nor sustain the others, so as to prevent the evil which has overtaken and (as it is generally believed) overwhelmed our whole race with ruin. Why was not Satan restrained, or his unsuspecting victims supported in that dark hour of trial? God, on that occasion as well as upon all others, acted on good and sufficient reason, as we must not doubt.

Let us now pass from the above difficulties, and see whether there are others which are no less stubborn. God is very merciful to his penitent children, is he not? "As a father pitieth his children, so the Lord pitieth them that *fear* him" (Ps. ciii. 13). From the account given in Genesis, it appears that Adam and Eve " heard the voice of the Lord walking in the garden," and God called Adam: " And he said, I heard thy voice in the garden and I was *afraid*, because I was naked, and I hid myself." Then, "as a father pitieth his children," so, on that painful occasion, God pitied "Adam and his wife," did he not? Were they not sorry for what they had done; and did they not believe in and fear God?

Then they believed, repented, confessed their sin, and feared the Lord. They were, therefore, as we are taught both from the Bible and the pulpit, just in that condition then to which we must all be brought before God will accept, forgive, and cleanse us from the pollutions of sin. "If we confess our sins, he is faithful and just to forgive us our sins, and to cleanse us from all unrighteousness" (1 John i. 9). Upon such godly fear, repentance, and faith God will pardon sinners, will he not? Then why did he not pardon them? Who will say, in this view of the case, that he did not then and there pardon them?

Is and was not Jesus Christ "the same yesterday, to-day, and for ever"? (Heb. xiii. 8.) By extending his pardoning love and cleansing power to Adam and Eve then, in the case supposed, would not all *the works of the Devil* have been destroyed? And would not the whole Adamic family have been as pure and holy as if that sin had not been committed in Eden?

That would have been a more easy and expeditious, as well as a far more successful, way for our blessed Redeemer to have not only destroyed "the works of the Devil," but to have restored our race to that purity in which we were originally created, than was the plan which he adopted, if that job in Eden was the only *bad work* which Adam and Eve and the Devil ever did — would it not? A simple act of the Divine will — a kind word, as "go in peace and sin no more" — would then have been sufficient. It would have been beyond comparison more expeditious, as but a moment of time would have been required, and it certainly would have been a more successful way by which to accomplish the purpose desired; for by so doing the whole race of Adam would have been redeemed from the effects of the Fall, and saved eternally.

Whereas, on the plan which was adopted, the labors and sufferings of the whole life, and the agonizing death, of God's only Son was required to inaugurate the plan, to prepare the way, by which we could be saved; some six thousand years, more or less (as the case may be), have been and will be devoted to the execution of the undertaking: and the best opinion as to the result of all these tedious labors and painful sufferings seems to be that the Devil hitherto has had and now has and holds possession and full control of, and will most likely be able to retain, and will finally be required firmly to hold and safely keep for ever, a very large majority of our *desperately wicked* or *most unfortunate family*, as the case may be.

If this life is but a continuation of the strife, rebellion, and war which originated in heaven, the scheme which was devised for the purpose of reclaiming all who were seduced into it by the Devil, and who repent their folly and wickedness, is such as none but an all-wise God could have planned, and as none but a God "whose mercy knows no bounds" would have conceded. In this view, the whole plan is perfectly symmetrical in all its appointments. It is complete — wanting in nothing. *It is perfect.* But, if we are an entirely new race of beings, and if this world was a new creation, and if Adam and Eve were made and put here for the purpose of propagating a new family of *eternal spirits* (!) " for the glory of God and our own happiness," as is the popular theory of our time, the whole undertaking has thus far proved, and must continue to the end, to be nothing better than a regular succession of the most signal failures and disastrous defeats on the part of our Maker, and a continuous series of triumphs on the part of his and our enemy! Is not this true?

If before we came into this world we were the servants of Satan, and had already been driven away with him from the presence of God and from the society of his holy angels, every sinner who repents in this life and returns to God is a trophy for Jesus Christ; for every change of allegiance which is perfected here constitutes another victory for him. And it was on account of this glorious truth that, when " the foundations of the earth " were laid (the plan of redemption perfected), " the morning stars (bright angels) sang together, and all the sons of God shouted for joy " (Job xxxviii.). And for the same reason still, " There is joy in the presence of the angels of God over one sinner that repenteth " (Matt. xv.).

With these suggestions and Scriptural authorities, the reader must be left for the present to answer for himself or herself, whether the war which is now in progress on earth between Christ and Satan, and their respective armies, is a new one, or is it the same war which was begun in heaven and has simply been transferred to this world?

No good reason has been nor can be given why our common Father should have rejected for ever one erring family, and then created another and put them immediately under the baneful influence of the same evil spirit who had led the first to revolt and ruin — can there? If such reason exists, what is it? And no authority is to be found in God's Word for saying that he did so — is there? If there is such authority, what is it, and where is it to be found? Then will we believe, without authority or reason and against both, that a God of so much goodness acted so cruelly, or that an all-wise and omnipotent Creator was foiled so completely as our God has acted and been foiled, if the popular theory under consideration be true?

No, that cannot be; and the time has come when some people must and will think and act for themselves. No system of religion will satisfy the craving appetite of a perishing generation of educated men and women, which is at once inconsistent with itself, with common sense, and with the Word of God.

Why is it that in this progressive age, and when every other branch of science is being so wonderfully developed and going on to perfection so rapidly, that theology alone is at a dead standstill? There is a cause for this; and it is so fully in view that every friend of Jesus Christ, who is capable of teaching, ought to see it. "Watchman, what of the night? Watchman, what of the night? The watchman said: The morning cometh, and also the night. If ye will inquire, inquire ye; return, come!" (Isa. xxi. 11, 12.)

The morning came with the Babe of Bethlehem. The night ensued the substitution of the CREED for the GOSPEL system of religion. This remark will be considered bold by many; it may prove offensive to some: but that it is true is a fact so palpable to every candid mind, that to argue it would be bootless.

Watchmen, you who stand on the walls of Zion, would it not be well for you — for each and all of you who have one — to give up your little sectarian creeds and confessions of faith to the bats and the owls, and go back to your common text-book? Facts of the first importance are plainly revealed there, but which appear to have been entirely overlooked for many dark and dreary ages. "If ye will inquire, inquire ye; return," come back to —

> "The Bible, the Bible, the dear, blessed Bible,
> The old-fashioned Bible that lay on the stand."

CHAPTER IV.

A brief Statement of the leading Facts revealed, and which constitute the Bases of the Christian Religion. — First Proposition considered. — A Creator; not chance. — A personal God. — Why Jehovah should assume a personal Form. — Opinions of Heathen. — Of the masses of Christians. — Locality of God.

THE following propositions are submitted for consideration, and which, as it is believed, embrace all the leading facts necessary to a brief but sufficiently comprehensive view of *natural* religion as revealed from heaven.

I. There is an all-wise and omnipotent Creator, and whose name is *Jehovah* or *Jah*.

II. He is a spirit, self-existent and eternal, separate and distinct from all other beings, and manifests himself to his holy, angelic creatures in a bodily form.

III. He is the Father of spirits, and Author of all things, and which were created for his glory in the obedience and happiness of his rational creatures.

IV. His home is in heaven; yet he is everywhere and at all times present in his knowledge and power.

V. Jesus Christ is the holy and most beloved Son of Jehovah-God, and like the Father he is an eternal spirit, separate and distinct from all other spirits, and who is revealed to us by his angelic name Michael, and as the Archangel, the Word, the Prince of Peace, &c.

VI. And the Holy Ghost is not another individual spirit, but the power and wisdom of God.

VII. Man is a spirit, eternal, immortal. This is not his primitive state nor his permanent condition; but he is here a prisoner of hope, clothed upon by a cumbrous body, and which serves the twofold purpose of a prison-house and the means of sense, thought, locomotion, and action.

VIII. Satan is also an eternal spirit, of great power and influence. And having been himself deceived (by his pride and vain ambition), and gone astray from the peaceful paths of love and obedience to the law of his Creator, he thereupon beguiled and seduced a host of others, and induced them to follow him into rebellion and war in heaven. And in that war "Michael and his angels fought against the dragon (Satan); and the dragon fought and his angels, and prevailed not," but were "cast out into the earth," and are "reserved in everlasting chains under darkness, unto the judgment of the great day."

IX. "The mercy of the LORD is from everlasting to everlasting upon them that fear him," as rebel angels did after their fall. (Ps. ciii. 17; Ezek. xviii. 23–32; Jer. ix. 24; and Jer. xxxi. 3.)

X. When those who had been so deceived and betrayed into sin, and cast out of heaven on that account, saw and realized their horrible condition, they became sorely penitent for what they had done; and therefore "as a father pitieth his children" in their afflictions, so the Lord pitied them, "because his compassions fail not" (Ps. ciii. 13; Lam. iii. 22); and hence a covenant was made between the Father and Son, and a plan devised by them for their (our) probation and redemption.

XI. Pursuant to which benign arrangement, Jesus Christ— the Son of God, the Word — prepared this world as the place, formed the bodies of our progenitors, became himself the propitiation for our sins, brings us into this life, and by the Holy Spirit teaches, warns, and offers each and every one pardon, full and free, who may prove worthy of such grace by repentance, faith, and obedience to the Divine will.

XII. And when all who are included in that divine covenant shall have had a term of probation here, then "the Son of man shall come in his glory." "And before him shall be gathered all nations; and he shall separate them one from another, as a shepherd divideth his sheep from the goats: and he shall set the sheep on his right hand, but the goats on the left. Then shall the King say unto them on his right hand, Come, ye blessed of my Father, inherit the kingdom prepared for you from the foundation of the world." And lastly, he will "say also unto them on the left hand, Depart from me, ye cursed, into everlasting fire prepared for the Devil and his angels." (See Matt. xxv. 31–34, and 41.)

Our first proposition is, that "There is an all-wise and omnipotent Creator, and whose name is Jehovah or Jah." The question whether there is such a God, or whether all things that exist are the fortuitous productions of blind chance, or of a great creative law of Nature, as others prefer to express it, has been so frequently, so fully, and so satisfactorily answered already by friends of the Bible theory of our being, that I do not think it worth while to recall the witnesses or reproduce the arguments in this work, by which that view is sustained. What we call accidents do sometimes happen; but to believe that the whole universe of worlds and the perfect system of laws by which they are governed, with all things rational and irrational that are known to be upon them, are the creatures of accident, or of a succession of accidents, requires a sort of credulity with which the God of Nature has furnished no man, and which can only be acquired at a cost of the most assiduous cultivation of a highly depraved mind, and which is guided by an equally perverse will. And therefore, without further remark, we will pass on.

The second proposition is, that "He is a spirit, self-existent, eternal, separate, and distinct from all other beings, and manifests himself to his holy, angelic creatures in a bodily form." That God is a self-existing and eternal spirit is so universally believed by all who admit his being, that it is not considered necessary to adduce either evidence or argument to prove it. But the latter part of this affirmation presents a subject which requires a very different treatment. In that we find the question squarely before us, Is there a *personal* God?

In approaching this sacred subject we should put off the shoes from off our feet, remembering that the place whereon we stand "*is holy ground.*" To treat of the *personality* of God is to tread upon not only holy but dangerous ground; and any attempt to teach or to know more of him or of his ways than he has been pleased to reveal in his written Word would be at once irreverent and impious! This will be carefully avoided; and it is with unfeigned diffidence, impressed with a sense of the most profound reverence and veneration, and in humble obedience to that which he feels to be an imperative duty, that the writer accepts the delicate task of so much as calling the attention of the Christian world to what the great Jehovah has revealed of himself as an individual.

To all who have *searched the Scriptures* with anxious desire, and for the holy purpose of knowing what is revealed there, and with no other motive than to avail himself or herself of the benefit of such heavenly knowledge, it can but appear amazing that such grave duty should have devolved upon the friends of Jesus Christ and of his cause in this enlightened age. In the earlier and purer days of the Church, Christians were wont to think, to talk, and to write about God the Father as the great Architect of the universe, the giver of all good, and as having a real personal existence.

It was long the province of the infidel to speak of God as nothing more than the first cause, or the great *creative principle* in Nature. But the deceiver is abroad *in the Church*, and it is now a painful fact that learned (?) ministers of the gospel are often heard to speak of Jehovah-God in about the same way; and further, as pervading the whole universe of worlds, and as being everywhere present at all times and in all things.

And it is moreover now held and taught by many, and who are accepted as Orthodox, that the soul, the spirit, which animated the body of Jesus Christ was human, and differed from the souls of other men only in this, that he partook more fully of the Divine nature; and that he ascended to heaven in his body, and is now there in his human form. And it is furthermore the common doctrine of so-called Orthodox Christians (and heterodox also) that the Holy Ghost is *a person*, equal with the Father and the Son, and yet that there are not three Gods but one only.

Before looking into the Book of inspiration to learn what has been revealed to us of our Creator, let us notice some of the principal reasons for believing that there is, or that there is not, a personal God. For the purposes of this inquiry, we must admit that there is at least an active, intelligent, first cause, or a great creative principle and power in Nature, and to which power all things whether animate or inanimate, rational or irrational, owe their being. And in this admission we deny that all things owe their existence to pure chance or accident, — or waive that question rather for the consideration of the other.

Now there being an active intelligent cause, or creative principle or power, which has brought every thing that we see, feel, or know to exist into the condition in which we find it, we must believe that great creative power could have made for himself a body in and by means of which he could have manifested himself to his rational creatures. That he *could* have done so, it is believed, will not be controverted by any one. Then, he could have made for himself a body for such benign purposes. Now is it more likely that he would or that he would not have done it? To answer this question satisfactorily, we must look first to the purpose for which such creatures were made. If God created them for his own glory, as held by some, is it not most reasonable to believe that he would have enabled himself to appear before them in a personal or bodily form? By that means he could have presented himself in person before them, and they could therefore have realized his being, his presence, his power, and his goodness to them more fully, and they could have felt and expressed their gratitude to him more perfectly. Is not this true?

And if the chief motive in the creation of holy angels and men, such as the redeemed of this world will be, was that they should be happy as well as holy, then would he not most likely have put it in his own power to appear in person before them, and to admit them to his sacred personal presence, that they might not only see him, but hold sweet converse with him face to face? Would not such angelic, intelligent creatures have desired such blessed privilege? And would such unspeakable joy and gladness be denied them?

But let us suppose that the ruling desire in the Divine

mind in all this creation was to render himself the more glorious by bringing into being such a host of happified and godlike creatures that he and they might live, rejoice, and dwell together in unity and purity (as most assuredly was the case), then is it not easy to believe that he did prepare a body for himself, and one for each of them also, and all in his own "*image*"? But again, it appears that many people of all heathen nations believe that there is a GREAT and GOOD SPIRIT (a personal God), who made all things, and who presides over and governs all his creatures. That certainly is the faith of such as make images representing — as they imagine — the form, parts, and features of the Great Spirit, and set them up in such manner that they can behold his likeness (as they suppose) while engaged in his worship.

And, furthermore, it is thought safe to say that as many as ninety-nine in every hundred of the great mass of unlearned Christians (and to include such as read the Bible and nothing else on religious subjects) now believe that God the Father sits *in person* on his throne in heaven, and that Jesus Christ sits on his right hand interceding for his people continually. Now how and from whence does such universal belief arise and possess the pious mind of so many people of different ages, countries, and conditions, and who can have had no other common teacher, and upon a subject of such sacred interest, if the Holy Spirit does not impress it there? And if so obtained, is not such opinion well founded?

In view of such facts and considerations, the most natural and reasonable inference (in the absence of all authority) is that there is a personal God. Is not this true? If we admit that there is a personal God, we cannot deny that he is at some particular place. For the very idea of person and that of place are inseparably connected; and every *person* in existence must be at some particular *place*.

And, therefore, if God is everywhere and in every thing at the same time, he is in no particular place nor in any particular thing at any time, and he can have no personal identity nor individual being. And if he is everywhere and in every thing in general, he is nowhere and in no particular thing; and, therefore, is as *no* thing. Now what is the difference between *no thing* and nothing? If there is any difference between the two, it is infinitesimal; and if searched for, it could not be seen with the aid of a first-class microscope.

Hence we learn that if there is no personal God, and if all things have sprung from nothing more than a great creative principle in Nature, as held by some Christian teachers, then the atheist is right; and he and all that class of Christians have agreed as to the nature and character of the Author of all things, and therefore they should quarrel no more about their religion. I will only remark further on this interesting branch of our subject at present, that all who hold that there is a God admit that he is a spirit; and they also admit that there are many other celestial spirits; and further that all the others have bodies, distinguished by size, form, and features. Is it not wonderfully strange, then, that all the eternal spirits have bodies but one, and yet that the only one who has no body should have been the Father of all the other spirits?

It may occur to some, as a first impression, that the idea of God's personality is inconsistent with that of his omnipresence. But a little reflection will suffice to remove that error; for if God is an individual essence, a being separate and distinct from all his creatures, and possessing the attributes of omniscience and omnipotence, he must have the power also of being everywhere present at the same time, and in some real sense. And here the question arises, how or in what sense is God everywhere present at the same time? If he is present everywhere and at the same time in such sense as to constitute omnipresence, as he certainly is, he must be so present either in person or in his knowledge and power. This being the case, is it more reasonable to believe that he is personally present everywhere and at once, or that he is in person always at some particular place (as is the case with men), and that his knowledge and power extend everywhere and to all things, so that he can search all hearts and understand all the "imaginations of the thoughts" of all men at the same time? And, in fine, is it not easier to believe that a God whose attributes and powers are all concentrated into a perfect spiritual body, should have and exercise all the wisdom, mercy, and power which our God is known to possess, than it is to believe that a mere creative principle, which it is said exists in all Nature and pervades all things, should have and exercise such power, wisdom, and mercy? These questions are left to find their own answers in the thoughts of all fair-minded readers.

CHAPTER V.

The same Subject continued. — Scriptural Proofs. — Was it the Soul or the Body of Adam that was made in the Image of God ? — Moses talked with God about his Body. — New Testament Authorities. — Spiritual and natural Bodies. — Conclusion.

HAVING already given such reasons for believing that there is a *personal God* as will, if no more, serve to prepare the mind of all readers, who are not so far gone in unbelief as to have become absolutely impervious alike to natural reason and to revealed truth, for a fair and unprejudiced consideration of what God has been pleased to reveal of himself, and for our good, we will now call attention to certain texts of Scripture which bear directly upon that subject. And in doing this we will begin at "the beginning."

In Gen. ii. 7, we are informed that " The Lord God formed man of the dust of the ground, and breathed into his nostrils the breath of life; and man became a living soul." And in the first part of the fifth chapter we learn that " In the day that God created man, in the likeness of God made he him; male and female created he them," &c. On these and other similar Scriptures, the question has been made whether it was the body or the soul, the spirit, the immortal part of man, that was made " in the likeness of God."

In the investigation of that question we should note carefully what is said there about the creation of both the soul and the body, as well as what is *not said* as to the creation of the soul. Of the body it is on record that "the Lord God formed man of the dust of the ground." Or was it the soul and not the body that was *formed* of the dust of the ground? That appears to have been all of man that was created on that occasion; and therefore we must believe either that the soul was *formed* of the dust of the ground, or that the body was made in the "likeness of God;" or we must reject the whole narrative as an unmeaning fable. Is there any way of escape from this conclusion? If so, where is it? In the absence of any revelation to the contrary, we must believe that it was the body that was intended as having been made "in the likeness of God," or reject the authority altogether. Is not this true?

But again, if the soul was made then, or if it was at that time as it was when originally created, we cannot admit that it was the soul of Adam which was made in the likeness of God, or like him, without denying the perfection of our Creator. For, according to that history, man was then not only imperfect, but he was subject to the delusive influence of Satan; and, as we learn there, he did in fact and soon thereafter yield to the subtle insinuations and temptations of the Devil (aided by Eve his wife), so far as to violate the positive command of his Creator, and which was, as it would seem, the only law or restraint under which he was placed. Was that god-like?

Observe, further, that there is not a word said in Genesis as to when, of what, or in what likeness, form, or image the soul of man was made. Yet we are there informed circumstantially of the time when the body was made, of the material of which it was *formed*, and in whose likeness it was made. These facts alone afford sufficient evidence on which to form the three presumptions (if nothing more) which follow: (1) That it was only the body of man which was made then. (2) That it was made in the likeness of God; and (3) That the soul was in being before that time.

As to what it was that is called "the breath of life," and which was "breathed into his nostrils," and distinguished man from all other animals, and which entitled him thereupon to be considered and called "a living soul," the Mosaic history does not inform us. He was not called the first, or the only, or even *the* "living soul," but "*a* living soul." Note that fact. Were there not many other "living souls" (spirits) at that time? If there were not, who or what were "all the sons of God (that) shouted for joy" when "the foundations of the earth" were laid? These considerations, unaided by others, afford material for such argument as could not be successfully answered, that it was the body and not the soul — the spirit, the immortal part of man — that was made in the likeness of God. Now the likeness, the form, the image of man we know. Then in what true sense could it have been said that the body of man was made in the likeness of God, if he has no likeness, no bodily form, and if he is nothing more than a creative principle which exists in Nature?

Let us now go back to Gen. i. 26, 27, and read and reflect on what is there said about the creation of man. "And God said, Let us make man in our image, after our likeness," &c. "So God created man in his own image, in the image of God created he him," &c. What do these Scriptures mean? If read and construed in that plain, common-sense sort of way in which we read and construe all other writings the meaning of which we want to get, we would understand from them that there were two or more persons present and together; that they had previously determined to make man; that they were then consulting as to the *form* in which he should be made; that one of the parties proposed to the other that they make him in their own image and likeness; that the proposition was accepted by the other party; and that man was created in that form or image which was common to both (or all) of those who were then present and concerned in his creation. Is not all that, and more, clearly implied in these two verses? We learn from them, also, that the two or more persons present and so engaged were both or all (as the case may have been) of the same image and likeness, and that man was made so as to have the same form and appearance which was the common one in which both or all of those present appeared — do we not? If we concede that it was the body and not the soul of man that was made "of the dust of the ground" (and who will say that it was not?), we must also infer from these texts that man, and all who were present at the time of his creation, were of the same personal form and appearance — must we not? In this view of these Scriptures, there must have been at least two individual personages then and there present, before the body of man was formed;

and Adam having been made in the same form, there were then at least three persons present, and all having the same general appearance — were there not?

It appears, also, that there was a conversation had and a consultation held between those who were present and co-operating in that work of creation. Who were the parties so engaged? This is a very interesting question; but we will not pause to consider of it further in this place, than to submit one thought for the benefit of such religious teachers as may profit by it. Those who hold the very common but unscriptural as well as unreasonable opinion, that God the Father, God the Son, and God the Holy Ghost are all one and the same, and that the three persons constitute but one God, must esteem that conversation as nothing more than a soliloquy, — God talking to himself!

Is not that view of the matter fearfully disrespectful to the Almighty? Any dogma which involves, as a necessary sequence, the necessity of believing that the great Jehovah was on that important occasion engaged in an idle conversation with himself, as crazy people sometimes do, should be discarded at once: and for that reason, if there were no others for repudiating it.

But as some may doubt whether the above texts have been properly construed, a few others are here given simply to sustain the interpretation offered of those already cited. "And Adam lived an hundred and thirty years, and begat a son in his own likeness, after his image; and called his name Seth" (Gen. v. 3). Now, in all seriousness, would any sane man suspect for a moment that the words "likeness" and "image," as used in this instance, have reference to the soul, the spirit of Adam, and not to his body? Such an idea is too absurd to admit of grave argument. And yet they are identically the same words which are so often used by the sacred writers in giving the resemblance of Adam to our Maker.

The following passage is also too clear to admit of doubt on this subject: "Whoso sheddeth man's blood, by man shall his blood be shed; for in the image of God made he man" (Gen. ix. 6). Would the meaning of this text have been any more plain if it had been written thus: "For *in the image of God* made he *the body* of man?" I think not.

We will now turn to a class of Scriptures which prove more directly (although not more conclusively) that God has a body consisting of form, size, and parts, as do the bodies of men, and that he manifests himself to his creatures in his bodily form.

In the thirty-third chapter of Exodus we have an account of a conversation between the LORD GOD (or God the Father) and Moses, "face to face, as a man speaketh unto his friend;" during which God concealed himself in "the cloudy pillar" which stood at the door of the tabernacle. Moses desired to see his God, "And he said, Thou canst not see my face; for there shall no man see me and live. And the LORD said, Behold there is a place by me, and thou shalt stand upon a rock. And it shall come to pass, while my glory passeth by, that I will put thee in a cleft of the rock; and I will cover thee with my hand while I pass by; and I will take away mine hand, and thou shalt see my back parts; but my face shall not be seen." (The last four verses.)

Remember that we are informed, on the authority of this same Moses (in Gen. v. 1), that man was created in the likeness of God. Is it not utterly impossible, therefore, to reconcile the above language of the Almighty himself *with the truth* upon any other hypothesis than that God did occupy a body on that occasion, and that it was "*in the likeness*" of the bodies of men? Particular mention is made there of *his face*, *his hand*, and of *his back parts*.

From this Scripture (as well as from others) it appears that God has forbidden any of us seeing *his face* in our present sinful state. Moses was anxious to see his God, who was present and conversing with him *face to face*, but who carefully concealed himself in the cloud; and Moses was denied the privilege of seeing more than *his back parts*. Now what are we to understand that Moses was to see under that promise? What did he expect to see? He certainly had reason to believe that he would see all the parts of the body of his Maker, as well as the size, form, proportions, &c., of each and of all of them together; just as he could see the several parts of a man walking from him. Is not this the plain meaning of the Divine promise? If so, Moses expected to see the *back parts* of the head, neck, arms, trunk, legs, and feet of THE DIVINE PERSON!— did he not? Would God have made Moses that promise if he had no such essential body that he could have shown him? Why conceal himself in a cloud, if God had no body that could have been seen without the cloud? To deny that he had such body would be blasphemy! (See Num. xii. 6-8, and Ps. xvii. 15.)

From the fact that God said to Moses: "I will put thee in a cleft of the rock; and will *cover thee with my hand* while I pass by," &c., we must infer that God's body is much *larger* than are the bodies of men; for he could not otherwise have so completely covered Moses and the *cleft of the rock* in which he was to be put *with his hand*, as to have concealed himself entirely from Moses until he should pass by and withdraw his hand.

This view is perfectly consistent with what is said in Genesis, that "God created man in his own image, in the image of God created he him; male and female created he them." By the word *image*, as repeated there, we must understand the general form and appearance of each as intended, and without any reference to the *size* of either. This is manifestly true, because the same word *image* is applied there to Adam and Eve both; and it is certainly the most reasonable supposition that their bodies differed in size and form just as the bodies of men and women now differ in these respects. And, furthermore, it was evidently intended to embrace the whole race of men — male and female — as being created in the image of God: and we are all of the same general form, likeness, and image, as compared to other animals and created things; notwithstanding the vast differences as to size, form, color, features, &c., which are well known to exist between men, and not only men of different races, but of the same race and sometimes of the same family.

Attention is again called to the proposition in Genesis: "Let us make man in our image, after our likeness." In the first chapter of St. John's Gospel we are informed that God the Father and God the Son ("the Word") were both present on that important occasion; and thereby we learn that the conversation, which is in part recorded there, was had between the Father and Son. And, as after that suggestion was made we are told that man was made in the image of God, we find that the bodies of God the Father and of Jesus Christ were in the same image and likeness; yet of the comparative *size* of the two we learn nothing there. But from these Scriptures the inference is irresistible that, after the body of Adam was *formed*, God the Father, God the Son, and man, their creature, were all three of the same *image* and *likeness*. Is not this true?

Before passing from this part of our subject, it may be well enough to remark further as to the size of the *Divine Person*, that it is reasonable to suppose that the body of the Creator is larger than are the bodies of his steadfast and holy angels. Because, if they too are of the same average size and in the common *likeness* of men, as we have abundant reason to believe that they are, it would be easier for them to distinguish him from one another by his great size than perhaps by any other means which wisdom could have devised. That is the way that God has provided to enable bees to distinguish their queen from each other, whether he has adopted the same convenient plan for his subjects to identify himself from other spirits or not. And simple as the case may appear, there is some reason for believing that the same means would have been employed to produce the effect desired in one case as well as in the other, and therefore that the same plan was adopted in both cases, and for the same purpose.

We find mention made of various other parts of God's body by the sacred writers, and in such way as we would not expect those good and holy men to have written if he has no body. For instance, we read of his *head, face, eyes, mouth, ears, arm, hand, feet,* and of his voice also; as in the following passages: "He put on righteousness as a breast-plate, and an helmet of salvation upon his *head*" (Isa. lix. 17). "The *eyes* of the Lord are upon the righteous, and his *ears* are open unto their cry. The *face* of the Lord is against them that do evil," &c. (Ps. xxxiv. 15, 16). "Blessed be the Lord God of Israel which spake *with his mouth* unto David my father," &c. (1 Kings viii. 15). "Hast thou an *arm* like God? or canst thou thunder with *a voice* like him?" (Job xl. 9.) "I will stretch out my *hand* and smite Egypt" (Exodus iii. 20). "I will make the place of *my feet* glorious" (Isa. lx. 13).

The Scriptures cited above have been taken chiefly from the Old Testament writers, as the careful reader must have observed. Let us now notice a few texts found in the New Testament, and see whether the same great truth is taught there. "So then after the Lord had spoken unto them, he was received up into heaven, and sat on *the right hand* of God" (Mark xvi. 19). See also Rom. viii. 34, and 1 Pet. iii. 22. From these passages, is it not the most natural inference that God the Father and Christ the Son are and appear to those about them as separate and distinct persons? And if we give implicit credence to what these writers said, must we not believe that both the Father and Son sat on the throne above, and side by side?

"God is a spirit" (John iv. 24). Now what is a spirit in the sense intended here? Observe, it is not said that God is *the* spirit, nor the Great Spirit, nor the Father of spirits; but that " *God is a spirit,*" as if there are other spirits "in the likeness of God."

The book of Revelation begins thus: "The Revelation of Jesus Christ, which God gave unto him to show unto his servants things which must shortly come to pass; and he sent and signified it by his angel unto his servant John." From this we learn that this Revelation *was given* by the Father to the Son, and that Jesus Christ " sent and signified it *by his angel* unto *his servant* John." Further on we are informed that the several messages to the churches were accompanied with the blessings of the Father — " the *seven spirits* which are before his throne " — and of Jesus Christ (Rev. i. 4, 5). From the tenth to the nineteenth verses St. John relates his vision of " the Son of man," describes his *personal appearance*, and states what Christ first said to him, &c. And by reading in connection Rev. xv. 5, 6, xxi. 9, and xxii. 8, 9, we find that the *angel* which St. John says "talked with" him was not only the same *angel* mentioned in the first verse, but that he was one of the *seven spirits* who sent their blessing to the churches, and one of the seven *angels* who "came out of the temple, having the seven plagues," &c.; and, furthermore, we learn that he was the redeemed spirit of one of our old prophets!

And it is evident that the *angel* — the *spirit* which appeared to St. John on that occasion — was so perfectly in that form which is called in Gen. i. 26 "our image," "our likeness," that St. John thought it was the Saviour who was still talking to him; for otherwise he would not have attempted as he did to worship him.

In these passages from Revelation the terms "angel" and "spirit" are repeatedly used (as by other Bible writers) as convertible, and meaning just the same thing. And in the seventh verse of the second chapter (and frequently thereafter) Christ is called "the spirit," but meaning the spirit whose message the angel was delivering. Hence we conclude that all angels are spirits, that the holy angels are "all ministering spirits," as St. Paul represents them as being, and that God is a spirit also; yet he is not an angel, but the Creator of angels — "*the Father of spirits*."

To constitute *a man* "a living soul," he must be "clothed upon" with a natural body; so an *angel* consists of an eternal spirit clothed with a "spiritual body," each being a spirit, and inhabiting a body adapted to his condition. As to the bodies of angels, no more can be necessary here than to refer to the frequent mention which is made of them by all the sacred writers both of the Old Testament and the New, and to call attention to the fact that they are uniformly spoken of as appearing in bodily form, and "in the likeness" of men. And, therefore, as "God is a spirit," he must have a body; for without it he would not be a spirit — would he?

Is it not impossible to form any well-defined conception or idea of such a thing as a spirit without a body? What sort of being would it be? It could not be seen either by angels or men, and therefore it could not have an *image* nor a likeness, could it? Such spirit or angel could be no more than some imaginary " principle in Nature," or " natural principle," as is the God of the atheist; a mere imaginary intelligence without size, form, feature, individuality, or locality — a phantasm! Is that the sort of something-nothing that Bible readers understand angels — spirits — to be?

But we must remember that it is insisted by those who deny the existence of a personal God, that it was the *spirit* and not the *body* of God "*in the image*" of which man was made; and that it was the soul, the spirit of man, and not his body that was made in the image of God. As to that I will only remark further in this place, that the early history of our race proves but too clearly that man was vastly inferior to Satan intellectually, and subject to the controlling influence of that evil genius in his actions. Was man in that respect like God? Is the great I Am inferior in capacity to Satan? or is he liable to be deceived and led into error by him, as man was when and as he was put in Eden? If God was not in any particular the inferior of his enemy the Devil, but had full power over him, and was not liable to err, man was not then like God spiritually, was he? And, therefore, as the soul and body together constitute the man, and if the spirit of man was not then like the spirit of God, man must have been like his Creator in his personal appearance (his body), if he was then made " in the image of God " in any true sense. Is not this conclusive?

Other Scriptures are no less conclusive on this subject; a few more of which we will now look into. St. Paul informs us that God sent " his own Son in the likeness of sinful flesh, and for sin condemned sin in the flesh " (Rom. viii. 3). And again, that man " ought not to cover his head, for as much as he is the *image* and glory of God " (1 Cor. xi. 7). Was it the spirit or was it the body of Jesus Christ that was sent into this world, and which was " in the likeness of sinful flesh "? If it is not the body of man which " is the image " of God, why is it that he " ought not to cover his head "?

"Let this mind be in you, which was also in Christ Jesus; who, being in the *form* of God, thought it not robbery to be equal with God; but made himself of no reputation, and took upon him the *form* of a servant, and was made in the *likeness* of men" (Phil. ii. 5–7). See also 2 Cor. iv. 4 and James iii. 9. Remember that spirits are *created*, and bodies are usually said to be *made*.

Now if we believed the sacred writings with that childlike confidence which is due from us to the revelations of God, we would be satisfied from this last quotation alone, and if the subject were nowhere else touched in the Bible, that God the Father and Christ the Son each appears to others about them in personal form, and that both are "in the likeness of men." Or will it be replied that it was the spirit of the Son, and not his body, that was "in the *form* of God" and "in the *likeness* of" the spirits of men? If that were true, would not our blessed Saviour have needed a redeemer as much as did those whom he came "to seek and to save"? Into what depths of folly and irreverence will not a bigot in religion go, rather than abandon a pet dogma!

The great apostle to the gentiles, in speaking of the Father and Son, uses these words in reference to the latter: "Who being the brightness of his glory and *the express image of his person*, and upholding all things by the word of his power, when he had by himself purged our sins, sat down on the *right hand* of the Majesty on high" (Heb. i. 3). Note carefully the language: "the express *image* of his PERSON "— "sat down on *the right hand* of the Majesty on high." It hardly will be contended that St. Paul meant to say that the *spirit* of Christ was the express image of *the person* of the Father, nor that the spirit of the Father was the "express image" of the *body* of the Son. But from the closing remark, that the Son "sat down on the right hand of the Majesty on high," the inference cannot be resisted that the apostle intended to be understood as saying that the image, the personal form and appearance, of the Father and Son were precisely alike; and that when Christ had finished the work assigned him in this world, he ascended to heaven and took his seat on Jehovah's throne, and on the right hand of his Father God.

With one other suggestion we will pass on. The very thought of a person is inseparable from that of a place. Every individual person must be at some particular place. If, therefore, God occupies a body distinct from all other bodies, he must at all times be at some one place, from which he can send abroad his agents, messengers, &c., and to which place they can return to his personal presence. Is he so provided with a place?

Let us see. King David says: "The Lord's throne is in heaven" (Ps. xi. 4). And again: "*From the place of his habitation* he looketh upon all the inhabitants of the earth" (Ps. xxxiii. 14). "The Lord is exalted: he *dwelleth* on high" (Isa. xxxiii. 5). The Saviour taught his disciples to pray to "Our Father which art *in heaven*" (Mat. vi. 9). Why address the Father as being *in heaven*, if he is on earth and everywhere else just as he is there? If we believe these Scriptures, we must learn from them, if we have not learned before from them or others of the same import, that God has a home, a "*place of habitation*," and that his throne is in heaven.

But that is not all. "There was a man *sent from* God whose name was John. The same *came* for a witness," &c. (John i. 6, 7). If God is *everywhere* at the same time, how could he send *a man from himself?* "I came forth *from* the Father, and am come *into the world ;*" again, "I *leave* the world and *go to the Father*" (John xvi. 28). Why should Christ have *left* the world to *go to the Father*, if God is everywhere? Or why say he was *going to the Father*, if the great Creator is everywhere, and has no individual being nor place of abode?

The following remarks are to be found in the ever to be remembered prayer of Jesus Christ, just before his arrest: "This is life eternal, that they might know thee the only true God, and Jesus Christ whom thou *hast sent.*" "*I came out from thee*, and they have believed that thou didst *send me.*" "And now I am no more in the world, but these are in the world, and I *come to thee.*" "And now I *come* to thee." "As thou hast *sent me into the world*, even so have I *sent them* [his disciples] into the world." "That the world may *believe* that thou hast *sent me.*" "These *have known* that thou hast *sent me* " (John xvii).

If Christ and the Father are one and the same — one in person, — and if God is everywhere (as some hold), how could our Saviour have said, "I am no more in the world"? If there is not a personal God, and who is at some place, how — with what meaning — could Christ have said to the Father and repeated the same words so often, " Thou hast sent me," and " I come to thee"? To those who really believe that Christ was sent into this world from the home of the Father, which is in heaven, and that, too, on account of his and their solicitude for those whom Jesus the Christ came to save; and that, in view of the awful death through which he had to pass so soon, that prayer was uttered in agony of soul, and that heaven was open to him, and he saw the Great Jehovah in all his loving-kindness looking down upon him, and as none but a God of love can look, — to such as so believe, I say, the language used on that dread and glorious occasion is not only perfectly natural, but it is easy to understand. " Father, the hour is come;" "I have finished the work thou gavest me to do;" "And now I come to thee." The whole of that divine prayer is at once childlike and Godlike. In sublimity, it is simple; and in simplicity, it is sublime.

If the Scriptures already quoted under this head are accepted as true, the question is settled: there is a personal God who created us, and a personal Mediator and Friend who has redeemed us. And under a firm conviction that the authorities which have been cited are sufficient of themselves to satisfy all who will take the trouble to examine them, and who may do so with a fervent desire to know the truth, that there is *a personal God*, I bring this part of our inquiry to a close. It cannot be necessary further to tax the patience of my readers, by pointing them to the host of other like Scriptures, all of which testify to the same divine truth, and upon the maintenance of which the whole system of Christian theology depends.

CHAPTER VI.

The Glory of God. — Happiness of his Creatures. — All were made as best for themselves. — God has a Home, a Throne, a Mercy-seat. — His All-seeing Eye penetrates the Universe. — He sees us, observes our ways, and by them tries us, proves us. — Closing Remarks.

OUR third and fourth propositions are: "(3) All things were created by him, and for his glory in the obedience and happiness of his rational creatures;" and "(4) His home is in heaven, yet he is everywhere present, and at all times, in his knowledge and power."

Both of these subjects have been partially treated in the preceding chapter. That course became necessary in our inquiries as to the personality of God; and it is for this reason that these two are considered together. And but few other remarks are intended with reference to either of them.

For those who admit, the existence of such a God as it has been insisted above that there is, no further authority nor argument is deemed necessary to prove that "all things were created by him." The sacred writers are too clear, and facts and things which are known and seen are too conclusive to the mind of all who so believe, to require any more evidence of that fact.

It may be well, however, to consider briefly the leading purpose which guided the Divine will in the creation of worlds and of rational beings to inhabit them. In speaking of man, by the prophet Isaiah, God says: "I have created him for my glory" (Isa. xliii. 7). As mind is more excellent than matter, so living spirits are more glorious than lifeless bodies. We may therefore conclude that happified spirits — holy angels — were the chief objects of desire moving our Creator in all his works, and that all other things were made with a view to his benign purposes concerning them, and to his foreknowledge respecting them. Hence it may be said, that, in some sense, God made every thing, whether animate or inanimate, rational or irrational, for purposes of his own glory.

But an important as well as a very delicate question arises here as to the way in which God derives his glory, his pleasure, from his works. And, as is usual in such cases, different and erroneous views are entertained upon that subject. The generally prevailing idea, even among Christians, seems to be that, as a man of unbounded wealth, high position, and of great power among men feels happy, even proud, of his large estates, official authority, and of the personal respect, not to say veneration, which is accorded him by his less favored countrymen, — so God, in looking over his domain of worlds, and contemplating his matchless power and wonderful works, and particularly in receiving the praise, thanksgiving, and adoration alike of men and angels, feels *about the same way!* Many good people have been punished for heresy, as all admit; but for what heresy which was half so disparaging to God or damning to men, as this certainly is, was ever a heretic burned, drawn, or quartered? Is God subject to the influences of pride and vanity as an egotistic man? When he who created all things looks down upon this sin-smitten world, and beholds the thousands and millions of his intelligent creatures hastening the downward road that leads to a yawning hell, does he delight in the scenes and prospect which lie before him? Does he look with pleased anticipation to that fatal day, when the blue flames from the depths of that burning lake shall come booming up and bound aloft, freighted with and bearing far away the plaintive cries and hideous groans of the lost, the eternally damned?

No, my Christian friend! the God of the Bible is a merciful God. *Love* is his first attribute, — the mainspring in all his works. "God is love;" "I have no pleasure in the death of the wicked," saith the Lord God; "Because he delighteth in mercy," says Micah. In speaking of the redeemed, Isaiah says: "Thou shalt also be a crown of glory in the hand of THE LORD, and a royal diadem in the hand of thy God," and "as the bridegroom rejoiceth over the bride, so shall thy God rejoice over thee."

Remember, our proposition is "That God derives his pleasure, his glory, from the obedience and happiness of his rational creatures." Then it may be asked, why he did not make us all so good, pure, and steadfast that none could fall into sin or rebellion, and go down to eternal death? If we admit the perfection of God in wisdom, power, and love, all such questions may be answered easily and simply by saying that he did make all *just as we were made*, neither better, worse, nor different; because that was the best condition, *for us*, in which we could have been created. Every known law and fact in Nature conspire in support of this hypothesis, and all good reason and fair Biblical construction tend to prove it. If we believe that God loves his creatures, as the Bible plainly declares that he does, and that his power is limited only by his own will, how can we doubt that he so made us?

"No failure in the success of any one of God's wise and beneficent schemes can fairly be inferred from the circumstance of a part of his holy angels having violated his righteous law, and gone so far into sin as to require their removal from the presence and association of those who remained steadfast. It is hazardous for erring man to essay any great penetration into the thick darkness that conceals from us many of the divine secrets which are connected with the wonderful providences of an all-wise God. It may not, however, be considered presumptuous to make a suggestion as to a probable reason why the Almighty permitted the Devil to deceive some of the angelic creatures, which were originally made holy and good, into sin and rebellion.

"That God could have restrained Satan and all his dupes from doing that, whatever it was, for which he and they have been, and are to be, severely punished, there need be no doubt, and will be none with those who admit the truth of the Bible. He did not, however, and for some good reason as we must believe, see fit to do so. Then the question arises, why did he not interfere to prevent the serious consequences of his and their conduct?

"Good and sufficient reasons may have existed, and of which we can form no sort of conception, why he did not interfere. But one reason occurs to my mind why he allowed Satan, and all who associated and co-operated with him, to pursue just such a course as each might prefer in the matter, and then held all parties, of every grade of capacity and social position, to strict account for whatever part each may have taken therein.

"Let us first notice the effect that the contrary course would have had. To have prevented Satan, for instance, from doing that which he desired to do, would have been inconsistent with that freedom of will which must be enjoyed by every rational creature to render him happy.

"If not free, he was a slave; and if a slave, and possessed of any very high order of intelligence, as he assuredly was and yet is, he would have been miserable. He could only be happy as long as he was free to act upon his own judgment, and pursue the dictates of his own will. God therefore saw fit to allow him to enjoy his unrestrained liberty, and to act in that way which pleased him most, as long as his conduct consisted with the peace and contentment of others who loved and kept his commandments. But when the time came that the quiet and happiness of others were seriously interrupted by the course which Satan and his followers were pursuing, he and they were driven out of heaven, and sent to a place of safety until they shall be finally disposed of, and where they could hinder the joys of none but themselves.

"Of course, God foresaw what the result of giving his holy angels the liberty of doing as they pleased would be when he made them. And as he could have made them either so perfect as to be infallible, or have restrained their conduct as he pleased, but did neither, we must conclude that he had some good reason for leaving them both fallible and free. We may therefore safely infer that such state of being is more conducive to the happiness of his creatures than any other would have been; and that, too, when we estimate all the consequences of our fall.

"It may be, and the presumption therefore is, that the aggregate amount of happiness enjoyed by his rational creatures, after making due allowance for the miseries suffered by

Satan and his adherents, is greater than it would have been if God had ordered his providence in any other way. Is not fallibility incident to freedom of the will?

"The loss of Satan, and of those who have and may elect to remain with him, may prove such wholesome warning to others as to prevent, during all eternity, another revolt from the just and liberal rules prescribed for the government of all the heavenly hosts. The most perfect freedom of will may in all probability be enjoyed by all others with entire safety. Those who finally may be redeemed on earth and restored to their former relations with those they left in heaven, having the privilege to mix and mingle freely with them (as it is most likely will be the case), must exercise a wonderfully healthy influence on others who have had no experience in the hardships of a sinner's career.

"There would be no risk in becoming the surety of any one of us who may be so fortunate as to make our way back to that fair and happy land, that we will keep the peace ever thereafter. Should any of the redeemed of earth ever witness another "War in Heaven," it will be only in the capacity of spectators. And the happiness of the whole celestial family will probably be highly intensified by the contrast of their own condition with that of those miserable, lost creatures who will ever stand as living witnesses to the vengeance of an angry God, and of the folly and danger of worshipping a creature rather than the Creator.

"If these views be correct, the very rebellion of Satan will redound to the glory of God, and increase the *quantum* of happiness enjoyed by his creatures. And the wisdom of his scheme will have been put to the test, and thereby proven to the satisfaction of all his rational creatures, Satan included, to have been the very best that could have been devised, and perfect in every particular."[1]

> "Faultless thou dropt from his unerring skill,
> With base power to sin since free of will:
> Yet charge not with thy guilt his bounteous love;
> For who has power to walk, has power to rove."[2]

[1] War in Heaven, p. 300.   [2] Arbuthnot.

We now come to the inquiry whether it is true that "God's home is in heaven; yet he is everywhere and at all times present in his knowledge and power." Having had occasion to notice the locality of God, in connection with his personality, it is not thought necessary to dwell at any considerable length on that part of our subject.

Micaiah said to the king: "I saw the Lord sitting on his throne, and all the host of heaven standing by him on his right hand and on his left" (1 Kings xxii. 19). See also 2 Chron. xviii. 18. Of Stephen, the first Christian martyr, it is said that, "He, being full of the Holy Ghost, looked up steadfastly into heaven and saw the glory of God and Jesus standing on the right hand of God" (Acts vii. 55). For our encouragement Christ said: "To him that overcometh will I grant to sit with me in my throne, even as I also overcame and am set down with my Father in his throne" (Rev. iii. 21). The man child, who was to rule all nations, "was caught up unto God and to his throne" (Rev. v. 12).

No comment of mine could make the meaning of the Scriptures last above quoted more plain than the inspired penmen have made them. The question, therefore, whether God has a home, a throne — a place at which he may be addressed by his people who are here, as "Our Father which art in heaven," and where he is seen by angel spirits — is one which depends altogether upon the trustworthiness of the sacred writings. For if we believe that the Bible is the Word of truth, we must believe that there is a place, a throne, a mercy seat, where God the Son and God the Father have been, now are, and will be seen hereafter.

That God is everywhere and at all times present in his knowledge, power, and loving-kindness will not, as it is hoped, be denied by any professed Christian. In speaking of the omnipresence of God, the Psalmist says: "If I ascend up into heaven thou art there; if I make *my bed in hell*, behold thou art there. If I take the wings of the morning, and dwell in the uttermost parts of the sea, even there shall thy hand lead me, and thy right hand shall hold me. If I say, Surely the darkness shall cover me, even the night shall be light about me; yea, the darkness hideth not from thee, but the night shineth as the day; the darkness and the light are both alike to thee " (Ps. cxxxix. 8–12).

It cannot be necessary to adduce other evidence on this point. No friend of the Almighty God will, as I trust, attempt to construe this Scripture as applicable to his personal presence; for none such would desire to have his home fixed, *his bed made, in the second place* named by King David, as one to which that presence which was intended by him extends. And notwithstanding that it is not thought worth while to offer any more proof of God's omnipresence " in his knowledge and power," yet it is important that we ever bear in mind the fearful truth that " The Lord *is in his holy temple*, the Lord's *throne* is in heaven; *his eyes behold*, his eyelids *try*, the children of men."

The all-seeing eye of him who created us is ever upon us, in every place and under every circumstance: day and night are one with him. He observes carefully all our ways, and will " without respect of persons " " *reward every man according to his works.*" Oh that every poor, ungodly sinner could fully realize his horrid condition in this life! Then would he repent! Then would he " return unto the Lord while it is called to-day! "

CHAPTER VII.

Fifth Division. — Jesus Christ a Spirit. — Distinct from all others. — And the Beloved Son of the Father. — The term Eternal defined. — John i. 1, 2, construed. — Proof of individuality of Son. — Apparent Biblical discrepancies reconciled.

WE have now reached the *fifth* division of our subject, and proceed to show that " Jesus Christ is the holy and most beloved son of Jehovah-God, and like the Father he is an eternal spirit — separate and distinct from all other spirits; and he is revealed to us by his name Michael, and as the Archangel, the Word, the Prince of Peace, &c."

If we admit that God the Father " is a spirit, self-existent, eternal, and separate, and distinct from all other beings," we will find it a necessary conclusion from that one fact that Jesus Christ is also a separate and distinct individual spirit. And we must admit that much as to the Great Jehovah, or deny the divine origin of the Bible, and thereby reject the only evidence we have of the main facts upon which the Christian religion is based.

But it is not the plan of this work to leave facts of such magnitude with no other support than mere conjecture or inference, however strong the conjecture or clear such inference may be. The writer does insist, however, upon the divine rule, "That in the mouth of two or three witnesses every word may be established." And, although that rule was given as applicable to the testimony of men, it is more safe, in the absence of any positive " thus saith the Lord," to consult " two or three " passages of Scripture before accepting as established any controlling or leading, yet controverted, fact. This necessity arises not from any want of confidence in the verity of revelation, but as a consequence of our own imperfections, and of the well-known fact that our translations of the Bible are all imperfect.

Now, with such cautious care, let us approach the delicately divine subject which lies before us, and see first whether "Jesus Christ is the holy and most beloved Son of Jehovah-God." The Psalmist says: "Thou wilt not leave my soul in hell, neither wilt thou suffer thine holy one to see corruption" (Ps. xvi. 10). As conclusive evidence that King David was not rejoicing in hope of a glorious future awaiting himself when he wrote that verse, but that his language was prophetic, and related to the coming Messiah, read what the apostle Peter said of it in Acts ii. 27–31. Moreover, it is said of Christ: "No man hath seen God [the Father] at any time: *the only begotten Son* which is in the *bosom* of the Father, he hath declared him" (John i. 18). And it is said that Abraham, in whose *bosom* Lazarus was seen, "offered up Isaac, *his only begotten son*" (Heb. xi. 17).

From these Scriptures we learn that Jesus Christ is the HOLY ONE, and to whom it was promised that his soul should not be left "in hell," and that his body should not "see corruption," and that he is the *only begotten* Son of the Father. Now, Christ being the only one who was assured before he came into this life, as men come into it, that he should not be exposed thereby to an eternal home in hell, and that his body should not *return to dust*, while all the rest of us come liable to the one fate and certain of the other, — the fair presumption is that he was and "is the holy and most beloved Son of Jehovah-God."

And inasmuch as the same words are used to express the relations which existed between Abraham and his son Isaac that are used to express the relations that exist between God the Father and God the Son, we should not infer that they are one *in person* because it is said that the Son "is in the *bosom* of the Father;" for, in speaking of Lazarus and of his condition after death, our Saviour himself said that "the beggar died, and was carried by the angels into Abraham's *bosom*" (Luke xvi. 22). But we ought rather to construe the word "*bosom*," as found in each of these cases, figuratively, and as meaning *heaven* — the place where Jesus is, and the place where Lazarus and all others of the redeemed are.

With a few more texts in reference to the first division of this subject, we will leave it and pass on. "And Jesus, when he was baptized, went up straightway out of the water; and lo! the heavens were opened unto him, and he saw the spirit of God descending like a dove and lighting upon him; and lo! a voice from heaven, saying, This is my beloved Son, in whom I am well pleased" (Matt. iii. 16, 17). See also Mark i. 10, 11. When Christ was transfigured on the mountain before Peter, James, and John, "A bright cloud overshadowed them, and behold, a voice out of the cloud, which said, This is my beloved Son in whom I am well pleased; hear ye him" (Matt. xvii. 5). The Great Jehovah never having given such manifestations of paternal affection for any other, the conclusion becomes irresistible that Jesus Christ is his most dearly beloved Son.

In the last two quotations above we have such evidence, likewise, as should satisfy all who feel any considerable reverence for God and for his revealed Word of the separate existence of the Father and Son. Those who receive the gospel truths and instructions with that child-like confidence which is enjoined by the Saviour, cannot doubt but that the "*voice from heaven*" in the first, and the "*voice out of the cloud*" in the other, were the utterances of the Father, made by him in the presence and hearing of, and concerning, his Son. To deny that would amount to a charge against our blessed Redeemer of a deliberate attempt to deceive those who were present on each occasion, and with the intention of deceiving them as to his individuality, and in regard to the personal relations existing between himself and his Father. Is there any way of escape from this dilemma; and, if there is, where is it?

If the Father and Son are *one in person*, as some hold that they are; and if "the Godhead bodily" dwelt in the Son, and in that sense in which St. Paul is (but most erroneously) understood as intending to say was the case,— then the "voice" which was heard at each of these memorable events must have proceeded from the Son, as ventriloquists cause sounds and words to appear as coming from persons and directions different from the true ones. Is there a Christian on earth who would purposely charge our Lord and Master with duplicity and deception, and that too in a matter so sacred? *There is not.* There were, most assuredly, *two parties* present both times, one of whom claimed the paternity of the other, and commended him as his " beloved Son." Is not this true?

Our next subject of inquiry is, whether, like the Father, the Son is an eternal spirit. The term "eternal" seems properly to denote continuance only. In this sense it is most frequently used by the sacred writers; when applied to the eternal Jehovah it should be understood as referring to his having neither beginning nor end of existence; as in Deut. xxxiii. 27: but when used in reference to men, nothing more than everlasting life or duration is intended; as in Mark iii. 29. In our proposition the word *eternal* is intended to be understood as meaning, in addition to continuance, about the same as the Scriptural expressions, "in the beginning," "from the foundation of the world," "before the foundation of the world," &c.

Now to prove that Christ is an eternal spirit in that sense is by no means difficult. The first two verses of the Gospel by John read thus: "In the beginning was the Word, and the Word was with God, and the Word was God. The same was in the beginning with God." As these two verses now stand in our Bible, the second has no meaning; for the first alone contains every idea that is expressed in both together; and the first verse, in its most literal construction, is made to represent the terms Word and God as synonymous: so that the two leading thoughts to be gathered from the passage as we have it are, that God the Father and the Word (Jesus Christ) are one and the same *in person* — one God, and that " in the beginning " he was *by himself.* In other words, St. John is represented as saying, in substance, that God was *with himself* and *by himself* at the time and place alluded to.

That there is some imperfection in the translation of these two verses is manifest; because as they now stand the second verse has no meaning, but is mere tautology. Is not this true? Now let us see if we can detect the error, from the construction and general intendment of the whole passage considered together, and find how to give both verses some reasonable meaning, and finally learn how to get the true sense of each. This can all be done simply by inserting between the last two words of the first verse the expletory words *the Son of*. The text would then read thus: " In the beginning was the Word, and the Word was with God, and the Word was *the Son of* God. The same was in the beginning with God."

The translators usually supplied words in this way, when necessary to give the sense of the original; and they uniformly *italicized* them in the same way, for the purpose of notifying their readers that such words are not in the original manuscripts from which our Scriptures were translated. This fact all well-informed readers know already. But by some means or from some cause they failed in this instance to supply these or any other words to preserve the meaning of St. John, in this the very first paragraph of his Gospel.

With the help of the above three little words we readily get an intelligible meaning, if no more, from both verses. And if the plainest, most natural interpretation of this Scripture is the correct one (as it unquestionably is), we have herein proof conclusive, not only that Christ is an eternal spirit, but of the separate existence of the Father and Son also.

Without stopping to give any thing like a full exegesis of this passage of Scripture, it is thought sufficient, for present purposes, to submit the remarks which follow. From the fact that the word " beginning " appears in both verses, we should infer that two different times or occasions and places are alluded to. One of the occasions intended may have been when the determination to create this world was made, and the other time evidently was when the world was made, and the place intended by the evangelist is the same of which we read in Genesis.

The great leading truths which St. John evidently intended first to record in his Gospel were that God the Father and Jesus Christ were both present at the time and place of the creation of this world; that the Father was and is the Author of all things; and that the Son, in virtue of the power vested in him by the Father, in his presence and pursuant to his instructions, formed this world and all that was then made. His purpose in that appears to have been to impress on the minds of his readers a true and appreciative sense of the divinity, power, and goodness of the Redeemer whom he preached to our fallen race. The enemies of Christianity, then as now, denied the divinity of Christ, and held that he was nothing but a man, and a deceiver at that.

It is generally conceded that the terms " Word " and " God," as found here, mean the same as Son and Father. And that the inspired writer intended to be understood as stated above will clearly appear by reading that chapter down to the thirty-fourth verse. The third affirms that " All things were made by him " &c. The tenth informs us that " He (the Word) was in the world, and the world was *made by him*," &c. In this connection see further Eph. iii. 9, Col. i. 16, and Heb. i. 2. None who read and believe the Scriptures already cited to prove that Jesus Christ is an eternal spirit can fail to be satisfied as to that point.

Here the question recurs, Is Jesus Christ a separate and distinct individual being; or is he one and the same with the Father? In citing Scriptural authorities to show the separate existence of the Great Jehovah, nearly or quite as much evidence was produced as would be necessary to satisfy any unprejudiced mind of the perfect individuality of the Son also. But as abundant proof lies in both the Old and New Testaments to establish either propositions separately, or both jointly, as may be preferred; and inasmuch as the question whether God the Father and God the Son are both but one and the same person, or whether they are two distinct individuals, is one of the first magnitude, — it is thought best to call the reader's attention to a few more Scriptures that bear directly upon it.

The Bible was evidently written for the sole and benign purpose of instructing honest and earnest inquirers in certain great facts and laws, which God was pleased to reveal and prescribe to and for the good of fallen man. And they were written in such way, that the class of readers for whom they were intended could with reasonable care and diligence understand them correctly, and avail themselves of the blessings provided therein. But no care was taken to avoid the criticisms of the mere caviler, nor the false construction of the shallow pretender in religion.

If, therefore, we really want to know the truth, for the love of truth, on any theological question, or on every one which it is important that we know and observe in regard to our present duties and eternal interests, we should first divest ourselves of every bias of mind and of all preconceived opinions, and then " search the Scriptures," comparing one with another as we proceed, with anxious desire to know the truth, the path of duty, the way to everlasting life; and we should proceed with a fixedness of purpose within us to walk in that way, regardless alike of the opinions of others and of the temporal consequences to ourselves. And all our reading and reflections should be mingled freely with fervent supplications to "Our Father which art in heaven," for light and knowledge; and ever bearing in mind the gracious promise, that " If any of you lack wisdom, let him ask of God, that giveth to all men liberally and upbraideth not, and *it shall be given him*" (James i. 5). Is that true? I believe it is true; and, if so, there can be no necessity for any difference in opinion among Christians as to the path of duty, or way to life.

Let us first look into such texts as are relied upon to prove that the Father, the Word, and the Holy Ghost are one. "There are three that bear record in heaven, the Father, the Word, and the Holy Ghost; and these three are one " (1 John v. 7). " He that hath seen me hath seen the Father " (John xiv. 9). "I and my Father are one" (John x. 30). These Scriptures, if nothing more were said on the subject, would establish the identity of the three as but one in person, clearly.

But let us look further, and read such texts as these: The Lord said to Moses, " There shall no man see me and live " (Exod. xxxiii. 22, 23). " No man hath seen God at any time "

(John i. 18). " My Father is greater than I " (John xiv. 28). " I can of mine own self do nothing ; as I hear I judge ; and my judgment is just, because I seek not mine own will, but the will of the Father which hath sent me " (John v. 30).

All these Scriptures must be believed by the learned Christian, or he cannot be accepted as a disciple of Christ; and notwithstanding, as read here, they make issues as complete as were ever submitted to a jury for trial. " I and my Father are one ; " " My Father is greater than I," — how can that be ? " He that hath seen me hath seen the Father ; " " No man hath seen God at any time ; " — and how is that ? Many had seen " God the Son." Contradictions more complete can nowhere be found ; and the Bible is full of such discrepancies. In Sam. xvii. 46, we read, " There is a God ; " and again in Ps. liii. 1, " There is no God." One or the other of these affirmations must be untrue.

It is, however, to the true believer a precious fact that all such Biblical issues, contradictions, and inconsistencies are made up very much in the same way by which we get the last one above. And that was done (as will be seen by turning to the two passages cited) about as it is said that a good old Puritan brother, when he wanted to preach a sermon against pride, fixed up his text, — " Top-not come down," — from Matt. xxiv. 17.

And I here repeat the remark that, when read and construed as all candid and capable people read and construe every other book, there is no contradiction nor any discrepancy whatever to be found in the doctrines taught from the first of Genesis to the last of Revelation. When such persons want to get the true meaning of any book or other writing, — and whether on the subject of public policy, religion, or any thing else, — they do not content themselves with reading a part of one verse, nor with any one sentence, paragraph, nor chapter even, and conclude that from such part they have found and taken in the entire views and intendments of the author upon the subject treated. So far from that, such students read the whole writing ; and if doubts arise as to the meaning of any part of it, they diligently compare such part with others, and if necessary with every other part, and thereby fairly get the real views of the author of the book or other writing as a whole.

Now let us adopt some such plan by which to get at the cause of such apparent conflicts arising from the texts of Scripture as quoted above. We will first compare them with other remarks taken from the same authorities, and try by that test to find wherein the errors lie. And let us take up in the first place the following words of the Saviour, "I and my Father are one," and inquire *in what sense* he intended to be understood as to the *oneness* of himself and his Father.

Just before his betrayal, Jesus in prayer said: "Holy Father, keep through thine own name those whom thou hast given me, that they may be *one* as we are." "As thou hast sent me into the world, even so have I also sent them into the world." "Neither pray I for these alone, but for them also which shall believe on me through their word; that they *all may be one;* as thou, Father, art in me and I in thee, that they also may be *one in us*." "And the glory which thou gavest me I have given them; that they may be *one*, even *as we are one*" (John xvii. 11–18, 20–22). Observe, the Son prayed that not only his disciples who were then following him, but that all who should believe on him "through their word," "may be one even *as we are one*." All are embraced in that divine petition who may believe and be saved during all subsequent ages of the world; and all are to be *one, as the Father and Son are one;* and the Father, Son, and all the redeemed are to become one. "As thou Father art in me, and I in thee, that they also may be one in us."

Is there any true and real sense in which it may properly be said that the Father and the Son, each being personally distinct from the other, and all the disciples of Christ, each of them also continuing individual persons, *all "may be one"?* There is just such sense; and that certainly is *the sense* intended by the Saviour every time he spoke of such unity: and that *oneness* is to be found in love, purpose, labor, success, and destination. The Father, the Son, and every disciple of his, each and all love one another; their purpose is one, and their labor is joint, " to seek and to save that which was lost ; " and the same result awaits the efforts of each as to the final salvation or loss of every sinner that comes into the world. And, above all, the Father, the Son, and all the redeemed of earth are destined to become members of one happy family eternally in heaven.

We will here notice a few other Scriptures in which the term *one* is used in a similar sense. In Gen. ii. 24, it is said that a man and his wife " shall be *one* flesh." That passage is quoted by the Saviour (Matt. xix. 5) in nearly the same language. And St. Paul, in speaking of man and wife, says, " And they *two* shall be *one* flesh " (Eph. v. 31). Such forms of expression are often found in the sacred writings ; but no sane man can believe that St. Paul (for example) desired to be understood as saying that a man and woman by marriage become absolutely " *one flesh* "— one body! That way of construing the writings or words of any one having common sense is ridiculous.

Man and wife are one while they *dwell in the " flesh "* in many respects. They are one, to a great extent at least, in their temporal interests, rights, hopes, fears, failures, successes, &c. But as eternal spirits they are altogether different ; one may serve God and the other obey Satan while here, and thereby each secure a permanent home far away from the abode of the other. And it is only in reference to their worldly relations of unity that we speak of them as one. The members of mercantile and other business firms are frequently spoken of in connection with their business interests as one.

And to reconcile all apparent conflict in the remarks of the Saviour, " I and my Father are one," and " My Father is greater than I," and again, " I can of mine own self do nothing," " I seek not mine own will, but the will of the Father which hath sent me," &c.,— it is only necessary to construe the first of these texts as we do the very same words, " *are one*," when applied to Christ and his disciples, to man and wife, to members of mercantile firms, &c. But if we insist that the Father and Son are one in person, or deny the separate existence of each (and which amounts to the same thing), it will be found impossible to reconcile these affirmations with each other on any reasonable hypothesis.

If the Father and Son are one, the same in every respect, how can either be *greater* than the other? Yet the Saviour said, "My Father is greater than I;" and again, "I can of mine own self do nothing." How is it that the Creator of the universe can of himself do nothing? If the Father and the Son are but one and the same person or spirit, how could the one have *sent* the other *from* heaven to earth, and remained above himself? Why should Christ have prayed to the Father that his disciples should all be one, as he and the Father are one, if they are but one and the same in every respect? Are all the disciples of Christ, the redeemed of our race, to be merged into and become one individual person?

As nonsensical as such thought must appear, we cannot otherwise construe the language of the Saviour, as quoted above, if he and his Father are literally but one person, — the same eternal spirit. In that view, to the holy angels in heaven there will ultimately be but one individual person or spirit seen there, and which will include the Father, the Son, and the whole family of the redeemed from this world — all having been swallowed up into and become but one! For, as we have seen, the Saviour prayed, "As thou Father art in me and I in thee, that they also may be *one in us.*" But again, how are we to understand these words of the Saviour, "I and my Father are one," in any other light than in the one already given? For if they are one in every sense, it is impossible that either can be the *father* of the other, — is it not?

The illustrations already given are deemed sufficient to explain the meaning of all the texts given above (including 1 John v. 7), and other similar ones, in relation to the unity of the Father and Son, and to show that there is no real conflict between them and others by which the individuality of each is plainly taught, — with but one exception, and we will now proceed to notice that one. In John i. 18, we read this: "No man hath seen the Father at any time;" and in John xiv.

9, we find these words: "He that hath seen me hath seen the Father." Here appears to be as plain and positive a contradiction as the most malignant enemy of Christ and his Church could desire to find. That "no man [*as such*] hath seen God [the Father] at any time," is a fact well sustained by other sacred authorities; and that nothing more was intended by St. John is evident. The difficulty arises in the mind of most readers as to the interpretation of the Saviour's meaning, when he said, "He that hath seen me hath seen the Father." To those who agree with the writer of this as to the origin of our race there is no sort of trouble about that; for I am well satisfied that we have all seen both the Father and the Son often before we came into this life. And that solemn truth was most likely uppermost in the divine mind when that remark was made, because in the same conversation (verse 7) the Saviour said to Thomas: "If ye had known me, ye should have known the Father also; and from henceforth ye know him and have seen him."

Note the phraseology each time: first, "From henceforth ye know him [the Father] and *have seen* him;" again, "He *that hath seen* me *hath seen* the Father." The past tense was used both times. Christ said to his disciples on another occasion, "Ye know not what manner of spirit ye are of" (Luke ix. 55); and to certain Pharisees at another time, and in the presence of his disciples, he said, "Ye are from beneath, I am from above; ye are of this world, I am not of this world;" "I speak that which I have seen with my Father, and ye do that which ye have seen with your father;" "Ye are of your father the Devil," &c. (John viii. 23, 38, 44). From these remarks it is very certain that neither the Pharisees nor his disciples knew then "what manner of spirit" (what family of spirits) they were of. It was nevertheless the prevailing belief with all Jews, at that time and before (the infidel Sadducees only excepted), that the souls of all men had lived (and in a better state than this) somewhere before coming into this life, and that we will live for ever.

The better opinion, therefore, is that his disciples understood the Saviour when he said, "He that hath seen me hath seen the Father," as having reference to the personal likeness of himself and the Father; and that they construed his language as if he had said, " He that hath seen me hath seen *the image of* the Father; " and that he so expressed himself intending to be understood in that way, and at the same time to excite doubts in their minds whether something more was not intended, and if so what it was, as he frequently did. That remark seems to have been generally so understood by Christian writers; and correctly, too, unquestionably.

The editors of an edition of the Bible with notes and references, published by the American Tract Society, make no comment on that verse; but for an explanation of the words now under consideration refer to Col. i. 15; and there the apostle in speaking of the Son says, " Who is *the image of* the invisible God, the first born of every creature." And in Heb. i. 3, St. Paul is still more clear and full on that point; he most indubitably understood the Son as if he had said, " He that hath seen me hath seen [the image of] the Father." And so we see that inspired and uninspired Christian writers alike agree as to the construction of that remark of the Son.

CHAPTER VIII.

The same Subject continued. — Prophecies of the Son consulted. — How they are construed in the New Testament. — Application. — Conclusion.

WE will now pass from the consideration of texts which, when read alone, seem to favor the view that God the Father and Christ the Son are one and the same in person, and notice other Scriptures from which the conclusion that they are entirely separate and distinct beings is irresistible. And for the purpose of preparing the reader's mind the better to understand what the Saviour said himself of the Father and of their relations each to the other, as well as what the evangelists and apostles said on that sacred subject, attention is called first to some of the prophecies in relation to the Messiah.

In Isaiah ix. 6, we have this: "For unto us a child is born, unto us a son is given; and the government shall be upon his shoulders, and his name shall be called Wonderful, Counsellor, The Mighty God, The Everlasting Father, The Prince of Peace." And it may be best to observe right here, that, inasmuch as subsequent sacred writers have nowhere called our Saviour "The Everlasting Father," as our translation makes Isaiah say he shall be called, we must understand him as intending to say that he (Jesus Christ) shall be called *the Son of* "The Everlasting Father." In that way we get the prophet's meaning, and reconcile that clause with other parts of the verse in which it is found, and with the whole Bible; just as we must construe the last clause of John i. 1, to give it any meaning.

But to return to the prophets. "Behold my servant, whom I uphold; mine elect, in whom my soul delighteth. I have put my spirit upon him: he shall bring forth judgment to the gentiles" (Isa. xlii. 1). This verse is cited in Matt. xii., with others following it, as applying to the Saviour: "Thou art my Son; this day have I begotten thee" (Ps. ii. 7). See also Matt. iii. 17 and xvii. 5, Acts xiii. 33. "I saw in the night visions, and behold, one like the Son of man came with the clouds of heaven, and came to the Ancient of Days, and they brought him near before him. And there was given him dominion and glory and a kingdom, that all people, nations, and languages should serve him; his dominion is an everlasting dominion which shall not pass away, and his kingdom that which shall not be destroyed." (Dan. vii. 13, 14.)

On these prophecies but few words in the way of application are deemed necessary. From the language of Isaiah ix. 6, "unto us a child is born, unto us a Son is given," &c., two parties must be intended. For to constitute a gift there must be two parties, — one who gives, and one that receives, and a subject of the gift — must there not? If so, in this case should we not understand that God the Father is the party intended as the giver, God the Son as the treasure given, and our race as the other party, and to which that precious gift was made? Is not this the most literal, reasonable, and Scriptural construction of the words used? Or will we believe that the prophet intended to teach that the Father who gave, and the Son who was given, were but one and the same individual being? How can it be said properly of any one that he is his own Son?

Our next quotation is from the same good old prophet (Isa. xlii. 1). There the Father designates the Son as "*my servant*," "mine elect;" and says of him, "I have put my spirit upon him: he shall bring forth judgment," &c. Would any man, woman, or child, who can read and understand the most plain and simple writing which can be found in any of our common-school primers, fail to perceive that two separate and distinct persons or parties are spoken of there? There is no chance for any unbiased reader to err so egregiously as to believe that but one person is contemplated in all that is said there, and applicable to the speaker and the party spoken of. But, on the contrary, all Christians admit that

God the Father through his prophet is the speaker, and that Christ the Son is the party spoken of. Nevertheless, it is insisted by some that the Father and the Son are but one and the same in person, and by others that they are likewise but one and the same eternal spirit.

Now if the Father and Son are the same in person or in spirit, what the Father said of the Son in form applies to himself in fact, — does it not? Then so to construe that Scripture involves at once the absurdity of holding that God is his own "*servant*," and the irreverence of saying that it is *himself* "in whom [his] soul delighteth"! Is not this conclusion on that construction irresistible? Where is the humble, or even the professing, Christian who is willing so to trifle with the sacred oracles of Almighty God?

Again, the Father has said of the Saviour, and repeated it too as shown above: "Thou art my Son; this day have I begotten thee." If they are the same, are not all such remarks calculated to deceive more than to instruct? I think so. We are informed by St. Paul that all Scripture is given by inspiration of God, and for our "*instruction*," &c. Satan is the deceiver!

We will now notice Daniel vii. 13, 14, and then come down to the gospel teachings upon this question: "Behold, one like the Son of man came with the clouds of heaven, and he came to the Ancient of Days, and they brought him near before him." In their edition of the Bible, the American Tract Society has this note: "13. *Like the Son of man;* this is a vision of the Messiah appearing in human form. *They brought him;* the ministering angels brought him to be invested by the Ancient of Days with universal dominion." And in their note on verse 9, where Daniel first employs the term "Ancient of Days," it is explained as meaning "*Jehovah.*" This authority, and which is entitled to profound respect, is referred to here for no other purpose than to show that the term "Ancient of Days," as used there, and as all Christians agree, is but another name for God the Father, and to avoid thereby the waste of time and space to prove that fact.

Here we have an instance in which the Father and Son

were both seen, and together. But it was "in the night visions" that the prophet was permitted to see "the Ancient of Days;" for no man is allowed to see the face of Jehovah with his natural eyes and live. And we are moreover informed here that *they* (the ministering angels) *brought him* (the Son of man) near before him (the Father). For what purpose was the Son brought *near* before the Father? The next verse, as if in anticipation of such question, answers it satisfactorily: "And there was given him dominion and glory and a kingdom, that all people, nations, and languages should serve him; his dominion is an everlasting dominion which shall not pass away, and his kingdom that which shall not be destroyed." No sincere inquirer for truth will need any comment on this revelation, so far as relates to the joint or separate existence of the Father and Son as taught here. For on that point the only question which can be made on this vision is one of credibility. Did Daniel really see two parties there, as he says he did? Was the one actually brought before the other, as stated? And did the Ancient of Days, in the presence of his prophet and of "*ten thousand times ten thousand*" ministering angels witnessing the ceremony, absolutely crown the Son of man king, and invest him with a kingdom, power, and glory, as Daniel says was done? If Daniel is right, the question is settled, — is it not? (See also Rev. iv. 2-9, and v. 1-7, &c.)

For the purpose of sustaining the views already given of the prophecies cited to prove the separate existence of the Father and Son, the following quotations from the New Testament are presented. Jesus said to his disciples: "As my Father hath sent me, even so send I you" (John xx. 21). His Father had sent him *abroad* on special and important business; even so the Son sent his disciples. Again, Christ said to them: "I ascend unto my Father and your Father, and to my God and your God" (John xx. 17). He *went up* to heaven. From this all must infer that God the Father held the same business relations to the Son that he (the Son) did to his disciples, — "My Father and your Father," "My God and your God." Jesus calls all godly men "my brethren"

(Matt. xxv. 40). "He [Christ Jesus] was in the world, and *the world was made by him*," &c. (John i. 10, and see v. 14). The Father "created all things by Jesus Christ" (Eph. iii. 9). "Who is the image of the invisible God, the first born of every creature" (Col. i. 15). One may have been made in the image of his Maker, but why should it be said of one who is identical with his Creator that he is "*the first born of every creature*"? Read in this connection Heb. i. 1–5 inclusive. The ninth verse of that chapter reads thus: "Thou hast loved righteousness and hated iniquity; therefore God, even thy God, hath anointed thee with the oil of gladness above thy fellows;" and that is a quotation from Ps. xlv. 7. Does this look as if Jehovah and Jesus are one and the same eternal spirit? "These things saith the Amen, the faithful and true witness, the beginning of the creation of God." "To him that overcometh will I grant to sit with me in my throne, even as I also overcame and am set down with my Father in his throne" (Rev. iii. 14–21). No explanation is necessary here; the facts revealed are too plain to be misunderstood. St. Paul says of Jesus (Heb. iv. 10): "For he that is entered into his rest, he also hath ceased from his own works as God did from his." Was the apostle then writing only of one or of two individuals? The *works* certainly seem to have been different. "Whosoever readeth, let him understand."

The paramount importance of the subject is offered as a sufficient apology for pressing still another class of authorities upon the reader's attention. And this is done for the purpose of explaining more fully the relations existing between the Father and Son, and of each to ourselves. The value of correct views as to these sacred relations cannot be overestimated, for they constitute the foundation upon which our whole religious edifice must stand or fall; and if we build upon a sandy foundation, when the rain descends and the floods come, "and the winds blow and beat upon that house," it will fall, "and great [will be] the fall of it."

"Ye are my witnesses, saith the LORD, and my servant whom I have chosen; that ye may know and believe me, and understand that I am he. Before me there was no God formed [or, as the marginal reading, *nothing formed of God*], neither shall there be after me. I, even I, am the Lord, and besides me there is no Saviour" (Isa. xliii. 10, 11). "I will not contend for ever, neither will I be always wroth; for the spirit should fail before me, and the souls which I have made" (Isa. lvii. 16). "And they fell upon their faces, and said, O God! the God *of the spirits* of all flesh" (Num. xvi. 22). "And Moses spake unto the LORD, saying, Let the LORD, *the God of the spirits* of all flesh, set a man over the congregation" (Num. xxvii. 15, 16). Should we not infer from the above texts that the Creator of spirits and the Maker of physical bodies are different? If we construe Isaiah xliii. 10, 11 in this way: that the Son (by the mouth of the prophet) is the speaker, and the words which follow as having been spoken by the Son, but for and as if by the Father in person, namely, "Ye are my witnesses, saith the LORD, and my servant whom I have chosen;" that the Jews were the "*witnesses*," and that the Son is the "*servant*" referred to; and if we consider all the rest of both verses as the language of the Son, and as relating to himself, — such inference will be greatly strengthened, will it not? If such is not the true construction, what does the Saviour mean by these words: "Before me there was no God formed," or "nothing formed of God"? The latter is the marginal, and most likely the best, rendering of the two.

The quotation from Isaiah lvii. 16, closing with "the souls which I have made," must be understood as the words of the Father by his prophet. And in Num. xvi. 22 we have the exclamation of the Israelites as a body, beginning, "O God! the *God of the spirits* of all flesh." And again, "Moses spake unto the LORD, saying, Let the LORD, *the God of the spirits of all flesh*," &c. (cited above). From such texts it would seem that Moses and the Israelites generally of his time, and Isaiah and his contemporaries, all considered God the Father as the immediate Creator of the *souls*, "the spirits of all flesh," or rather of the spirits which *dwell in flesh* (as men) — would it not? And yet, as we have already seen, it is evident that this world, the bodies of men, and every thing else here at least were made mediately, and by the Son Jesus Christ.

The following Scriptures, carefully studied, may prove to some as "a light that shineth in a dark place." In Heb. xii. 9, we find this: "We have had *fathers of our flesh* which corrected us, and we gave them reverence; shall we not much rather be in subjection unto the *Father of spirits*, and live?" "For there is one God and one Mediator between God and men, the man Christ Jesus" (1 Tim. ii. 5); and who is said to have been "the beginning of the creation of God" (Rev. iii. 14), "The first born of every creature" (Col. i. 15), "The image of him that created him" (Col. iii. 10, and Eph. iv. 24), "And the world was made by him" (John i. 10, and Heb. i. 2).

The apostle Paul informs us that there is "one Lord, one faith, one baptism, one God and *Father of all*," &c. (Eph. iv. 5, 6). St. Peter exclaims, "Blessed be the God and *Father of our Lord Jesus Christ* (1 Pet. i. 3); and the great Creator of all is mentioned as "*the God of our Lord* Jesus Christ" (Eph. i. 17). And in the third verse of the same chapter St. Paul began his expression of gratitude to the "Father of spirits" in this way: "Blessed be the God *and Father of* our Lord Jesus Christ." The Saviour said to Mary, "Go to *my brethren*, and say unto them, I ascend unto *my Father* and *your Father*, and to *my God* and *your God*" (John xx. 17). "For both he that sanctifieth and they who are sanctified are all of one, for which cause he is not ashamed to call them brethren" (Heb. ii. 11).

Men having the same father are called brothers, now as then; and as Christ who sanctified, and men who are sanctified, "are all of one" *family* (as the apostle evidently intended to be understood as saying, and as was originally the case, beyond all room for doubt or question), he and they are properly said to be "brethren." But if he who sanctified and they who are sanctified are not of the same family, he and they are not brethren, are they? If Christ is the Son of God, and he "by whom also he [God] made the worlds," and if we are new creatures, having had no previous existence, but are brought into being for the first time, with and as our bodies are formed, or when we are born into this life, — in what good sense are we and Jesus Christ, who made the world, said to be brethren? And in that case, and if Jesus and Jehovah are one and the same, how can he (Christ) and we men be "all of one"?

Some good people, as we must believe them to be, hold that God the Father and Christ the Son are one and the same eternal spirit; while others believe that Jesus Christ was but a man. And the latter class of thinkers differ again among themselves; some saying that Jesus was a very good man, that he partook largely of the divine nature, &c., and others pronounce him a shallow pretender! In matters about which men differ in opinion so widely, it is often the case that the truth lies between the extreme views of opposing disputants, and that both parties are wrong. And if St. Paul was right when he said, "All Scripture is profitable for instruction," both of said contending parties — as classed at first, and as subdivided too — are in error on this vital point of revealed truth. For if the Scriptures above cited — first, to prove the distinct personality of Jehovah-God, and, lastly, to identify and establish the divinity of our blessed Redeemer — are to be relied upon, and in their most plain, natural, and literal meaning, they put the truth of both propositions beyond the reach of doubt. And if the Scriptures, when construed in that way, *deceive* and lead us into error, they are not profitable for *instruction*, are they? And moreover, as all will find who try them, it is utterly impossible, without violating every rule for the construction of language, so far to bend, warp, or *wrest* all the Scriptures which have already been referred to for these purposes as to make them consistent with either of their theories.

And that is not all, nor is it the worst feature of their case, for their whole system of theology is based upon erroneous views of our Maker, of our Redeemer, and of ourselves; and it is therefore and necessarily not only based upon error, but it is at the same time inconsistent with itself, with natural reason, and with revelation. This stubborn fact is now being clearly exposed to the gazing and exultant hordes of the enemy; and it is actively and efficiently used to the confusion of the friends of Jesus Christ and his Church, and to the delight of Satan and his followers!

Oh that good men, learned men, and great men too, and of every denomination (as many of our ministers and priests really are), could and would lay aside all prejudice against one another, and get out from under the crushing weight, the incubus, of their severally beloved sectarian dogmas, and humble themselves as *little children* at the feet of Jesus, and there seriously and prayerfully review their respective homemade creeds — comparing them carefully with the Bible as they proceed! A few short months of such sweet and godlike work would suffice to bring all Christians into " one faith," and all would then " be of one mind."

But, oppressed with a sense of the sad truth that all such elysian thoughts are too visionary upon which to risk one fond hope of realization while in this wicked world, let us meekly accept the situation, and hopefully though painfully deal with men and things as we find them.

If all teachers who "live of the gospel" were to agree upon the " one faith " that is taught therein (and there is but *one* on any point of faith), how long would it be until all Christians would " be of one mind," and " live in peace " as one happy family? If the time required under such circumstances to effect so much would be short — say one year at most, — when the Judge returns to reward " every man *according as his work shall be*," will the glorious plaudit, " Come, ye blessed of my Father, inherit the kingdom prepared for you from the foundation of the world," greet the ears of those who are mainly answerable for all the schisms, divisions, and persecutions of the Church? Take due notice, brethren, and govern yourselves accordingly!

CHAPTER IX.

Of the Holy Ghost. — His Office. — Is he a Person, or a Power of God? — Doctrine of a Trinity of Persons in one considered. — Its Origin. — History of. — Evil effects of. — Inconsistent, Unreasonable, Unscriptural.

BELIEVING that the authorities which have been presented in the preceding pages will prove sufficient to satisfy every unprejudiced reader that the great Jehovah-God is a spirit, self-existent, eternal, and distinct from all other spirits; and that Jesus Christ is his most dearly beloved Son, "the first born of every creature," "the bright and the Morning Star," and by whom [God] made the worlds, — we will now look into the same old Book, and see what is revealed there in relation to the Holy Ghost.

That the Holy Spirit of God has an important work to do in the redemption of man is manifest to all Bible readers. After his resurrection from the dead, Jesus came to his disciples "and spake unto them, saying, All power is given unto me in heaven and in earth. Go ye, therefore, and teach all nations, baptizing them in the name of the Father, and of the Son, and of the Holy Ghost," &c. (Matt. xxviii. 18, 19). There must have been some good reason why that particular formula should be observed and used in the administration of the holy rite of baptism, or it would not have been required, would it? If baptism was designed as the ordinance, the ceremony, by which the recipients thereof should be initiated into the Church, the kingdom of God on earth, as it is generally believed to have been, and evidently was intended to be, — why should it not have been administered in the name of "Our Father which art in heaven"? We are taught so to address our prayers; and he is our Creator, and the source of all power. Or, as he is our Redeemer, why should not baptism have been administered in the name of "Our Lord and

Saviour Jesus Christ"? Or why not baptize in the name of both, the Father and the Son? — in the name of the Father as our Creator and of the Son as our Redeemer?

The Father created us pure and holy; but under the influence of Satan we fell into sin, and have been driven away from the personal presence of the Father, the Son, and the entire family of the holy gods (or angels, as we are wont to call them), and are doomed to eternal banishment unless we repent and seek salvation in this life. Then what more do we want than a Redeemer? Whether we *want* it or not, we *need* something more than that. Of what value would a Redeemer be to us if we could not find him? It is true that the Saviour calls continually, "Come unto me," &c. But the condition of a lost sinner here, and in that respect, is about as would be that of a blind mute if lost in a deep wilderness, of a dark and stormy night. He could not see nor hear a friend, nor know that one is calling him. And such a one would therefore need the help of one who would take him by the hand and lead him back to his home, his family, and his friends, would he not?

Just so it is with the wandering children of God. They need a friend, a teacher, one who can and will instruct them of the dangers which surround them; and who " will bring the blind by a way that they know not, and will lead them in paths that they have not known, and will make darkness light before them;" and who will lead them back and up to the mercy-seat, where they can find the Saviour. That is the office of the Holy Ghost. (See Isa. xlii. 16.)

And it is therefore eminently appropriate that the penitent believer in Jesus Christ should be baptized in the name of the Father, and of the Son, and of the Holy Ghost. For we thereby take upon ourselves the most sacred of all obligations that we will adore the Father as our *Creator*, revere the Son as our *Redeemer* and friend, and venerate and obey the Holy Spirit as the *Voice* of God and our *Teacher* and *Guide* in the way to eternal life. "To-day, if ye will hear his *voice*, harden not your heart" (Ps. xcv. 7, Heb. iii. 7). "The Comforter, which is the Holy Ghost, whom the Father will send in my name, he shall *teach* you," &c. (John xiv. 26).

Here the question comes squarely before us, Is the Holy Ghost a separate and distinct person, or is that merely a name given to the *voice* of God, certain manifestations of *power* exercised by him for his glory and our good? This question has vexed the Christian world sorely for many dark ages. But we have no evidence of any difference of opinion on that subject during the days of the apostles, nor before their time. And certain it is that the Old Testament Scriptures cannot be misunderstood, in that respect, by any competent and devout reader.

The authorities and suggestions already adduced and offered to prove that God the Father and Christ the Son are personally as distinct from one another as were Abraham and Isaac his son, should obviate the necessity of further evidence or argument here as to the personality of the Holy Ghost. For to hold that the Father and the Son are different persons, and that the Holy Spirit is another person, distinct from the Father and from the Son, yet of equal power with the other two, would be equivalent to affirming that the Father, Son, and Holy Ghost are all three separate persons, all distinct from each of the others, — *three Gods!* And while such proposition would be equally unscriptural, it evidently would not be half so unreasonable as is the popular (orthodox?) belief, namely: " There be three persons in the Godhead, — the Father, the Son, and the Holy Ghost; and these three are one true eternal God, the same in substance, equal in power and glory, although distinguished by their personal properties."

I am aware that the advocates of the doctrine of " *the Holy Trinity,*" as they call it, complain of those who insist that such thing is impossible; and therefore I will not do that, but proceed to show, (1) That it is inconsistent with itself; (2) That it is unreasonable; and (3) That it is unscriptural. And I honestly think that proof conclusive of these three propositions ought to be sufficient to wean off the most confirmed bigot or dupe, as the case may be, from any form of belief that is not older, nor better sustained by reason or authority, than is this ingeniously mysterious invention of *priest-craft*.

And as the evidence to prove the last of the above propositions is so clear and conclusive that no candid and unbiased reader can fail so to consider it, I will be brief on the first two. A few preliminary remarks are deemed necessary however. As to the age of this delusive enigma, I will only add here, to what has already been said on that subject, that no trace of such thought can anywhere be found previous to the death of the last one of the apostles.

The term "trinity" is not a Scriptural form of expression, and that word cannot be found in the Bible. But the name of that doctrine and the theory itself were both introduced about the time when a few priests determined to do all the thinking for their flocks, and commenced the business of manufacturing so-called religious creeds of faith for the people to believe. The greatest difficulty in their way was to induce Christians generally to approve and adopt their views, and to waive their natural right to think for themselves in such matters. Every available plan was resorted to for that purpose; and that which was perhaps the most successful one was to impress the Christian mind with the idea that the Bible is a mysterious book, exceedingly difficult to understand; that to err in faith is dangerous or damning; and therefore it is more safe for the membership to accept the deductions of the ministry from the Bible as to all important doctrines, rites, and ceremonies as indubitably true and correct, and to act upon them in all their meditations and devotions.

It was claimed, also, that the Church when assembled in ecumenical council could not err; that the Holy Spirit would direct her in all truth, &c. No argument, however, could be produced that could satisfy some liberty loving Christians that so much should be conceded to the clergy; and therefore the latter soon began to enforce the most strict conformity, not only on the part of the laity, but by recusant priests and other officials of the Church also. That was done at first by decrees, edicts, bulls, &c. But that sort of coercion having failed of success in many cases, the most cruel tortures were invoked; and at length the penalty of death was prescribed and freely inflicted, and in some cases in the most horrible and brutal manner that the Devil could invent, for that unnatural and ungodly purpose.

These persecutions commenced soon after Constantine the Great relieved Christians from their heathen persecutors, and about the year A.D. 313. And it was but a short time thereafter until Christians were persecuting one another, for opinion's sake, far more extensively and cruelly than the heathen had ever done.

To enable the clergy to get and hold the perfect mastery of the lay members of the Church, and as far as possible to ease the restive consciences of the unruly, they so shaped their articles of faith as to render them perfectly unintelligible on some of the most vital points. They likewise brought to their aid the traditions of the Church, as they called them, and introduced such pompous, mysterious, and solemnly impressive forms and ceremonies for public worship as would completely overawe the superstitious and timid; and by such means they finally brought them down to the most servile submission to every behest of their masters.

And it is to these changes, so effected, and the transitions from the simple faith, rites, and forms for worship which are so plainly taught in the Gospel, that the world is indebted (if a debt it be) for the wonderful doctrines of the "Holy Trinity," "Transubstantiation," and others of the same sort, as well as for the magnificence, mystery, pomp, and splendor now displayed by the mother Church in her public worship.

The Church of Christ should feel abundantly grateful to the Almighty, it is true, for the inestimable reforms which have already been effected by Luther and his associates and successors, and by others since his time. Yet it must be confessed that the good work which was then commenced has not yet been finished, but that much still remains to be done. And neither Christian ministers nor competent laymen should ever feel satisfied, nor cease their labors in that direction, until the doctrines, ordinances, and worship of the Church shall have been fully restored to their primitive simplicity and purity.

Feeling well satisfied that the preceding remarks are not too strong, but that they are true, and that it is necessary to say that much, if no more, of the evil consequences of what is commonly and properly called *priestcraft*, as it existed previous to the Reformation and to a great extent still exists, — the writer considers it equally due to the cause of truth that we confess the other painful fact, that Protestants generally have left behind them some well founded and highly beneficial observances of the mother Church. Nor is it pretended that officials of the Catholic Church who participated in so distorting plain and natural truths as revealed from heaven, nor that even those who went so far as to approve the bitter persecutions that ensued, were all bad men. The human mind is "wonderfully and fearfully" constituted. There is no safety in saying what an enthusiast cannot believe. The truth is that, in matters of religion, all men believe *just what they want to believe*. And strange as it may appear at this time, the writer, if no other, firmly believes that many of those who are now so bitterly denounced as hypocrites or fiends, or as both together, sincerely believed that they were rendering the cause of "the meek and lowly Jesus" a good and acceptable service in persecuting, even to the tortures of the Inquisition and to death, those whom they most erroneously considered heretics.

That was the great error of that dark age. And it was not confined to the Catholic Church; but Protestants did the same thing then, and in fact since the Reformation of Luther was fairly under way, where they had the power. In the year 1648 the British Parliament, under Protestant influence, published an ordinance against heresy, and in which the penalty of death was provided for and against persons guilty of either one of the several heresies specified therein; one of which was for "denying the Trinity in any form."

The article on the subject of the "Trinity," which is now under review, was copied here from the confession of faith of the same family of Protestants which then ruled the government of England. If, therefore, an Englishman had expressed the opinion "in any form" in that comparatively modern age of the Church, which the writer is now trying in all seriousness and honesty of purpose to impress upon the Christian mind, he would have incurred the penalty of *death* under the law of that great and professedly free and enlightened country!

These facts are not brought to the reader's attention for the purpose of stirring up anew old prejudices between Catholics and Protestants; nor is it done to offend either party, nor in any way to hinder the prosperity or influence of either for good. But they are recalled to mind by a friend of the glorious cause of Jesus Christ, and one who loves all his friends, and therefore desires to promote peace, harmony, and concert of action as far as possible among all Christians and of every name. And it is done with a fervent desire thereby to benefit all parties, and to promote our common interests as one entire family. In fact, the only reason why these unpleasant remembrances are brought up here at all, is to show to all how and by what means this now comparatively old, unnatural, and unreasonable dogma of the Church was originally introduced, and has been preserved in its present form so long. For it is a fact which all should know, that, on this as well as on some other important religious subjects, the Christian mind has been held in a state of vassalage for hundreds of years, and has not been free to act, investigate, and "go on to perfection" in theology as in other natural sciences.

While the human mind has been left free to investigate every other subject, and the learned have been not only permitted but earnestly encouraged to publish the results of all their researches for the benefit of their fellow-men, theology alone has been kept at a dead standstill. That was done, as we have seen, by the enactment of the most stringent laws against, and inflicting savage penalties upon, nonconformists, and all who should dare to offer one thought (drawn from the Bible) in advance of the darkness which enveloped the fourth century.

And since the civil authorities have interfered, and prevented Christians (!) from destroying each other (as no other animals in the world have ever been known to hunt down and wantonly kill others of their own species), other penalties have been devised by ecclesiastics which are but little less efficient in preventing any and all advancement in Biblical science.

Suppose the Pope of Rome himself, or a cardinal, bishop, or priest of his Church, should to-day " deny the *Trinity* in any form," how long would he or any one of them hold his place in the Church? What minister of any leading Protestant and trinitarian sect (but one) would dare venture a doubt as to the correctness of their doctrine of the " Holy Trinity" as they term it? Should any one act so rashly, he would soon have occasion to repent his *folly*, although he may never have repented of his *sins* — would he not? And what would become of the mere lay member of the Catholic Church, or of any one of the creed-observing Protestant Churches, in such case, which would so deal with their highest dignitaries?

I knew a man who read the Bible for himself, and formed his faith upon that olden Book while yet a member of a church that had a human creed (the best one of the kind), and who dared to speak and write about the sacred truths he found revealed from heaven, and to contrast them freely with the mystic relics *sure* of the worst work of once unsaintly *popery*. In that, of course, he showed more zeal than prudent care for self or ease, or slavish fear of priestly power. He had luck, — of course he had. But of what sort it was but few would ask, and to what length it went some may not care to know, and hence I will not stop to tell. His luck, however, of whatsoever kind it may have been at first, has much improved since then, and, as he humbly trusts, will be far better still during the vast and safe hereafter. (Matt. v. 11, 12.)

Seeing, then, that the doctrine of the Trinity in the present form has been held too sacred to admit of examination for the past fifteen hundred years, we should therefore consider it *an open question*, and one which demands the careful consideration of all who venture to teach the Christian religion, and of all who love the truth; for it is a well-known fact that hundreds and thousands of intelligent and well-informed people during all these centuries have been driven to doubt and disbelief of our holy religion, because they did not believe this mysterious and unreasonable tenet of the Church. And yet both priests and ministers have told and still tell them that they must so believe or be eternally lost! The Devil in dealing with skeptics uses this article of Christian faith as an all-sufficient argument by which to hold many of them aloof from the Church of God and from faith in Christ, and so to retain them in his confidence.

Let us, therefore, in the fear of the Lord and love of truth, proceed to examine this delicate subject fairly, freely, yet reverently and prayerfully, in the light of reason and of revelation; and just as we should examine every other point of religious faith which is a subject of doubt or disputation.

Remember that three objections are made to the doctrine of a trinity of persons in one " *Godhead*," as held in common by the mother Church and by most Protestants: (1) That it is inconsistent with itself; (2) That it is unreasonable; and (3) That it is unscriptural.

The force of the first two objections will be more readily seen by copying questions 8, 9, and 10, with the answers to each as found in the catechism from which the article was taken, and which are as follows: " Q. 8. *Are there more Gods than one?* — A. There is but one only, the living and true God. Q. 9. *How many persons are there in the Godhead?* — A. There be three persons in the Godhead, — the Father, the Son, and the Holy Ghost; and these three are one true, eternal God, the same in substance, equal in power and glory, although distinguished by their personal properties. Q. 10. *What are the personal properties of the three persons in the Godhead?* — A. It is proper to the Father to beget the Son, and to the Son to be begotten of the Father, and to the Holy Ghost to proceed from the Father and the Son from all eternity."

The proposition respecting the Trinity is a compound one, and consists of five distinct parts or affirmations, taking no notice at present of the term " *Godhead* " as used there. The first of which is that " There be three *persons* in the Godhead, — the Father, the Son, and the Holy Ghost;" the second is that "These three are one," &c.; the third is that all three of these persons are "the same in substance;" the fourth is that they are all three "equal in power and glory;" and the fifth is that they are all three "distinguished by their personal properties."

Are all of these affirmations respecting the Deity consistent with each other? I hold that they are not. According to Webster, a proposition is inconsistent with itself which contains "such opposition or disagreement as that one proposition (or affirmation) infers the negative of the other, such contrariety between things that both cannot subsist together," or "so that the truth of one proves the other to be false."

Now does not the proposition that there are "three *persons* in the Godhead" infer the negative of the other that "these three are one"? How can *three persons* be but *one person?* In any natural or literal sense such thing is impossible, — is it not? We may conceive of three or more principles or powers in Nature which may so harmonize as to co-operate as one principle or one power; but we cannot properly predicate the same *oneness* of three individual persons, — can we?

Jesus Christ frequently speaks of himself and the Father as being one in *purpose*, but he nowhere says that they are one in *person*. But where does the Saviour say that the Father himself and the Holy Ghost are one in any sense; or where does he say that the Holy Ghost is one with the Father or with himself? He nowhere says any thing like that, but much to the contrary.

And again, does not the predicate that the one is the Father of the other logically imply that the latter is the Son of the former? It most assuredly does so imply: then is not that inconsistent with the proposition that they two are one *in person?* Who will say that it is not? And it is also affirmed that the three persons in the Godhead are one; and again that they are all three "distinguished by their personal properties." Have we not here an irreconcilable inconsistency? If they have personal properties so different from one another that each may be distinguished from the other two by such personal dissimilarities, they are not one in person, are they?

We now come to our second objection to the "form of doctrine" that is usually employed to express the relations supposed to exist between the Father, Son, and Holy Ghost; and which is that it is utterly *unreasonable*. And the first logical fact to which attention is called here is, that every inconsistency which the main proposition contains as between its several parts affords conclusive evidence that the whole is unreasonable. For no inconsistent proposition is a reasonable one, — is it? And, therefore, all that has been said under the first head applies with equal force here.

The best thing that its warmest friend can truly say of the present popular theory of the Trinity (that three persons in this instance constitute but one person) is that it is a paradox; for it certainly appears to be unreasonable as a first impression, — does it not? And therefore it devolves on the advocates of that form of belief to prove that it is nevertheless reasonable and true. This they adroitly try to avoid, simply by saying that it is all right, but that it is mysterious and we cannot understand it. That is sufficiently satisfactory to the most indifferent and credulous; but there are some people who want better evidence of the safety of an old boat, and which looks so rickety, before risking their eternal all upon it. And yet we are told that we must believe all that, or we cannot be saved. How many are driven into hopeless infidelity because they cannot believe that which their own good sense condemns as false!

But to return. It is sufficient for the present purpose to show this view of a Trinity to be apparently untrue; because no proposition that appears on its face to be false can be accepted *per se* as true, — can it? And, therefore, whatever appears to be false must stand condemned as unreasonable until proof of its verity is adduced. Is not this good logic?

If the Father and Son are the same person, that *person* must be at once *his own Father and his own Son!* — must he not? Certainly it must be so. And if one is the Father of the other, of course the latter must be the Son of the former;

and then they must be different persons. Is not this conclusive?

But to be good Trinitarians, we must furthermore believe that the Father, Son, and Holy Ghost, all three, sprang into being simultaneously, each of his own energy and will; and that all three are precisely " equal in power and glory." If true, that was a wonderful event, was it not? Three Gods all bounding into life at once, and each of his own accord and unaided energy; and, which is more amazing still, all just happened to be exactly " equal in power and glory"! It certainly cannot be necessary to make any labored argument to show that such a proposition is utterly unreasonable and untrue. It is thought at least safe to say that such thing never occurred before, and will not happen again. May not any one venture to affirm that much of the past, and to prophesy to that extent for the future?

The whole of those three questions and answers were copied above chiefly for the purpose of enabling the reader, by comparing the eighth and ninth answers together, to see their inconsistency at a glance. The eighth is well sustained by the Bible, but the ninth must rest on no better foundation (originally) than priestly fancy, and in a darker age than this; although it now has the all powerful support of the bigotry and dogmatism of both priests and preachers, with but relatively few exceptions, and is backed alike by the superstitious fears of themselves and of their flocks.

The answer to the tenth question has one redeeming virtue; it is unquestionably true in point of fact (saying nothing about the propriety of so using the word "*proper*"). But the latter clause, by which we are informed that it is "*proper*" " to the Holy Ghost to *proceed from* the Father and the Son from all eternity," is decidedly damaging to the preceding answer; for if the Holy Ghost *proceeds from* the Father and the Son, he cannot be one and the same with them, — can he? Is it not unreasonable to believe that one person proceeds at the same time from two other persons, and that continually? And is not the belief that the Holy Spirit proceeds from the Father and the Son inconsistent with the idea that he has a real, distinct, personal existence? And is it not indicative of the fact that he "is the power of God and the wisdom of God"? And in fine, if the Holy Ghost (the Comforter) is one with and equal in power and glory to the Father and the Son, how is it that he is subject to the control of each of them, and in fact is sent on errands of mercy by either of them at will? (See John xiv. 26 and xvi. 7.)

CHAPTER X.

The same Subject continued. — Doctrine of Three Persons in One unscriptural. — Trinity, Triune, &c., not Bible language. —The word " Godhead " noticed. — 1 John v. 7, 8 examined. — Many other Texts cited. — The Holy Ghost a Power exercised both by the Father and the Son. — The Holy Ghost has no Name ; has never been seen, &c.

OUR third and last objection to the popular theory among Christians, that there are three persons in the Godhead, is that it is unscriptural. And having already noticed the individuality and personality of the Father and of the Son, it is now only necessary to " search the Scriptures," and learn there the relations which exist between them and the Holy Ghost, and the nature and office of the latter.

The question between the writer and Trinitarians (I repeat) is not " whether there be any Holy Ghost," but it is whether the Holy Ghost is a *person* emanating from God, or whether he is the *power* of God. And notwithstanding the way which leads to the divine truth for which we are about to go in search is a plainly marked one, yet there has been a good deal of rubbish thrown in it, which with your indulgence, my friend, I will go before and remove, so that you may have a pleasant walk from the slough of Error to the rock of Truth.

The terms *trinity, triune, trinitarian,* &c., and the word " Godhead," demand our first attention in this connection. Of the first three, and of all others like them, no other mention need be made than to remind the intelligent reader that no such terms or words as *trinity, triune,* or *trinitarian* are anywhere to be found in the Bible. All such terms and words have been invented since the apostolic age. And such enlargement of the vocabulary became necessary, because the new idea (of a trinity of persons in the Godhead) could not conveniently and fittingly have been clothed and presented to the admiring gaze of the credulous multitude with any words or forms of language known to the sacred writers.

The word "Godhead" appears to have been used by but one of the inspired penmen, and but three times by him. And I here give the three verses in which it is found, with the notes on each which were made by the authority of the American Tract Society. In Acts xvii. 29, we read: "For as much then as we are the offspring of God we ought not to think that the Godhead is like unto gold or silver or stone graven by art and man's device." *Note,* — "29. *We ought not to think;* that Jehovah is like material objects of any kind." The same apostle next used that word in this way: "For the invisible things of him from the creation of the world are clearly seen, being understood by things that are made, even his eternal power and Godhead; so that they are without excuse," &c. (Rom. i. 20). *Note,* — "20. *From the creation;* ever since the creation. *His eternal power and Godhead;* his divinity, and worthiness of being loved, adored, and obeyed. *Without excuse;* having no reason for disobeying him." And the third and last time we find it is in Col. ii. 9; there, in speaking of Jesus Christ and of his claims upon our confidence, St. Paul says: "For in him dwelleth all the fulness of the Godhead bodily." *Note,* — "9. *Godhead bodily;* God incarnate, or dwelling in human nature."

Notwithstanding the frequent use made of that term by Trinitarians, as containing something favoring their notion, it is believed that no learned advocate of that theory would be willing to affirm that the word "Godhead," as found in either of these texts, contains any evidence that the Father, the Son, and the Holy Ghost, being three persons as they agree, are "the same in substance, equal in power and glory; although distinguished by their personal properties." There certainly is nothing of the kind intimated in the above notes, as given by the high Protestant authority which made and approved them. And it is a note-worthy fact, that in the Douay (Catholic) edition of the Bible the word which reads *Godhead* in our Bible is rendered "divinity" in each of the two verses first copied above; and that although it is translated "Godhead" in Col. ii. 9, in the next verse the word *complete*, as in King James's edition, is rendered *filled*, so as to make the meaning of the whole passage clear, and showing also that, as the mother Church understands it, no reference to the doctrine of the Trinity is found there.

Dr. Malcom, in his Bible Dictionary, defines that term thus: "*Godhead* means the nature or essence of God," and cites the three texts already noticed as containing it. And Webster defines it in this way: "*Godhead*. 1. Godship; deity; divinity; divine nature or essence; *applied to the true God, and to heathen deities*. 2. A deity in person; a god or goddess." And, as it must be observed, no argument in favor of the Orthodox (?) doctrine of a trinity of persons in the *Godhead* can legitimately be drawn from the simple fact that St. Paul used that word as he did, and which has been so translated.

But should any one feel inclined to think differently, such an one is advised to read all his epistles carefully, and see whether he anywhere else said any thing from which we should infer that he entertained such opinion; and to note particularly these words of his: "There is one body and one spirit, even as ye are called in one hope of your calling; one Lord, one faith, one baptism; one God and Father of all, who is ABOVE all, and through all, and in you all" (Ep. iv. 4, 5, 6). Did he believe that the "God and Father of all, *who is above all*" (as he says), and who (by his spirit) is "through all and in you all," has any equal? And did he intend to inform his readers that the *spirit* and *Lord* (the Son), and the *God and Father*, mentioned there, are all but one and the same? If they are all three the same, how could one of the three be *above* the other two? So to *wrest* that Scripture would make the apostle directly to contradict himself! — would it not?

The authority on which Trinitarians usually and mainly rely, however, to sustain that theory is found in 1 John v. 7, 8. And it may safely be said that there is no other passage in the whole Bible, which as fairly construed affords them a shadow of evidence in support of what they call the doctrine of "the Holy (or Adorable) Trinity." It is the one to which they uniformly refer for support; and then they usually cite some other texts, all of which when examined, as it is found, either do not touch the question at all, or are on the other side.

Here is that authority: "For there are three that bear record [*in heaven, the Father, the Word, and the Holy Ghost; and these three are one. And there are three that bear witness in earth*], the spirit and the water and the blood; and these three agree in one." On this passage it may be best to remark, that we have the authority of the learned Dr. Tischendorf that the words which are included here in brackets, and printed in Italic letters, are not in either of the three old manuscript copies of the Bible, upon one or the other of which all Christians rely for a correct version of that good Book. See Tischendorf's New Testament at that place.

And it is furthermore said of the same words that there is now an old manuscript copy of the Bible, in a library at London, in which they are found *as a marginal note*. If that is their first appearance in writing, we should esteem them as of no more value than the mere opinion of the copyist. Be that as it may, if Dr. Tischendorf is right (and I have never seen or heard the correctness of his notes disputed), the words in question are but an interpolation into that passage of sacred Scripture, and in that case should not be allowed to render that mysterious which without them is plain. And as an evidence that he is right, attention is called to the circumstance that in their translation of the Bible, with notes, the American Bible Union omit precisely the same words, and make this explanatory note: "The words omitted are wanting in all ancient copies."

And yet when the only safe rule of construction is applied to the whole passage quoted, the result is found the same as if we reject the part italicized altogether: for pursuant to that rule, it must be construed so as to make it consist with the other Scriptures which relate to the same subject. And to do that we only have to interpret it as intending no more than that "these three are one," *in love, purpose*, and labor, "to seek and to save that which was lost" — our race. And that construction renders it consistent with all other passages and texts of Scripture, except that it represents the Holy Ghost as one with the Father and Son, and which we find done nowhere else in the Bible.

Let us now look into the authorities, and see whether the Scriptures teach that by the term Holy Ghost *a person*, or the teaching, warning, sustaining power, "the voice of the Lord," is intended. The Saviour says: "The sheep hear his voice; and he calleth his own sheep by name, and leadeth them out," "and the sheep follow him, for they know his voice" (John x. 3, 4). Is not the *voice* here intended the same that is referred to in Deut. iv. 30, 31? There the promise is, "When thou art in tribulation, and all these things are come upon thee, even in the latter days, if thou turn to the Lord thy God, and shalt be obedient unto *his voice* (for the Lord thy God is a merciful God), he will not forsake thee, neither destroy thee, nor forget the covenant of thy fathers," &c. And is not that the same *voice* which is mentioned in Ps. xcv. 7, 8? The Psalmist there says: "For he is our God, and we are the people of his pasture and the sheep of his hand. To-day, if ye will hear *his voice*, harden not your hearts," &c. Is not the Holy Ghost the power, "the voice," by which God calls us to himself? In calling the attention of his Hebrew brethren to that sacred admonition, St. Paul said: "Wherefore, as the Holy Ghost saith, To-day, if ye will hear *his voice*, harden not your hearts," &c. (Heb. iii. 7). Observe, he does not say that King David *saith*, but he says, "the Holy Ghost saith." Did not the apostle understand that the Holy Ghost is the teaching power, "the voice," which inspired that Psalm? He certainly so believed; for he could not otherwise have represented it as the language of the Holy Ghost.

And again, we find mention of the Spirit of God made in the following texts and in other forms. God said to Moses: "I will come down and talk with thee there, and I will take of the spirit which is upon thee, and will put it upon them" (the seventy elders), &c. (Num. xi. 17). "And the Lord came down in a cloud and spake unto him, and took of the spirit that was upon him, and put it upon the seventy elders," and " they prophesied," &c. (Num. xi. 25). And in Neh. ix. 30 we have this: " Yet many years didst thou forbear them (the wicked Jews), and testified against them by thy spirit in thy prophets." In these two places we have the idea of the same spiritual gift expressed in three different ways: first, I will " put it [the spirit] upon them;" second, he " gave it unto " [the seventy] ; and lastly it is spoken of as " thy spirit in thy prophets," or as abiding in them. Now is not the same thing intended in each of the above instances, which is elsewhere expressed by the term " gift of the Holy Ghost "?

We find the Holy Spirit mentioned in Gen. i. 2, in this way: " And the earth was without form and void; and darkness was upon the face of the deep. And the spirit of God moved upon [*brooded* or *hovered over*] the face of the waters." Here it is evident that something other than God himself was intended, as that which " moved upon the face of the waters." It is commonly understood that it was the Holy Ghost — the third *person* in the Trinity — who so moved over the waters preparatory for the work contemplated. This opinion is just half right. It unquestionably was the Holy Ghost — the almighty power and wisdom of God — which passed over the chaotic mass of matter, of which this world was about to be made, and prepared it for this use. But it is no less certain that it was not any one person who went over all the immense body of matter and so prepared it. (See Luke i. 35.)

We must come to this conclusion for two reasons: first, because it would have required more thousands of years for any one person to have gone over and prepared the materials than it did take days to make all the preliminary arrangements and complete the whole work as it was done; whereas the Almighty Creator (and who has promised to " create new heavens and a new earth ") could readily have applied his creative power all over and all through the vast mass as it then was, and in that way have prepared it instantly for this or for any other use he might have designed to make of it.

The Christian mind in our time seems to be impressed with a vague notion, if it amounts to no more, that the Holy Spirit has only been engaged in his work for the redemption of man since the ascension of the Saviour. And it is firmly believed by many that he now confines his labor of love to those only who have the gospel preached among them. Passing by, for the present, the question whether the Holy Spirit visits those to whom the gospel has not been preached, let us see whether he has not been engaged in his heavenly work to save our lost race ever since man has been on the earth. And it may be well to remark here, and by way of parenthesis, that the pronoun *he* is applied to the Holy Spirit for the same reason that it is applied to the sun.

We have already seen that St. Paul understood that King David wrote under the inspiration of the Holy Ghost. Now we will look into a few other kindred Scriptures. In Gen. vi. 3, God says: "My spirit shall not always strive with man." Must we not believe from this that his spirit did strive with man then? Did not Moses and David and Isaiah believe that the Spirit of God did strive with the people of their respective ages? Among the last words uttered by the Psalmist on earth were these: "The spirit of God spake by me, and his word was in my tongue" (2 Sam. xxiii. 2). Was it *a person*, or the power and wisdom of God, that he said "was in my tongue"?

Remember, our question relates to the personality and not to the existence of the Holy Ghost. In Isaiah lix. 21 we have this: "As for me, this is my covenant with them, saith the Lord: My spirit that is upon thee (Isaiah), and my words which I have put in thy mouth shall not depart out of thy mouth, nor out of the mouth of thy seed, nor out of the mouth of thy seed's seed, saith the Lord, from henceforth and for ever more." From the language employed here it would seem that the blessing promised — the gift of the Holy Spirit — was a present one, and which was to be enjoyed by all the family of Jacob, from Isaiah down, who "turn from transgression," as expressed in the preceding verse; and which divine promise of the Holy Spirit to *abide in them*, as elsewhere it is said, appears to have been assured to all such persons from then to the end of his work. Nearly the same promise was made, perhaps equally extensive, in Isaiah xliv. 3: "I will pour my spirit upon thy seed, and my blessing upon thine offspring." The prophecies abound with references to and promises of the Holy Spirit (but to cite all of them could benefit no one, for those already quoted are as full, clear, and comprehensible as could be desired by any one who believes them), sufficient to show that the Holy Spirit of God has been in the world, and engaged in teaching men the way to life eternal, from the earliest ages to the present time. And it may be safely said that nobody who has not been taught to believe that the Holy Ghost is *a person* — an individual spirit — would come to any other conclusion, from reading all the Old Testament writings, than that he is the power of God, the wisdom, "the voice of God," by which he teaches men of spiritual things.

Having already noticed the leading texts of New Testament Scripture, which are relied upon as furnishing evidence that the Divine Spirit is a person, the third in that trinity of persons of which those called Trinitarians hold that the Godhead, as they interpret that term, consists, — attention is now invited to another class of Scriptures, and to other Scriptural terms and forms of expression found therein, which bear on the other side of this question. The angel that visited the virgin Mary said to her, "The Holy Ghost shall come upon thee, and the *power* of the *Highest* shall overshadow thee; therefore also that holy thing which shall be born of thee shall be called the Son of God." Was it the third *person* in the Trinity, or any other *person*, that came upon and overshadowed the virgin on that occasion? or was it not the "*power* of the Highest?" See Luke i. 35, and answer these questions with due respect for the virgin mother, and proper reverence for the Son of God, my Christian reader, and you cannot err in your answers thereto.

The Saviour warned his disciples that, for his sake, they would be "brought before governors and kings," and for their encouragement said to them: "But when they deliver you up, take no thought how or what ye shall speak: for it shall be given you in that same hour what ye shall speak. For it is not ye that speak, but the spirit of your Father which speaketh in you" (Matt. x. 19, 20). And by turning to Luke xxi. 14, 15, you will find the same counsel and encouragement given them in this form: "Settle it therefore in your hearts, not to meditate before what ye shall answer. For I will give you a mouth and wisdom, which all your adversaries shall not be able to gainsay nor resist." Observe here, their speaker was to be one that was in themselves. And St. John says (1 John ii. 14) to those " who have overcome the wicked one," that " the *word of God abideth* in you;" and St. Paul speaks of " his spirit that *dwelleth* in you" (Rom. viii. 11). Now is it not evidently true that " the spirit of your Father which speaketh in you," as in Matthew, and the " mouth and wisdom," as in Luke, both refer to the same helper? And is not the " word of God [that] abideth in you," from 1 John, and " his spirit that dwelleth in you," from Romans, the same indwelling spirit and power which is intended in each of the four passages? And is not the Holy Ghost that teacher and power? It is confidently believed that no earnest seeker for truth will answer either one of the last questions above negatively.

Assuming that much, the inquiry arises, Do the expressions *in you, mouth and wisdom, abideth in you,* and *dwelleth in you,* indicate that the Holy Ghost, to which they are applied, is a person — an individual spirit? I think not. To deal frankly with such question, what could be more absurd than to affirm that any being having the qualities of individuality and personality can be in two different places at the same time? Any such proposition must savor of the absurd somewhat, as we must confess. But what should be said of the Trinitarian theory, — that the Holy Spirit is the third person in a trinity of persons (three in one), and that he is not only in two places at one time, but that he is in the heart of *every Christian all the time!* Those who *talk* that way freely admit that they cannot understand it, but insist that it is nevertheless true; and, worse than all, they teach the confiding, giddy multitude that they must believe it or, for their stubborn unbelief, they will be doomed to eternal burning in hell!

And, which is more criminal, Catholic and Protestant chiefs and leaders in matters of religion have alike, but in different ages as we have seen, procured the enactment of municipal laws providing the penalty of death for every one who should dare deny their human doctrine of " The Holy Trinity," as they term it. How many pious, truth-loving Christians have suffered death under such laws can only be known to us at the great day! Would not such fiendish cruelty seem more befitting a set of "unwashed devils," than the professed followers of the meek and lowly Jesus?

Let us notice the ensuing references to the Holy Ghost with regard to the question whether he is an individual spirit, as we are assured that God the Father and Christ the Son each is, or whether he is the power of God, our teacher, an instrumentality of the Almighty. Notice the figurative terms found in the several texts which follow: " Ye were *sealed with* that Holy Spirit of promise " (Eph. i. 13), — as we seal packages *with* a wafer or bit of wax! " He [John the Baptist] shall be *filled with* the Holy Ghost, even from his mother's womb" (Luke i. 15). "And they were all *filled with* the Holy Ghost [on the day of pentecost], and began to speak with other tongues as the spirit gave them utterance " (Acts ii. 4). The Holy Ghost acted the part of their teacher, and of one who excelled all other teachers; for he taught those unlettered fishermen instantly to speak languages of which they knew nothing before. Each one of them must have had his own instructor, or they could not have learned so much within a time so short, — could they? In the thirty-third verse of that chapter, it is said that the Divine Spirit was on that occasion "*shed forth*" by our risen Saviour. From Acts v. 3, it appears that Satan also has power to *fill the hearts* of some people with his evil spirit. Instances of persons having been *filled with* the Holy Ghost are frequently reported in the sacred writings, and in so many different forms of language that to cite others here could do no good.

Other figures are used for the same purpose. " I will *pour water upon* him that is thirsty, and floods upon the dry ground; I will *pour my spirit upon* thy seed, and my blessing upon their offering" (Isa. xliv. 3). "I will *pour out of* my spirit upon all flesh," &c. (Joel ii. 28). And see Acts ii. 17. The term *pour out,* as we pour water, is likewise used in that connection, and frequently, all through the Bible. Is that fact favorable to the idea that the Holy Spirit is *a person?*

According to King James's translation of the Bible (and that is the one uniformly cited and quoted in this work when no other is mentioned), John the Baptist said that, "He [Christ] shall baptize you *with* the Holy Ghost and *with* fire" (Matt. iii. 11). Here the Divine Spirit is analogized to, if not said to be used as, a baptismal font and to fire. And this view is still more clear as the passage is rendered both in the Douay, and in the American Bible Union, editions. The first of which gives it thus: "He *shall* baptize you *in* the Holy Ghost and fire." And the other in this way: "He *will immerse* you *in* the Holy Spirit and fire." Observe, the first of the three represents the baptism intended as administered *with,* and the last two as *in,* the good Spirit. There are also many other passages of Scripture in which similar mention is made of baptism and the Holy Ghost, but the above are deemed sufficient for present purposes.

The apostle Paul speaks of the Corinthian church as being "the epistle of Christ ministered by us, written not with ink, but *with the spirit* of the living God; not in tables of stone, but in fleshly tables of the heart" (2 Cor. iii. 3). The spirit of God certainly is the best possible *writing fluid* when the impression is to be made on the Christian's heart and read in the light of his life; but if the apostle had believed that the Holy Spirit is a person, he surely would not have employed that figure by which to have conveyed his meaning in that instance, — would he?

The Saviour promised to send his disciples another Comforter, after he should cease ministering to them in person or as a man, and who should abide with them for ever. "Even the spirit of truth, whom the world cannot receive, because it seeth him not, neither knoweth him; but ye know him, for he dwelleth *with* you and shall be *in you*" (John xiv. 17). Now is it not simply impossible that the Holy Ghost, if a person, an individual spirit, can *dwell with* and *be in* all and each of the disciples of Christ at the same time? Bear in mind that a spirit has personality and individuality as well as men and other animals have such qualities. And in 1 John iv. 13 it is written that, " Hereby know we that we dwell in him [in God] and he in us, because he hath given us *of his spirit.*" That is, he has brought us, if we are truly his children, *partially* under the influence of the Holy Spirit. It was not so with Jesus, the Christ, however; for of him it is said that, " God giveth not the spirit *by measure* unto him" (John iii. 34). Such expressions as "*of his spirit,*" and "*the spirit by measure,*" do not indicate the thought that the spirit which is so apportioned is an individual, a person, — do they? All such remarks may nevertheless be predicated of *a power* most appropriately, as all must see.

St. Paul said to his son Titus, God " saved us by the washing of regeneration and renewing of the Holy Ghost, which he *shed on us abundantly* through Jesus Christ our Saviour" (Tit. iii. 5, 6). What are we to understand by the words "renewing of the Holy Ghost"? If the Holy Ghost is a person, and the third of a holy trinity of persons, he did not need *renewing*, — did he? We certainly have no evidence that he engaged in sin and rebellion against God, as it is said that some misguided spirits (angels) under the lead of Satan did. Then do not the expressions, "washing of regeneration and renewing of the Holy Ghost," apply to fallen man? And if so, is it not thereby affirmed by implication strong that we have at some time been *clean*, and submissive to the Divine will, having no need of *washing, regeneration,* nor of a "renewing of the Holy Ghost" within us? When were we submissive to the promptings of the Holy Ghost before regeneration through the intercession of Jesus Christ? Before we arrived at the period of discretion, it cannot properly be said of us that we were submissive to either the Good or the Evil Spirit since we came into this life, — can it? But to avoid digressing too far, we must conclude that by the words "renewing of the Holy Ghost," as the apostle used them there, he intended no more than that the constraining, preventing, and saving power of God was renewed, brought into congenial action again, within them. And we should not overlook another noteworthy remark which is found in the text before us. It is likewise said there of the Holy Ghost that it was "*shed on us abundantly* through Jesus Christ our Saviour." People often *shed tears* in this world of woe; the sun *sheds* his light "abundantly;" and St. Paul furthermore says, "The love of God is *shed abroad* in our hearts by the Holy Ghost *which is given* unto us" (Rom. v. 5). "Whoso readeth, let him understand."

According to Acts x. 44, 45, while St. Peter was preaching to Cornelius, his family, and assembled friends, "the Holy Ghost *fell on all* them which heard the word," and those who went there with him were astonished, "because that on the gentiles also was *poured out* the gift of the Holy Ghost. From this Scripture we learn that during the first gospel sermon which had ever been preached to that congregation, something *fell on* every one of them, and whatever it was that fell on them was *poured out*. Now was it *a person*, or *a power*, which was so *poured out* and *fell on* that assembly? A correct answer to this question must settle the main one now under investigation. If, reader, you conclude that it was *a power* which produced such astonishment on that occasion, and desire such power, you can learn from Luke xi. 13 that God has promised to *give* that saving power to them that *ask him* for it. And from Acts viii. you may find that it is a treasure of great value, and can be had simply by asking for it; and yet that it cannot be bought with money. That is also strange, — is it not?

St. Paul exhorted his brethren, saying, "If we live in the spirit, let us walk in the spirit" (Gal. v. 25). And St. Peter informs us that, "God *anointed* Jesus of Nazareth *with* the Holy Ghost and *with* power" (Acts x. 38). In the first of these texts, we are informed that the Holy Ghost is something *in which* Christians could and should *live* and *walk;* and in the other, that God *anointed* the Saviour with the same thing, whatever it may have been. That the language of each one of the apostles last quoted is figurative will not be denied;

but when applied to the power and love of God, as each intended, the figures are both apt and beautiful. What should be said of such figurative expressions if intended to apply to any sort of *a person*, is left for the answer of some learned (?) one, who may find it necessary to wrest the Scriptures to sustain a favorite dogma of his.

That the Holy Ghost is a gift, and the crowning gift of God to those who return to his love through faith in Jesus Christ, and not a personal being, is manifest from such texts as the following: "Then said Jesus to them again, Peace be unto you; as my Father hath sent me, even so send I you. And when he had said this, he breathed on them, and saith unto them, Receive ye the Holy Ghost" (John xx. 21, 22). This was after the resurrection. "Then Peter said unto them, Repent, and be baptized every one of you in the name of Jesus Christ, for the remission of sins, and ye shall receive the *gift* of the Holy Ghost" (Acts ii. 38). That was said to the amazed, alarmed, and penitent multitude of wicked Jews, on the day of pentecost, who had crucified the Son of God. And lastly: "This only would I learn of you, Received ye the spirit by the works of the law, or by the hearing of faith?" (Gal. iii. 2.) The only comment deemed necessary, in the way of application of those Scriptures, as intimated above, is simply to call attention to what St. John says as to the relations which exist between God and those who have "put on Christ:" "If we love one another, God dwelleth in us, and his love is perfected in us. Hereby know we that we dwell in him, and he in us, because he hath given us of his spirit" (1 John iv. 12, 13).

It may be well enough, before passing from this branch of our inquiries, to say, that the *divine power* which is called indifferently "The spirit of God," "The Holy Spirit," "The Holy Ghost," &c., is one that may be and is exercised alike by the Father and the Son. The Saviour has informed us that the Father is greater than himself, and that in and of himself he can do nothing; but that all power is given unto him in heaven and in earth by the Father; and particularly, that the Father has given him power on earth to forgive and to save us from eternal death. These endowments necessarily include the power to confer the gift of the Holy Ghost upon his disciples, to abide with and dwell in them. And it is in reference to this benign work of redemption, that our Saviour has informed us that he and the Father are one. They are one in love, purpose, and power to save penitent sinners.

But as some may doubt whether the power to confer the gift of the Holy Ghost may be and in fact is exercised by both the Father and the Son, the following evidence is submitted to show that such is the case. In John xiv. 16 we find this: " And I will pray the Father, and he shall give you another Comforter, that he may abide with you for ever; even the spirit of truth," &c. And in the twenty-sixth verse of that chapter the Saviour further says: " But the Comforter, which is the Holy Ghost, whom *the Father will send* in my name, he shall teach you all things, and bring all things to your remembrance, whatsoever I have said unto you." And again the Son says: " But when the Comforter is come, whom *I will send unto you* from the Father, even the spirit of truth, which proceedeth from the Father, he shall testify of me," &c. (John xv. 26). The instance of the exercise of that power by the Son, which is recorded in John xx. 21, 22, and which has already been quoted in another connection, is conclusive proof of his power to confer that divine gift.

A remark of the Saviour, in relation to the " Comforter," appears to have been misunderstood by some : " Nevertheless, I tell you the truth. It is expedient *for you* that I go away ; for if I go not away, the Comforter will not come unto you; but if I depart, I will send him unto you " (John xvi. 7). That verse should be construed as if the third clause read thus: " For if I go not away, the Comforter will not come [from me] unto you." When so read, the truth of the remark is self-evident, and it is full of meaning and comfort. And his intention certainly was to console his disciples in their grief on account of his near departure from them, by assuring them that it was best for themselves and for the cause in which he and they were engaged, that he should return to the Father ; for he could then minister to them, teach and comfort them, as well as all other probationers on earth, more perfectly as their God and the mediator in heaven, than he could while here, living as a man, in the flesh. This, or some like construction, is necessary to reconcile that remark with the whole tenor of that conversation. For he had already told them that the *Comforter* to which he alluded " is the Holy Ghost," " even the spirit of truth ; " of the nature, office, and power of which " Comforter " he had also informed them, and which Holy Spirit was already with them, as they well knew.

It should be observed, also, that the Holy Spirit is nowhere else in the Bible called the " Comforter," except in that one conversation. And when the Saviour spoke of him as " another Comforter," he evidently intended no more than a more efficient manifestation and exercise of the *divine power* by a crucified, risen, and glorified Redeemer, than could be effected by him while here as he then was. This view is confirmed by the consideration that none of the other evangelists saw fit to notice the descriptive term " Comforter " (" Paracletus ") as there used by the Saviour, in any way. But if a new and different sort of *Comforter* had been intended, they surely would all have recorded the promise, — would they not?

The Scriptural evidences which have been given above to prove that the manifestations of Almighty power, wisdom, and grace, which is called in the Word of God the Holy Ghost, &c., is not a distinct person as the Son of God is, must impress the mind of every unbiased reader as conclusive upon that question. And the truth is, that evidence more clear and irresistible could not have been given of that sacred truth, without having said directly and positively that the spirit of God is not an individual creature of his, but a name given to certain manifestations of his power and love. And to one who would not be satisfied with any evidence short of such divine declaration, it could not be proven that " the voice " of a man is not a person distinct from himself; for the Bible nowhere says, and in so many words, that it is not, — does it?

There are several negative arguments against the personality of the Holy Ghost, and which strike the mind of the writer with much force. Wherefore, he offers a few of them to his readers for what they are worth. The first is drawn from the fact that in the agonizing prayer of Jesus Christ, just before and in full view of his betrayal, and while he made frequent mention of his then present and future disciples, and of the relations between himself and them, and of the personal relations which had previously, did then, and would thereafter exist between the Father and himself, and which runs through the whole chapter, — no reference whatever is made to the Holy Ghost. If it be true that the Holy Spirit is the third person in a holy trinity of persons, and equal in every respect with the Father and the Son, is it not amazing that, while the Saviour said so much about the Father and himself, and of his disciples too, not a word was said of the Holy Ghost? See John xvii.

And would any intelligent and conscientious man of the Trinitarian faith have written the verse which follows? "But I would have you know that the head of every man is Christ; and the head of the woman is the man; and the head of Christ is God" (1 Cor. xi. 3). In this enumeration of *heads*, no place is left for the Holy Ghost either as *a head* or *an equal*. And if the modern doctrine of the Trinity be true, the best we can say for the good old apostle who wrote that letter is that he was sadly mistaken in that important particular.

Another evidence that the Holy Ghost is not a person — an individual spirit — may legitimately be drawn from the fact that *he has no name*. The Father, the Son, and other celestial spirits have names; as Jehovah, Michael, Gabriel, &c. But who ever heard or read of any such proper name of the Holy Ghost? On the contrary, he is uniformly designated by words of description such as "the Holy Ghost," "the spirit of God," &c.

And another negative argument against the belief that the Holy Ghost is a person, as God the Father and Jesus Christ are, is to be inferred from the fact that *nobody has ever seen him;* and we have no evidence that he purposely conceals himself from our sight. We are fully informed that the great Jehovah uniformly concealed himself as in a cloud or in fire from the view of Moses and others, whenever he had occasion to speak to him or them; and that at one time he permitted Moses to take *a back view* of his person. And Daniel saw " in the night visions " the Father and Son together; and St. John also saw them together; and the Son has been seen often: yet no one up to this late age of the world, and as far as we are informed, has ever seen the Holy Ghost. Why? All who have carefully examined the authorities given in the preceding pages, must come to the same conclusion as to the reason why the Holy Spirit of God has never been seen; and it is for the all-sufficient reason that he is not a personal being, and therefore he has no body either as a man or an angel, which could be seen.

In view of all the authorities to be found in the revealed Word of God which bear upon the subject (but few comparatively of which have been noticed in these pages however), the writer has come to the same conclusion at which St. Paul arrived (but by a much shorter process in his case), and which is that there is " one God and Father of all, who is above all," &c. (Eph. iv. 5). And further, that, by the term Holy Ghost, that sovereign wisdom and power is intended by which God, knowing all things, effects all his purposes, — such as to create worlds and to govern, teach, reward, &c.; all of which he may do, either directly or by such instrumentalities as he may prefer.

I do not wish to weary the reader by belaboring this subject longer. It cannot be necessary to press the matter further; for the Scriptures are too full, clear, and plain in this regard to admit of mistake or doubt by any one who really desires to know the truth. If, however, men want to believe that there is " one true and living God *in three persons*, Father, Son, and Holy Ghost," and yet that the Son is " of *one substance* with the Father" (as expressed by Pope Pius IV.), they will believe it still, and as firmly, without evidence and against evidence and reason too, as if sustained by both. Hence it can do no good to offer argument or proof to those who " will not believe " any evidence when produced. Every one who will look into this whole matter with the care which its importance deserves, must come to the conclusion that the notion that there are three persons in one, as applied to the Deity, originated not from the Bible but in *priestcraft* alone, and that it lives on the superstitious fears of a priest-ridden people, whether they be Catholics or Protestants.

For, as we have seen, during long ages men were compelled so to believe (or say they did) on pain of death; and now to question " in any way " the Trinitarian doctrine, as held by Catholic and Protestant teachers, subjects the recusant member to all the anathemas of the former and to exclusion from most of the latter churches. Let others incline as they may, for myself I prefer the guidance of " the spirit of truth which proceeds from the Father," and of his written Word, through this dark and dreary world, rather than listen to the " fables " and follow " the commandments of men that turn from the truth."

It is easy to believe that there is one God and Father of all; that Jesus Christ is his Son and our Saviour; that they, although one in *purpose*, are as distinct *in person* as were Abraham and Isaac his son; and that by the term " Holy Ghost " that power is intended which proceeds from the Father, and teaches, warns, and encourages probationers in this life, as we are taught in the Bible.

A theory which is at once so natural, reasonable, and Scriptural as that is, could at any time have been sufficiently impressed on every Christian mind, without the infliction of temporal pains and penalties for that purpose.

CHAPTER XI.

Concerning Gods, Devils, and Angels. — "There be Gods many and Lords many." — "God of Gods." — Prophets, Apostles, and Judges called Gods. — "Sons of God." — All to become Gods or Devils. — All to be called Angels. — The lost Song.

THE fact that the Father and Son are alike called God, and that many other spirits are called gods also, deserves some attention here. We are informed by St. Paul that "there be gods many and lords many. But to us there is but one God, the Father, of whom are all things, and we *for* him; and one Lord, Jesus Christ, by whom are all things and we by him" (1 Cor. viii. 5, 6). That being true, as all Christians must admit, it becomes desirable to know who or what *creatures* he calls gods. Looking no further than to the above passage, we see that some creatures of God are called gods. For he there says that "there is but one God, the Father, of whom are all things," and "one Lord, Jesus Christ, by whom are all things," &c.; and therefore all other beings which he calls *gods* must be creatures of the Father.

Of the word lord or "lords" as used by the apostle there, I will only remark that it is one of very general application, and merely denotes a superior. Thus, Jehovah-God is called "the Lord God," and he is above all other beings. Jesus Christ is called "the Lord," and he being next in dignity and authority to the Father is superior to all else. The members of the upper house of the British Parliament are called "Lords," and hotel-keepers and others are called "landlords."

In Deut. x. 17, it is said that "The Lord your God is God of Gods." (See also Josh. xxii. 22, and Ps. cxxxvi. 2, and lxxxii. 1.) From these texts it is clear that the same idea of "gods many" was entertained by the Old Testament writers. Now were these "gods many" citizens of heaven? or were they denizens of earth? or were they to be found both in heaven and earth? From Job we learn that when "the foundations of the earth" were laid, "the morning stars sang together, and all the sons of God shouted for joy" (Job xxxviii. 4–7). Who are they that are called "morning stars," and who sang together on that interesting occasion? In Rev. xxii. 16, Jesus Christ is said to be "The bright and morning star." We must conclude, therefore, that he is the first, the brightest, the ruling star of that seraphic host who sang praises to the Father God for that goodness and mercy which were manifested by the grace in which "the foundations of the earth" were laid; and the holy angels of heaven, yet those who are not of such as are designated by the term "morning stars," are "the sons of God" who "shouted for joy." What a glorious time was that!—singing and shouting in heaven! But that happy throng are not done rejoicing on that account yet; for "there is joy in heaven *over every sinner* that repenteth."

But to return; may not all the morning stars and sons of God, who sang and shouted on that gladsome event, with propriety be called gods? That they may well be so called will hardly be denied. And there is another class of Scriptures from which it appears that quite a number of denizens of this world are likewise called gods. In Exodus xxii. 28, this command is found: "Thou shalt not revile the gods (or judges), nor curse the ruler of thy people." And in Psalms lxxxii. 6, we find this: "I have said, Ye are gods, and all of you are children of the Most High." The Saviour quoted that passage, and made the remarks which follow on that subject, namely: "Is it not written in your law, I said, Ye are gods? If he called them gods unto whom the Word of God came, and the Scripture cannot be broken, say ye of him whom the Father hath sanctified and sent into the world, Thou blasphemest, because I said I am the Son of God?" (John x. 34–36.) "The word of God came" to the prophets and apostles, and through them to us. Should we not therefore infer that the Saviour considered all the true prophets and apostles entitled to be called gods?

And again, it is said in John i. 12 that, "As many as received him [Jesus Christ], to them gave he power to become the sons of God." And St. Paul says, "As many as are led by the Spirit of God, they are the sons of God" (Rom. viii. 14). "Sons of God," that is, faithful disciples — Christians. And, as already suggested, all the sons of God may properly be called gods, just as men of superior wealth or position are called lords, — may they not?

If, then, all who "are led by the Spirit of God" may with propriety be called gods, what should they be called who "are led by the spirit of" the Devil? — Devils, of course. And, kind reader, if you will examine the whole matter in the light of revelation, you will find the truth of the case to be, that there are but two classes of eternal spirits. There is one great Creator of all whose name is Jehovah; and one Redeemer whose celestial name was Michael; and there is one arch-deceiver whose name is Satan. And all the servants of God and his Son Michael (Jesus Christ) are called gods, and all the servants of Satan are called devils; and by one or the other of these two names, all of each of the two families of spirits will be called and known during all eternity.

The term *angel* seems to have been applied indiscriminately to all the family of Jehovah, of whom we learn any thing in the Bible from the first of Genesis to the last of Revelation. Michael, who is also (and usually in the New Testament) called Christ, is called the Archangel (Jude ix. and Dan. xii. 1); Satan is spoken of as an angel (2 Cor. xi. 14), and mention is made of "the angel of the bottomless pit" (Rev. ix. 11). And all who were engaged in that "war in heaven," of which we read in Revelation xii., and on either side, are called angels. The disembodied spirit of the old prophet, who was sent back from heaven to deliver that important message to St. John, is called an angel (Rev. xix. 10, and xxii. 8, 9). We may fairly suppose that, inasmuch as the messenger who was so employed was called an angel, others who are redeemed here and return to heaven will likewise be called angels, — may we not? At the judgment of the great day, all who are not restored to the Divine favor will receive the awful sentence, "Depart from me, ye cursed, into everlasting fire prepared for the Devil and his angels"

(Matt. xxv. 41). And all that miserable host will ever remain the angels of the Devil, — will they not? So as it must be observed by every one, all eternal spirits have been, now are, and will continue to be known as and called angels, whether they ultimately go up to heaven or down to hell.

By way of digression, I beg leave to recall the reader's attention to the following summary of the above facts, and to make a suggestion in relation thereto. Observe, that those who were driven from heaven with Satan, and they who remained there, were all called angels; the redeemed here who have or may return there are and will be called angels, and those who continue in the service of Satan will also be called angels. Then we all have and will retain the same old family name. How is that, if we and they are of entirely different families?

In the warfare which is progressing here we have the same leaders as before; but Michael is now called Christ, and his soldiers are called Christians or saints, and Satan is now called the Devil, and his soldiers are called devils or sinners. Those who were cast out with Satan are held as prisoners here until the final judgment (Jude 6), and then they and we are all to be judged at the same time; and all who are then judged, except those who are redeemed in this life, will be sent to the same place of punishment, and for the same term; and that place is the same which was "prepared for the Devil and his angels." Were the sins of those who were cast out of heaven so nearly the same as are the sins of men in this life, that we and they should receive precisely the same punishment? Are we and they so similar in our nature, and our offences so much alike, that the same sort and degree of punishment is adapted to the nature and due for the crimes of each? Are we to believe that the same evil genius has been permitted to deceive, betray, and ruin two distinct families of God's children, — one in heaven, and another on earth? Is not all this wonderfully strange if true? — as it must be, if we and they are of no kin!

But we are wandering too far. A few years ago our children were taught in Sabbath-schools to sing, "I want to be an angel," and which they did with gleesome delight. Christians generally have entertained pleasurable hopes that they will sometime get to be angels; and our homespun sort of preachers, who are led more by the Holy Spirit in their investigations of the sacred oracles and reflections about the world to come than by any human creed of religion, have ever encouraged such sweet anticipations, believing them to be well founded. But while that angelic song was in the zenith of its popularity, I was pained at hearing the pastor of a church, in preaching to his flock, say and insist that we (as a race) are not, never were, and *never will be angels;* and I regretted much more, a short time thereafter, to see an editorial article in one of our best Sabbath-school magazines, in which the very same opinion was expressed and advocated.

In our present condition, they were both technically correct in saying that we are not angels now; for in our present condition we are called and known as men, women, and children. But, if we are of those who were cast out of heaven with Satan, we certainly have been angels; and all who finally make their home in hell (as we have seen) will no less certainly be angels hereafter, whether they have been of that class of spirits heretofore or not. So that there can be no doubt as to the fact that all our race will hereafter be angels, except the comparatively few who will ultimately reach the home of the angels of God. And as some who have preceded us are angels in heaven now, we have the best sort of evidence that, if we should be so fortunate as to be numbered with the redeemed of the Lord, we too will be angels, and so continue to be classed and known for ever. It is therefore undeniably true that both of the ministers alluded to, and all who so teach, are deceivers, — " false prophets."

CHAPTER XII.

The Atonement. — Scriptures relating thereto clear, when viewed as applying to Fallen Angels. — Antinomianism a device of the Devil. — A change of opinion produced, how. — Texts relied upon to sustain Predestination noticed. — Other Scriptures contrasted with them. — A certain Class elected. — Another Class rejected. — All to be judged by our Works.

THERE are but few questions, if any, in regard to which Christians differ in opinion, that would be more affected by the common approval of the theory "that the souls of men are of the fallen angels," than those which relate to the nature and extent of the atonement which was made by Jesus Christ for our race; for if we admit that we are of those who were cast out of heaven with Satan, for sin and rebellion under his deceptive influence there, and that we are brought into this life for any sort of probationary purpose, we must believe also that the grace which brought us here has provided for all who come some chance to be profited by our coming. This is the most reasonable inference from that state of facts, — is it not?

It is not likely that any fair-minded man or woman, who sincerely believes that we owe our origin to that "*war in heaven*," will ever adopt the antinomian view of the Atonement; because, to do so would be equivalent to a charge against our all-wise and omnipotent Creator and indulgent Father, not only of gross partiality in his manner of dealing with his creatures, but of mocking at the fears and laughing at the calamities of his own (once dearly beloved though now erring) children! — *unheard of mercy!* By bringing us here, and putting the Bible in our hands with all the blessed assurances found therein (such, for instance, as the following: "Come unto me, all ye that labor and are heavy-laden, and I will give you rest;" "Jesus was made a little lower than the angels, that by the grace of God he should taste death *for every man;*" "Whosoever will, let him take the water of life freely,") fond hopes of "a better day a-coming" are naturally excited in the mind of all who read the "glad tidings" contained in that good old Book. All who believe that there is a God, a Devil, a heaven, and a hell (as most people in all ages and countries have and do believe), and who have read or may read those precious promises, must at some period of life feel encouraged to hope for a personal interest in them. Is not this true? Then, if the future destiny of all was settled, unalterably fixed, before the world was made, are not all of those (if there be any) who are doomed already to eternal punishment in hell, deceived?—honestly, naturally deceived?—deceived by what they read in the Bible! And are not all such deluded men and women (if such there be) subject to be mocked, laughed at, and ridiculed by all bad men and devils who behold them and know their horrible condition?

If such be our nature and origin, and if some of us have no interest in the salvation which was purchased by Jesus Christ, and therefore have no chance to avoid a home in that place of final punishment which "was prepared for the Devil and his angels," why are we all here? Why were not those for whom no pardon was provided sent on to their eternal home at once? Or why were they not kept in Tartarus, "in chains under darkness," until the contemplated work of redemption was completed, and then sent on to their permanent home? In any view of the case, what good reason can be given why any one should have been brought into this life who must go to hell at last, and without regard to any thing that he may desire or do in this world? And certain it is, that the all-wise and omnipotent Being who created the universe has not done and will not do any thing without a good and sufficient reason for so doing. Who will deny this proposition?

Next to that of a trinity of persons in the Godhead (and which has been so fruitful of infidelity), the doctrine of absolute and unconditional election and reprobation has, as it is believed, been the means of the damnation of more men than any other scheme which the Devil has invented. That is the specific remedy which Satan administers to every sin-sick soul, and which by far too frequently proves effectual; and it is the most successful bait that he has yet procured with which to seduce the unwary Christian from the path of duty, and finally to entrap him again. When the Holy Ghost has aroused the ungodly sinner to a fearful sense of the danger to which he continually stands exposed, and of the necessity of repentance and obedience to the plain and simple requirements which the gospel makes of all who believing in Jesus Christ want to be saved by him, up comes the deceiver with his quack medicine, and whispers in his listening ear: "Be not alarmed; God will do right. You cannot save yourself: if you are one of the elect, he will save you in his own good time and way; and if you are not, you cannot reverse the decree of the Almighty," &c.

All that is literally true. God will do right: we cannot save ourselves; if of the elect we will be saved, and we cannot reverse the decrees of heaven. But it is the same sort of truth by which he deceived our mother Eve. "The serpent said unto the woman, Ye shall not surely die, for God doth know that in the day ye eat thereof, then your eyes shall be opened, and ye shall be as gods, knowing good and evil." She took his counsel, eat of the fruit, and the consequences were just what God and the serpent both had said they would be. They (Adam and Eve) became "as gods knowing good and evil;" and while it is true that she did not die a natural death, as she had previously supposed she would if she should violate the Divine command, yet she did die a spiritual death, which was incomparably worse. And so she was deceived into sin and death, not by direct falsehood, but by a perversion of the truth, — the worst sort of lying.

And just so it is that the same archfiend deceives all who come within his reach and power. When he tries to lull the fears of the penitent sinner or of the unwary Christian, he tells such an one that all the elect will certainly be saved. And so they will be: but in that he takes advantage of an error into which he had previously betrayed his victim, with respect to the *reasons* which had guided the Divine will in determining whom he would save and whom destroy; and therefore he simply perverts the truth.

The Devil does not inform his disciples here in this life that God has predestinated to eternal happiness in heaven all who believe, repent, and keep the commandments, and that he has predestinated all who do not repent to eternal punishment in hell. Of course he does not; for were he so to teach, the last one of them would abandon him and return to God without delay, would they not? But he adroitly impresses the mind of all who learn of him that: "Those of mankind that are predestinated unto life, God, before the foundation of the world was laid, according to his eternal and immutable purpose and the secret counsel and good pleasure of his will, hath chosen in Christ unto everlasting glory, out of his mere free grace and love, without any foresight of faith or good works, or perseverance in either of them, or any other thing in the creature, as conditions or causes moving him thereunto; *and all to the praise of his glorious grace.*" The counterpart of that article of faith is in these words: "The rest of mankind God was pleased, according to the unsearchable counsel of his will, whereby he extendeth or withholdeth mercy as he pleaseth, for the glory of his sovereign power over his creatures, to pass by, and to ordain them to dishonor and wrath for their sin, *to the praise of his glorious justice.*"

> Then, if a thing so strange be true,
> Man has but little here to do
> More than to serve, as best he may,
> His own desires while here we stay.
> And when the saved shall meet in heaven,
> God's praise must all up there be given;
> For those who go to that hot place
> Will not perceive "*his glorious grace!*"

Will they?

The above are the fifth and seventh sections of the third chapter of the Presbyterian confession of faith; and they are copied here from the same volume from which the article on the *Trinity* was taken for examination in a preceding chapter. There the writer paid that old, intelligent, and pious Christian family a well-merited compliment; and here he must offer them the best apology of which the truth will admit, for having introduced the above articles of their faith as a result of the false impressions which are made on the minds of men by the Devil. In the first place it is remarked, that it should be sufficient to remind my learned brethren that the Devil "deceiveth the whole world." That includes all men of every degree of capacity, whether Christian, pagan, or infidel. We are all deceived by him in some respect; we are all imperfect, and therefore liable to err. Great and good men doubtless so hold and teach; and the writer of this so believed until some thirty years old, and as firmly as he ever believed any thing. But for the change of my views as to the origin and nature of the human soul, the presumption is that I would have been of that opinion still. But on reading the Scriptures which bear upon the doctrine of election as applying to rebellious angels who were cast out of heaven with Satan, and who had been in his service long before coming into this life, my mind has undergone a radical change relative to the questions of Election and Free-will.

And if the same cause uniformly produces the same effect; and if the reader will "search the Scriptures" as earnestly and laboriously as the writer did, to learn the true origin of our race as revealed therein, — he or she will reach the same conclusion about that matter. And then we will differ no longer as to the nature and extent of the Atonement; for in that view of ourselves the whole matter is too plain, natural, and simple to admit of any doubt. It is nevertheless true, however, that the Word of God clearly teaches that all men are invited, and may *repent and be converted*, whether we interpret that Word as applicable to fallen angels, to spirits which are first brought into being when and as their bodies are, or to such as are created at the time their bodies are born; if there be such.

In the first part of the fourth chapter of this work the following belief is expressed: "That Jesus Christ brings us into this life, and by the Holy Spirit teaches, warns, and offers each and every one pardon, full and free, who may prove worthy of such grace by repentance, faith, and obedience to the Divine will." That form of faith antagonizes directly and fully the views presented by the two articles above quoted; and it is now proposed to look into some of the evidence contained in the Bible which is applicable to this issue, but in a brief way.

We will first notice the Scriptural texts which are cited in that confession, in support of the belief there expressed, and which are the following : —

"(2.) Eph. i. 4, 9, 11 : According as he hath chosen us in him, before the foundation of the world, that we should be holy and without blame before him in love. Having made known unto us the mystery of his will, according to his good pleasure, which he hath purposed in himself. In whom also we have obtained an inheritance, being predestinated according to the purpose of him who worketh all things after the counsel of his own will. — Rom. viii. 30 : Moreover, whom he did predestinate, them he also called; and whom he called, them he also justified; and whom he justified, them he also glorified. — 2 Tim. i. 9 : Who hath saved us, and called us with an holy calling ; not according to our works, but according to his purpose and grace, which was given us in Christ Jesus before the world began. — 1 Thess. v. 9 : For God hath not appointed us to wrath, but to obtain salvation by our Lord Jesus Christ. — (3) Rom. ix. 11, 13, 16 [These verses are only so cited, but they are as follows] : For the children being not yet born, neither having done any good or evil, that the purpose of God according to election might stand ; not of works, but of him that calleth. As it is written, Jacob have I loved, but Esau have I hated. So then, it is not of him that willeth, nor of him that runneth ; but of God that showeth mercy. — (4) Eph. i. 6–12 : To the praise of the glory of his grace, wherein he hath made us accepted in the Beloved ; that we should be to the praise of his glory, who first trusted in Christ."

The above are the authorities cited in support of the first

branch of the proposition now under review; and the following are those offered to sustain the other: —

"Matt. xi. 25, 26: At that time Jesus answered and said, I thank thee, O Father, Lord of heaven and earth, because thou hast hid these things from the wise and prudent, and hast revealed them unto babes. Even so, Father, for so it seemed good in thy sight. — Rom. ix. 17, 18, 21, 22: For the Scripture saith unto Pharaoh, Even for this same purpose have I raised thee up, that I might show my power in thee, and that my name might be declared throughout all the earth. Therefore hath he mercy, &c. Hath not the potter power over the clay, of the same lump to make one vessel unto honor and another unto dishonor? What if God, willing to show his wrath and to make his power known, endured with much long-suffering the vessels of wrath fitted to destruction? — 2 Tim. ii. 20: But in a great house there are not only vessels of gold and silver, but also of wood and of earth; and some to honor and some to dishonor. — Jude 4: For there are certain men crept in unawares, who were before of old ordained to this condemnation; ungodly men, turning the grace of our God into lasciviousness, and denying the only Lord God, and our Lord Jesus Christ. — 1 Pet. ii. 8: Being disobedient; whereunto also they were appointed."

That God did foreknow all things from the beginning we must admit, or reject the authority of the Bible. Then when Eden was planted, he knew what would be the final destiny of all our race. And from the Scriptures above quoted (and there are many others of similar import) we should also believe that God did elect and predestinate some of us to eternal life in heaven, and that he did likewise predestinate that all others should depart to the place "prepared for the Devil and his angels." This fundamental and fearful truth is plainly taught in God's Word; but the question before us is, On what principle, for what *reason*, did God so *elect* to save some men and women, and to reject others? Was that Divine choice made " without any foresight of faith or good works, or perseverance in either of them, or any other thing in the creature as conditions or causes moving him thereunto," as it is so affirmed that it was? Or was it made in full view of the fact that some would believe, repent, and obey "the law of the Lord," and that others would not; and with regard to the conduct, in that respect, of each one in this life? Or, more briefly, did God arbitrarily and (as we would say of men) capriciously, and without any good and sufficient *reason*, "predestinate" some certain men to a home in heaven, and to damn certain other men eternally? Or was it his purpose to try us all fairly and impartially, and to prove us; and then to save all who believe, repent, and obey, and to reject all who refuse so to do?

In the last form we have the true issue, and one that is intelligible and tangible. And the writer has "elected" to take the negative or last mentioned side of that question, and with St. Peter to insist "that God is no respecter of persons; but in every nation he that feareth him and worketh righteousness is accepted with him."

As the reader must have observed, all the authorities but two, that are cited or quoted in support of the affirmative (as we will hereafter call it) of this question, are taken from the writings of St. Paul; and the other two can have but little if any bearing upon it. We will therefore look first into some other remarks which he made in the same letters, with an occasional italicizing and parenthesis in the way of emphasis and explanation; and then offer some thoughts for the purpose of removing all appearance of conflict in what that learned and faithful apostle said therein, or elsewhere. And both for purposes of fairness and brevity we will take them as they come, in each epistle, quoted on the other side.

In the first chapter of Romans, 21–32, we have this, and more: "And even as they *did not like to retain God* in their knowledge, God gave them over to a reprobate mind, to do those things which are not convenient. Who knowing the judgment of God, that they which commit such things *are worthy of death*, not only do the same, but have pleasure in them that do them." And see the same, ii. 6–13: "God will render to every man *according to his deeds;* to them who by patient continuance *in well doing*, &c., eternal life; but unto them that are contentious and *do not obey* the truth, but obey unrighteousness, indignation and wrath. For there is no *respect of persons* with God. For not the hearers of the law are just before God, but *the doers of the law* shall be justified." Ibid., iii. 28: "Therefore we conclude that a man is justified [made just] by faith, without the deeds of the law." (A gentile is justified by means of faith in Christ, "without the deeds of the" Jewish law.) Ibid., v. 13: "For until the law, sin was in the world; but sin is not imputed where there is no law." Ibid., vi. 16: "Know ye not, that to whom *ye yield yourselves* servants to obey, his servants ye are to whom ye obey, whether of *sin* unto death, or of *obedience* unto righteousness?" (Is there no volition implied here?) Again, ibid., viii. 13: "For if ye live after the flesh, ye shall die; but if ye through the Spirit do mortify the deeds [the desires] of the body, ye shall live." (Are there no *conditions* affixed to our fate?) We are told (verse 17) that we shall be "Heirs of God, and joint heirs with Christ, *if so be* that we suffer with him."

After the passages that are quoted from Rom. ix. to sustain the affirmative of our question, St. Paul says (verse 32): "Wherefore? [Why were Jews, who follow after the ceremonial law, cut off?] Because they sought it [righteousness] not *by faith* [in Christ], but, as it were, by *the works of the law*." Ibid., x. 4–13: "For Christ is the end of the law [or put an end to that law] for righteousness to every one that believeth. Moses describeth the righteousness which is of the law. That the man which doeth those things *shall live by them*." (Were not all men saved who did *the works of the law* under the Jewish dispensation? But now it is said that) "There is no difference between the Jew and Greek; for the same Lord over all is rich unto all that call upon him [as directed in the Gospel]. For whosoever shall [so] call upon the name of the Lord shall be saved." Ibid., xi. 2: "God hath not cast away his people [the Jews] which he foreknew" (would believe, repent, &c. He foreknew everybody, did he not?). Ibid., xiv. 18: "For he that in these things [the things taught in the Gospel] serveth Christ is acceptable to God and approved of men."

The above texts, found in the letter to the Romans, are deemed sufficient to excite a suspicion in the reader's mind, if no more, that those taken from that epistle and relied upon to sustain the belief of an absolute and personal election and reprobation are misunderstood. We will now notice similar remarks which are contained in Ephesians, to show that the same is true with regard to the authorities taken from that letter, and relied upon also to sustain the same unnatural error.

On reading that epistle, we may all profit by observing and heeding the exhortation of the apostle, that: "Till we all come in [into] the unity of the faith, &c., we henceforth be no more children, tossed to and fro and carried about with every wind of doctrine, *by the sleight of men* and cunning craftiness [as by getting up so-called confessions of faith or creeds of religion], whereby they lie in wait to deceive; but, speaking *the truth in love* [we], may grow up into [a knowledge of and faith in] him in all things, which is the head, even Christ" (Eph. iv. 13–15).

In the sixth chapter of that epistle (verses 1–8), St. Paul teaches and warns thus: "Children, obey your parents in the Lord; for this is right. Honor thy father and mother, which is the first commandment *with promise*, &c. Servants, be obedient to them that are your masters, &c. With good-will doing service, as to the Lord, and not to men; knowing that whatsoever *good thing any man doeth*, the same shall he *receive of the Lord*, whether he be bond or free." Here we learn that God will reward us even for doing our duty to other people. Then if we fail to discharge a duty to him, will he reward us all the same? If not, the Divine blessings depend *somewhat* on our conduct, do they not?

In the next verse the apostle concludes that branch of his subject with the other admonition and declaration: "And, ye masters, do the same things unto them for bearing threatening; knowing that your Master also is in heaven: *neither is there respect of persons* with him" (Eph. vi. 9). And then he opens his concluding remarks in this way: "Finally, my brethren, be strong in the Lord, and in the power of his might. Put on the whole armor of God, that *ye may be able to stand* against the wiles of the Devil," &c. What! is there danger that any Christian may fall?

Much reliance appears to be placed upon 2 Tim. ii. 20, in support of the affirmative. All the comment deemed necessary to a just appreciation of that evidence is simply to give that verse, with the preceding and following ones. And here they are (verse 19): "Nevertheless, the foundation of God standeth sure, having this seal: The Lord knoweth them that are his. And let every one that nameth the name of Christ depart from iniquity." Verse 20: "But in a great house there are not only vessels of gold and of silver, but also of wood and of earth; and some to honor and some to dishonor." Verse 21: "If a man therefore *purge himself* from these [the things just enumerated], he shall be a vessel unto honor, sanctified and meet for the Master's use, and prepared unto every good work." But if a man *purge not himself* "from these," how then? Does this look as if God chose his elect "without any foresight of faith or good works"? But of this more anon. And to prevent suspicion that there is something wrong about the allegation that St. Paul speaks of a man "purging himself" from sin, attention is here called to the last verse of that chapter, which is this: "And that they may *recover themselves* out of the snare of the Devil, who are taken captive by him at his will" (2 Tim. ii. 26).

While it is true that the apostle to the gentiles wrote more of the foreknowledge of God, and of election and predestination, than any other inspired writer, he also taught that salvation is purely of grace through faith, and dependent upon obedience to the requirements of the gospel, as fully and clearly as did any other evangelist or apostle. He was a bold writer, one whose sole purpose was to serve God faithfully, and to benefit his fellow-men. And with that view, he wrote so that such as sincerely desire to learn the truth can do so, but regardless of the mere caviler's objections, as well as of the craftiness of those who wish to pervert what he said for selfish purposes, "men of corrupt minds and destitute of the truth, supposing that *gain is godliness,*" as he describes them. But of the duty to observe and do the works appointed in the gospel (as well as of the danger of falling away), and of the value of such works, he wrote perhaps as fully and strongly as did any other.

In addition to the remarks of that apostle which have been referred to already, he said of good works and their value as conditions to salvation: "Wherefore, my beloved, as ye have always obeyed, not as in my presence only, but now much more in my absence, *work out your own salvation with fear and trembling;* for it is God which worketh in you both to will and to do of his own good pleasure" (Phil. ii. 12, 13). Again: "For *in doing this*, thou shalt both *save thyself* and *them that hear thee*" (1 Tim. iv. 16). "Wherefore, let him that thinketh he standeth take heed *lest he fall*" (1 Cor. 10–12). "Stand fast, therefore, in the liberty wherewith Christ hath made us free, and be not *entangled again* with the yoke of bondage" (Gal. v. 1). "For *if we sin wilfully*, after that we have received the knowledge of the truth, there remaineth no more sacrifice for sins, but *a certain* fearful looking for of judgment and *fiery indignation,*" &c. (Heb. x. 26, 27).

The exhortation, "*work out your own salvation* with fear and trembling," if considered alone, would be found as strong as any, if not the strongest, authority contained in the Bible in favor of the idea that we can save ourselves by our own individual efforts; but, when read in connection with other language of his, and with an honest desire to get his views on that subject, we find that St. Paul (as well as every other inspired writer) has taught us to believe (as stated above) that salvation is purely of grace through the instrumentality of faith, — not *in virtue* of our works, — and that God is not partial in his dealings with us, but that the same grace is freely offered to all, and upon the same conditions, namely, of our repentance and obedience to the law of Christ as contained in his gospel.

There is a reason why the apostle to the gentiles wrote more fully than did other inspired writers of the foreknowledge of God, of his providences, the time when and how the grace by which we may be saved was given us, &c. And it is simply because he was more fully instructed in such secret things than was any other of his time, or (as far as we are informed) who had lived here before him. This is manifest from the fact that he wrote more about such things, more fully, and in a manner very different from the other sacred writers. But as to his superior information concerning secret things we are not left to conjecture alone. In 2 Cor. xii. 1–9, we have a key to all that mystery. We are there informed that "a man" was "caught up to the third heaven," — "into paradise, and heard unspeakable words, which it is not lawful for a man to utter." That "man" unquestionably was the apostle himself, as it is clearly intimated there.

As the writer has had occasion to show in a former work,[1] the apostle Paul was fully informed of the nature and origin of our race, and why and for what purpose we are here; and he indirectly or casually made frequent allusion to such "secret things" in his epistles, and about in the same way, or rather to the same extent, that the Saviour spoke of them himself. And notwithstanding all the inspired writers knew that we have lived somewhere and in some way before we came into this life, yet we have abundant evidence that they — or at least that the immediate disciples of Christ — did not know to what class or family of pre-existent spirits we belong.

That it was well understood, however, by the disciples of Jesus Christ, that both he and they had lived before, will sufficiently appear from the two conversations between him and them which follow: "Whom do men say that I the Son of man am? And they said, Some say that thou art John the Baptist; some Elias; and others Jeremias, or one of the prophets" (Matt. xvi. 13, 14). All appear to have known that Christ had lived before. "And as Jesus passed by, he saw a man which was blind from his birth. And his disciples asked him, saying, Master, who *did* sin, *this man* or his parents, that he was *born blind?*" To which question Jesus Christ answered, in substance, that it was not on account of

---

[1] War in Heaven, chap. xii.

his nor of his parents' sins that the man was born blind; but that he should have that opportunity to make known his miraculous power. He did not, however, say that the blind man could not have sinned before he was born into this life, as the disciples evidently thought that he might have done. If those who were learning wisdom of Jesus had been in error on a matter of that importance, would he not have corrected them? See John ix. 1–3. And at another time the Saviour said to certain unbelieving Jews: "Ye are *from* beneath; I am *from* above. I speak that which *I have seen* with my Father; and ye do that which *ye have seen* with your father. Ye are of your father, the Devil," &c. (John viii. 23, 38, 44). So it appears that the Redeemer and the redeemed all come from somewhere else into this world, and that this is merely a common meeting-place, and not the pristine home of any of us.

And that just before the crucifixion the disciples did not know what family or class of spirits they were of, we have the best sort of evidence. For when some Samaritans refused to entertain our Saviour and his disciples, James and John asked leave to "command fire to come down from heaven and consume them, even as Elias did;" but Jesus "turned and rebuked them, and said, *Ye know not what manner of spirit ye are of*" (Luke ix. 51–55). But, as we learn in Revelation, one of them (St. John) was thereafter fully informed in regard to that matter; and which had hitherto "been kept secret from the foundation of the world."

CHAPTER XIII.

The same Subject continued. — How to reconcile all Scriptures touching Election. — For whom Christ died. — A Class and not Individuals elected. — Texts relied upon by Antinomians noticed. — Who are the Elect. — The Central Bible-Truth. — "Top-not come down." — The case of Jacob and Esau. — St. Paul and Pharaoh. — Temporary blindness. — The Potter and his Clay. — Origin of Election-dogma. — Injurious effects thereof, &c.

IF we construe all that St. Paul said (and which has been cited in the preceding pages, first in support of the affirmative, and last of the negative side of our question) as applicable to new creatures, we involve him in such inconsistency as cannot be reconciled. But if we read all his writings as relating to such as have lived and sinned before coming into this present life, we will find no discrepancy whatever in all we have of his writing. And the same is true of all the other sacred Scriptures.

Take for illustration the two passages that follow: "For the Scripture saith unto Pharoah, Even for this same purpose have I raised thee up, that I might show my power in thee," &c. (Rom. ix. 17). And this: "Jesus was made a little lower than the angels, that by the grace of God he should taste death *for every man*" (Heb. ii. 9). Did Jesus "taste death for" Pharaoh? Here appears to be a contradiction. But if we understand the writer of each text as having believed that Pharaoh was one of the most wicked, hardened, and impenitent sinners that was cast out of heaven with Satan, the difficulty all vanishes into nothing; for in that view we would construe what is said about raising Pharaoh up for a specific purpose as meaning that God, knowing his evil nature, raised him up from his imprisonment in Tartarus, and put him upon the Egyptian throne, for the purpose of inflicting the proper chastisement on that wicked people for their cruel treatment of the Israelites, through him as their stubborn and ungodly king. And that most assuredly is the true and the only satisfactory solution of the problem. The declaration that Jesus should "taste death for every man" is a positive one; and the only question which can properly be made upon it is one of credibility: Is that Scripture true? If it stood alone, and were inconsistent with other passages, that question might with propriety be made. But that glorious affirmation is not only consistent with every other fact that is taught in the Bible, but it finds support in every other remark which can be found in God's Word on that sacred subject, when rightly understood; and it is equally consistent with our best views of natural reason and of divine justice.

The argument that is offered against that precious gospel truth is not only sophistical in itself, but it finds no countenance in the Scriptures, save such as palpable perversion and the most violent wresting can afford it. And yet it is held and insisted that if Christ died for all men, then all must be saved, or he died in vain as to the lost. But a sufficient reply could be made to that assumption, simply by saying that he did not die to save any particular individual, but to provide for the salvation of all who come to him penitent for sin as a class. His invitation is: "Come unto me, *all ye* that labor and are heavy laden, and I will give you rest."

It cost the Redeemer no more time, labor, nor suffering to make provision for all who are called than it would have cost him to provide only for those who do come and are saved by him,—the elect few. And yet by providing for all who would come to him, and inviting all to come who will,—as he did and does,—he cuts off all just ground of complaint on the part of those who neglect or refuse the proffered pardon and salvation. And at the same time he manifests the divine sympathy and tender mercy for all our race, and proves that "God is no respecter of persons, but in every nation he that feareth him and *worketh righteousness* is accepted of him."

Let us now see whether there is any conflict between the texts cited on the opposing sides of our question, or whether there is any evidence contained in the Scriptures cited on the part of the affirmation that God made his election of some to eternal life, and of others to death, regardless of what any one may desire or do while in this life.

The first authority introduced by them consists of Eph. i. 4, 9, 11, which severally read as follows: "4. According as he hath chosen us in him, before the foundation of the world, that we should be holy and without blame before him in love." Observe, first, that this epistle was addressed "to the *saints* which are at Ephesus, and the *faithful* in Christ Jesus," some of whom were Jews and others gentiles. That verse informs us that Jesus Christ and all of our race were in being before the world was made, — does it not? Of course it does; for it says that the Father "hath chosen us [Christians] in him [Christ] before the foundation of the world," &c.; and that could not have been done if he and we were not then in being, could it? But nothing is there said as to whether that choice was made with or without reference to what God foreknew we would do while here.

Their next authority is this: "9. Having made known unto us the mystery of his will, according to his good pleasure which he hath purposed in himself." This does not in any way touch our question.

Lastly, we have this: "11. In whom also we have obtained an inheritance, being predestinated according to the purpose of him who worketh all things after the counsel of his own will." Here we learn that there was some sort of predestination concerning us, yet we find no intimation that there was the least partiality exercised against any one, in selecting those destined to be saved or to be *passed by*.

Then comes the following: "Moreover, whom he did predestinate, them he also called; and whom he called, them he also justified; and whom he justified, them he also glorified" (Rom. viii. 30). This letter was addressed to Christians also, thus: "To all that be in Rome, *beloved of God*, called to be *saints*," — of whom some were Jews and some Romans; heathens, as considered by the former. In this verse it is not stated that none but those who were to be *glorified* were called; and if we construe it as intending to say that they were predestinated to eternal life, without regard to any foresight of faith or obedience on their part, we make the apostle contradict what he had already said in that letter about God being no respecter of persons, — that he will render *to every man* " according to his deeds," &c.

To get the meaning of that verse we must first read the preceding one. Then we have substantially this: " For whom [God] did foreknow [would repent, &c.], he also did predestinate," &c.; " whom he did predestinate, them he also called," &c. When the apostle wrote that chapter, he evidently had in his mind's eye the great purpose which moved the " Father of spirits " to the creation of this world and the redemption of the penitent lost. He foreknew who would and who would not repent, with the privilege intended to be offered in this life, although the offer was to be made to all alike; and, therefore, those whom he foresaw would repent were and are the beneficiary objects in all this glorious work, — the " elect of God." Hence St. Paul says: " For whom he did foreknow, he also did predestinate *to be conformed to the image of his Son*, that he [the Son] might be the first *born* among many brethren " (that is, their Prince, Lord, and Saviour); and having many who, as his brethren, should be joint heirs with him to his kingdom of heavenly glory. And it is not alone true that all whom he foreknew would repent are *called;* but, as St. Paul elsewhere says, God not only calls but he commands " *all men everywhere to repent*, because he hath appointed a day in the which he will judge the world in righteousness," &c. (Acts xvii. 30, 31). And those who obey the call, and yield themselves perseveringly to the friendly influence of the Holy Spirit, are they who are sanctified and saved; while all who reject the call and persistently refuse to obey the divine command, — " repent," &c., — are they whom God has predetermined " *to pass by*." And this is, in substance, the convergent point, the central truth, the golden text, in which all the divine teachings meet and harmonize.

Next to Rom. viii. 30, we are offered this: " Who hath saved us, and called us with an holy calling, not according to our works, but according to his own purpose and grace, which was given us in Christ Jesus before the world began" (2 Tim. i. 9). The meaning of this verse does seem too plain to admit of doubt, to any one who has read the twelfth chapter of Revelation. If we believe that the grace by which we have been or are to be saved "was given us" "before the world began," as this Scripture says it was, we must believe also that we were then subjects of God's mercy, and capable of receiving that precious gift; neither of which could have been the case if we were not in existence at that time, — is not this true? Then, whether we are of the fallen angels, or are newly created spirits, that grace which brought us here, "and called us with an holy calling" (to repentance and faith) after we came into this life, could not have been "according to our works," but must have been "according to his own purpose and grace." For if we are of those who were cast out of heaven with Satan for our sins, such grace, then, was "not according to our works," was it? And if we are new creatures, and were never in being before, we could not have done any sort of work prior to our birth, could we?

But we have not the least intimation that God does not offer that grace to every one who comes into the world, nor that he made his election without reference to any foresight on his part of what any of us would do or desire while here, — have we? "For God hath not *appointed us to wrath*, but to obtain salvation by our Lord Jesus Christ" (1 Thess. 5, 9). The last remark above applies as well to this verse as to the preceding one; and, therefore, with no more than the emphasis given the words "appointed us to death," we will pass on.

We now come to the ingeniously patched-up and extraordinary bit of revelation (?) which was prepared in the most approved style of the art of *creed-making* from St. Paul's epistle to the Romans, — "*Top-not come down!*" Here it is: "(For the children being not yet born, neither having done any good or evil, that the purpose of God according to election might stand; not of works, but of him that calleth). As it is written, Jacob have I loved, but Esau have I hated. So then it is not of him that willeth, nor of him that runneth, but of God that showeth mercy. Therefore hath he mercy on whom he will have mercy, and whom he will he hardeneth" (Rom. ix. 11, 13, 16, 18).

Observe, first, that the above scraps are all taken from the same letter in which the following is found, a part which has been already, but not so fully, cited above: "Who [God] will render to every man *according to his deeds;* to them who by patient continuance *in well-doing* seek for glory and honor and immortality, eternal life; but unto them that are contentious, and *do not obey the truth,* but obey unrighteousness, indignation and wrath, tribulation and anguish, upon every soul of man that *doeth evil,* of the Jew first, and also of the gentile; but glory, honor, and peace to every man that *worketh good,* to the Jew first, and also to the gentile; for there is no *respect of persons* with God. For as many as have sinned without law shall also perish without law; and as many as have sinned in the law shall be judged by the law: (For not the *hearers* of the law are just before God, but the *doers* of the law shall be justified. For when the gentiles, which have not the law, do by nature the things contained in the law, these, having not the law, are a law unto themselves; which show the work of the law *written in their hearts,* their conscience also bearing witness, and their thoughts the meanwhile accusing or else excusing one another). In the day when God shall judge the secrets of men by Jesus Christ, according to my gospel [that is, the gospel which he preached]" (Rom. ii. 6-16).

The preceding remarks are not made up of garbled extracts; but they are copied here just as found in that letter, but *italicised* by myself. And these, with his other and similar remarks, to be found in the first part of that epistle, should be considered as introductory to and explanatory of what he was preparing to say of the foreknowledge and eternal purposes of God concerning our race.

There is something wrong in this matter, as all must see; for the apostle is evidently misrepresented by one or the other party, or he is utterly inconsistent with himself in what he there wrote. But the fault is not to be traced to St. Paul: he knew whereof he wrote. And to every capable man and woman who will read, compare, and study not only all of that letter but all that we have from that inspired penman, as intended by him to instruct pre-existent spirits, while here on probation, in the way that leads to eternal life, and also of the other way which ends in death, — by every one who so reads, I say, it will be found that all he wrote is at once perfectly consistent with itself, and plain and easy to understand. And it will furthermore be found, by all who so read, that it was likewise a leading desire on the part of the apostle at the same time to declare and defend the undying mercy and uniform justice of God in his dealings with all his rational creatures.

A little further on we find these words: "But now the righteousness of God *without the law* is manifested, being witnessed by the law and the prophets; even the righteousness of God which is by faith of Jesus Christ unto all, and upon all them that believe; for *there is no difference*, for *all have sinned* and come short of the glory of God; being justified freely by his grace, through the redemption that is in Christ Jesus, whom God hath set forth [fore-ordained] to be a propitiation through faith in his blood, to declare his righteousness for the remission of sins *that are past*, through the forbearance of God: to declare, I say, at this time, his righteousness; that he might be just, and the justifier of him which believeth in Jesus" (Rom. iii. 21-26).

Note his words: "There is *no difference;*" "all *have sinned;*" "for the remission of sins that *are past.*" What meaneth such language? "Sin is the transgression of the law;" "where no law is, there is no transgression." If in this life we have our first chance to sin, why is it said "there *is no difference,* all *have sinned,*" and that the propitiation was made "for the remission of sins that *are passed?*" Would any man who had due respect for the truth, and who believed that this is our first *real life,* have said that I — or you, reader —" *have sinned*" near two thousand years before we were born? Would he?

In that case, what law had or could we as individuals have transgressed? Was there a law in force at the time of the temptation and fall in Eden, that the children — all descendants *ad infinitum* — should be held accountable for the sins of their parents? If there was such law, it has not been revealed to us; but it has been "kept secret from the foundation of the world." Certain it is that Ezekiel never heard of it: see the eighteenth chapter of his prophecy. Yet it is said (not by the Bible however) that our God will hold you and me, and all others of our day, to account for the sin of the *father of our flesh* in Eden, so far as to punish every one of us eternally in hell for it, who does not severally seek and find pardon for that sin while in this life! Must not the judgment of intelligent and so-called educated ministers of the gospel be fearfully perverted, who so hold "and teach men so"? Can such an one feel that he is honoring our benign Creator in so representing him to his rational creatures? But these are merely side-bar remarks; let us return to the matter before us.

It would be sufficient for present purposes to say that there is no evidence contained in any of the above passages, as taken from the ninth of Romans, that the *election* therein spoken of was made " without any foresight of faith, or of good works, or perseverance in either of them, or any other thing in the creature as considerations or causes moving him [God] thereunto," as so held by the opposite party. But the case of Jacob and Esau, which is there relied upon to prove that God " is a respecter of persons " without regard to their conduct, proves clearly that the Divine choice, in their case at least, was made with a full knowledge of the two men; for it is there said that "the children being not yet born," had not (of course as men) "done any good or evil." And it also proves that God "worketh all things after the counsel of his own will," and in such way as always to have " the right man in the right place "; and yet so as to do no injustice to any one, but on the contrary to deal mercifully with all. The very fact that God manifested no partiality for Jacob (whom he had evidently chosen as his instrument by which to effect a very important purpose), but offered that boon to Esau in causing him to be the first-born, proves that he does work all things in his own way, and that his uniformly is the best way.

In that instance, Esau — the unsuccessful brother — had no cause of complaint on account of Jacob having been made the happy head of God's favored nation; for he gave him the legal right of primogeniture, but Esau "despised his birthright," and sold it to Jacob for a mess of pottage: and that he did at home, in his father's house, where there could have been no danger of starvation, nor of serious suffering for food. But he preferred the gratification of his sensual desire for one dish of that "savory pottage," *right then*, to the glorious heritage which God had proffered him! Many such men have lived in all ages of the world, and now live, as the judgment will doubtless prove.

After Esau had sold his birthright so freely though foolishly to his brother, and confirmed the title *with an oath*, he tried to defraud Jacob out of all the benefit of that right by procuring from their old, blind, and dying father the blessing which appertained to it; and, as it appears from the sacred history of that extraordinary family, he certainly would have succeeded in doing so, but for an ingenious artifice of their mother. She interfered — as in such cases mothers will — to protect her youngest and most deserving son in the enjoyment of that right which he esteemed so highly, but which Esau had "*despised*," and so ungratefully trifled away. In his after life, Jacob proved to be a devoutly pious man, a worthy successor to Abraham and Isaac in godliness, and fit to be called a patriarch of God's chosen people. Esau, on the other hand, became the father of the Edomites, whose once fair and fertile land now lies a dismal wilderness, under the righteous curse of God for the wickedness of that nation.

The scheme which God had devised for our probation required that two sons should be born to Isaac, and that they should be as different in their natures as were Jacob and Esau. One he wanted to become the head of the Israelites, and the other to head the Edomites. And well knowing the moral proclivities of each, "before the foundation of the world," they two were chosen; and no doubt with a full knowledge of precisely what each one of them would do in this life. In this view we can readily see what was intended by the remark, " Jacob have I loved, but Esau have I hated," — and whether made before their birth or after their death. It was the faith and obedience of Jacob that God loved, and the unbelief and wickedness of Esau that God hated; all of which he clearly foresaw from the beginning. Christians ought not to believe, *nor to teach*, that God *hates* any of his own creatures *without regard to their conduct*, — should they?

The preceding is believed to be a sufficient reply to the argument sought to be drawn from the texts now under consideration, and which were offered as evidence to prove that the eternal future of all men was unconditionally fixed and settled before we were born. But it is due alike to the memory of St. Paul and to the glorious cause of gospel truth, that another and equally satisfactory reply be made to that argument. By turning to that chapter it will be found that the verse immediately succeeding that in which reference is made to what God said to Rebecca before her children were born, is this: " It was said to her, The elder shall serve the younger," — but which is there omitted, and the verse next below it is given, so as to represent the apostle as saying that God said to Rebecca, before her children were born, " As it is written, Jacob have I loved, but Esau have I hated." This last remark was not made to Rebecca at all (so far as the record shows), but it was made to Malachi, the last of the Old Testament prophets, and some thirteen hundred years (as it is generally believed) after both Jacob and Esau were dead, and all their works as men had passed before the all-seeing eye of an unerring Judge (see Gen. xxv. 23, and Mal. i. 2, 3). In relation to this matter I will at present only further say, that we have in this case a fair example of the manner in which human creeds of religion are hatched and fostered.

In the case of Jacob and Esau we are furnished with a beautiful illustration of the manner in which God orders his providences, so as to effect all his benevolent purposes concerning our sin-smitten race; and by which means he so manages as to deal kindly and impartially with all up to the time of repentance (by all who will repent), and throughout our several lives to deal with equal liberality and impartiality with all the penitent as a class, and with all the impenitent as another class: so that when we all meet at the judgment, and are all judged, and rewarded or punished, *every man according to his works*, there can be no complaint even by those who are finally lost. And furthermore, so that, as it will then appear to all, the mere fact that God foreknew from the beginning precisely who would repent and be converted, and who would not; and the other fact that he did elect to eternal life all who would repent and keep the commandments, and determine to reject all who would not do so, — can work no injustice to or hardship upon any one; for, as far as we are concerned, the case of each one of us will then stand just as it would have stood if God had known no more of the result of our probation than we knew about that, on the day of our birth into this world. And a third fact — that before regeneration none of us can know whether we are of those who are to be saved or not — fully counterbalances and neutralizes the effect of the other two facts (as to the foreknowledge of God, and who will and who will not accept salvation); for our conduct cannot be affected in any way by a Divine foreknowledge of things to come, but of which events we are totally ignorant.

The sixteenth verse of that chapter is next presented: "So then it is not of him that willeth, nor of him that runneth, but of God that showeth mercy." This needs no explanation; for it is not pretended by the writer that we can save ourselves, either by a mere act of the will nor by our own good works; but it is purely of divine grace that any of us are saved.

And lastly we have this: "Therefore hath he mercy on whom he will have mercy, and whom he will he hardeneth." This presents two questions: first, on whom is God pleased to have mercy? and last, who or what class of people is it that "*he hardeneth?*" Let that sainted apostle answer both of these questions for himself. In the preceding part of that epistle we have his answer to our first inquiry, where he says that God "will render *to every man* according to his deeds," &c., — Rom. ii. 6-16, which is fully copied above. Is it not amazing and equally painful that so great and good a man as St. Paul was, and who was so careful to explain his views so fully and clearly on all practical questions, as if possible to avoid all danger of misconception by any earnest inquirer for truth, should have been so wofully misunderstood? He frequently refers to this subject, as he evidently esteemed it one of the first magnitude; and in divers places and different forms he labored to make himself understood, as to the offices of faith and works, by all who regard the truth. But inasmuch as the above extract from that one letter must be sufficient to satisfy all who want to know who or what class of people St. Paul has taught us to believe that God has predestinated to eternal life, we will pass on.

Now let us see, on the other hand, who or what class of men it is said that God "*hardeneth.*" In the very first of Romans we are informed that some people do not "*like to retain* the knowledge of God in their hearts," and that he gives such "over to a reprobate mind," &c. Does God harden such? Let us see. In 2 Thess. ii. 10, 11, 12, we learn that some "perish" "because they received not *the love of the truth,* that they *might* be saved. And *for this cause* God shall send them *strong delusion,* that they should *believe a lie;* that they all might be damned who *believed* not the truth, but had *pleasure* in unrighteousness." From this it appears that some persons, after having been brought to a knowledge of the truth, the manner of life we must live if we would be saved, love not that way of living; but take "pleasure in unrighteousness," — prefer to walk the broad way that leads to death; "and for this cause" God sends them "strong delusion," &c. Are they not hardened, "their conscience seared [as] with a hot iron" (1 Tim. iv. 1, 2)? And is not that done for a sufficient *cause?* Here we may learn whom it is that God "*hardeneth,*" and why they are hardened; and that those who *love not the truth* after having been brought to a knowledge of it (converted?), but who still take pleasure in sin (*little sins,* of course!), are they who are *hardened;* and it is done on that account. They are gone!

But in the abundance of caution let us hear the apostle further about that hardening process, and see whose fault it is that any are hardened. In Heb. iii. 12–15, we find solemn warnings like the following: "Take heed, brethren, lest there be in any of you an evil heart of unbelief, in departing from the living God. But exhort one another daily, while it is called to-day; lest any of you be *hardened* through the deceitfulness of sin. For we are made partakers of Christ, *if we hold the beginning of our confidence steadfast unto the end;* while it is said, To-day, if ye will hear his voice, *harden not your hearts,*" &c. Hence we learn that *through* " an evil heart of unbelief," and the "deceitfulness of sin," we may be hardened; and we are exhorted not to harden our own hearts. Therefore we should conclude that whether it is said that we harden our own hearts, or that God hardens us, the same thing is intended; and that in either case, if we are hardened at all, it is because we do not love the way of truth, but take pleasure in sin.

Hear what the wise king says on this subject. In Prov. xxviii. 14, xxix. 1, we find the following: "He that *hardeneth his heart* shall fall into mischief;" again, "He that, being often reproved, *hardeneth his neck,* shall suddenly be destroyed, and that without remedy." Solomon's view of the matter most assuredly was that, if a man's *heart* or his *neck* be hardened (which are but different forms of expressing the same condition), such hardening is his own fault, and therefore he is appropriately punished for it. And the case of the Egyptian king fully sustains him in his opinion. For Pharaoh was "often [and awfully] reproved;" yet his heart, naturally hard, became harder still, as the Divine reproofs were repeated and intensified, and certain it is that he was suddenly "destroyed and that without remedy." And upon Pharaoh's case it may well be remarked further, that if the fault were not his, the punishment would not have been inflicted upon him as it was, — would it?

Mention is made both in the Old and New Testament Scriptures, and often, of men becoming "*hardened*," "*stiff-necked*," "blinded," &c.; and in some instances it is done in such way as to leave the impression on the reader's mind that God had caused them to become so "hard-hearted," &c., and in others that they had "hardened" their own hearts, &c. In Isaiah xlv. 6, 7, we find a key to the whole matter. God has there said: "I am the Lord, and there is none else; I form the light, and create darkness; I make peace and create evil; I the Lord do all these things." So we see that God has taken to himself the responsibility of all that is done in heaven, earth, and hell. And, bearing this fact in mind, we find no difficulty in reconciling all that the Scriptures say about the hardening of hearts, &c., not only with one another, but with all that is said therein of the power, wisdom, omnipresence, goodness, and mercy of God. For, being the source of all power, God must of course *do* or *permit* all that is done; and consequently it may properly be said of every thing that is done, that (in some sense) "this is the Lord's doing," although it may appear "marvellous in our eyes." To harmonize the Scriptures, if the thing done be an evil act, we must believe that God merely *permitted* the evil spirit — the enemy of God and man, Satan — to do it.

Men often become hardened, blinded, tempted, to do evil, &c. But in such cases we have the following caution and instruction: "Let no man say, when he is tempted, I am tempted of God; for God cannot be tempted with evil, *neither tempteth he any man;* but every man is tempted, when he is drawn away of his own lusts and enticed." "Every good gift and every perfect gift is from above, and cometh down from the Father of Lights, with whom is no variableness, neither shadow of turning" (James i. 13, 14. 17).

The blindness, hardness of heart, temptations to evil, &c., to which we are here subjected, all tend to lead us away from the narrow path that leads to life, and expose us to eternal death, and therefore must be classed with the evils of this life; and hence we should consider them as the doings of the enemy, and as such strive to avoid them. For we are reliably informed that "The Lord is not slack concerning his promise, as some men count slackness; but is long-suffering to us-ward, not willing that any should perish, but that all should come to repentance." Again, and from the same: "Of a truth, I perceive that God is no respecter of persons; but in every nation he that feareth him, and worketh righteousness, is accepted with him" (Acts x. 34, 35). And, lastly, let us again hear St. Paul, who was represented at Westminster as the apostle of fatalism; though dead he still lives, and says: "But we see Jesus, who was made a little lower than the angels for the suffering of death, crowned with glory and honor; that he, by the grace of God, should taste death for every man" (Heb. ii. 9). And the gainsaying world is challenged to show that he (Paul) ever wrote a line which is not perfectly consistent with the last verse quoted from him.

There are, however, certain facts, and particularly some circumstances connected with the remarkable history of St. Paul, and some remarks made by him, which favor the belief that for special reasons God sometimes does, of his sovereign will, but partially and temporarily, blind the eyes and harden the hearts of men. The devotional nature of the apostle to the gentiles, his capacity to judge of men and things, his ardent love of truth and self-denying fidelity to her cause, as understood by him at the time, — when considered in connection with his opportunities to learn of the Messiahship of Jesus Christ, — all conspire to prove that his eyes were purposely blinded, and the truth withheld from him, to prevent his earlier conversion. For that, good and weighty reasons are now manifest to all who have made themselves acquainted with Bible history. God had special use for just such a man as he was; "and in very deed for this cause" God "raised [him] up," as he did Pharaoh to the place for which the latter was as well adapted as St. Paul was for his office. Each of these extraordinary men exactly filled an important place, which God in his economy had need of a man to fill; and just at the time and place where each was wanted, then and there he was found. And the most reasonable presumption is that both were benefited in some way by the employment to which they were respectively assigned, — one in this and the other in the glory world.

The remarks of St. Paul to which allusion was last above made are recorded in the eleventh chapter of Romans. He there says, among other things of like import, that: "Blindness [or hardness] in part is happened to Israel, until the fulness of the gentiles be come in; and so all Israel shall be saved," &c. Note, he does not say that blindness is happened to the *Jews*, "in part," or altogether; nor does he say that *all Jews* shall be saved; but it was *Israel* that was in part (some of them) blinded, and it is *Israel* that he said should all be saved. By the term "Israel" he evidently intended such of the Jews as were ultimately brought to faith, repentance, and salvation in heaven, and who now constitute a part of the "Israel of God," — just as do such gentiles as were converted and saved. Many of those who were so blinded were, as we may reasonably believe, brought to light on the day of Pentecost, soon after the crucifixion. If no special means had been employed to hinder or delay the faith of devout Jews who were then in Jerusalem, and many of whom had witnessed or been informed of the miracles wrought by Christ, could he have been crucified there? Failing in that, he could not have fulfilled the mission on which he came, and the prophecies concerning him. And such temporary blindness on the part of such as he knew would believe and repent, and whom he fully intended to save *on that account*, could have proved of but little injury to them; and it is more likely that it was made a means of their enhanced and eternal joy in heaven. Hence the divine prayer, "Father, forgive them; for they *know not* what they do."

Attention is now invited to Rom. ix. 21: "Hath not the potter power over the clay, of the same lump to make one vessel unto honor and another unto dishonor?" Of all the perversions and wrestings of Scripture which have yet been attempted to bolster up unreasonable, unscriptural, and soul-destroying human creeds of religion, few if any excel in reckless mendacity the ungodly use which is made of this text. One who has sufficient regard for revealed truth to induce him to read the preceding part of that letter, if no more, cannot fail to detect the sophistry which is perpetrated in the use that is made of it. For the construction that is put upon it in that confession (and in others of that sort) is in direct conflict with all the hope-inspiring and love-giving instructions which are contained in that same letter; and also with such assurances as the following: "As they *did not like* to retain God in their knowledge, God gave them up to a reprobate mind," &c. (i. 28); "Who [God] will render to *every man* according to his deeds" (ii. 6); to them that continue in well doing, &c., "eternal life," but unto them that do not obey the truth, but obey unrighteousness, "indignation and wrath," &c. (ii. 7, 8). Read the whole letter, and compare all its parts the one with the other, and you cannot fail to see the glaring injustice done its author.

That epistle, as already observed, was addressed to all Christians then in Rome, some of whom before their conversion were Jews, and others gentiles. A leading purpose of the apostle appears to have been to declare the loving-kindness and universal goodness of God toward all men; and at the same time to impress on the mind of his readers a true sense of his omnipotence, and of the equal but unyielding justice, always tempered with mercy, which he does and will render to all. Wholesome wooings and warnings are likewise given therein, alike to all classes both of Jews and gentiles.

The thought contained in the verse before us seems to have been taken from Isaiah lxiv. 8: "But now, O Lord, thou art our Father; we are the clay and thou our potter; and we all are the work of thy hand." The prophet and the apostle both fully recognize the unlimited power of God, and call attention to it not as a terror, but a source of comfort and encouragement, assuring us that he is not only willing but fully able to deliver and to save all who confide in and obey him. And each of them illustrates his conception of the Divine power over men by analogizing it to that which a potter has over his clay. The analogy is appropriate. But neither one of them seems to think, nor to fear, that because

God has as much power over his rational creatures (men and angels) as a potter has over his wares, that he will send nine-tenths of us, more or less, to hell (without regard to what any of us may do or desire), and simply because He could do it! There is nothing in the language there used, either by Isaiah or Paul, which could, without violence to every established rule of construction, be construed as meaning that God will save a chosen few, and commit all others to hell, there to burn for ever, without regard to our conduct, "*and all to the praise of his glorious grace!*" — is there?

There is one view of the matter, and but one, in which we can conceive of the reason why any one ever so understood that Scripture; and that is to be found in the hypothesis that those who so construe it believe that God derives his *chief pleasure* from witnessing *the miseries* of his creatures! If there is any other solution of the problem, what is it? If that opinion as to the nature of our Creator were true, then we could understand how the preservation of any one from the common purpose of our creation is to "the praise of his glorious grace;" and how the salvation of each man (or angel) so spared, and therefore of the highly favored few, will for ever stand as so many monuments "to the praise of his glorious grace." For if such were the nature of the omnipotent Creator of the universe, and had he consulted his own preference alone, he would have had the gratification (!) of seeing all his rational creatures writhe and scream and burn in the flames of torment for ever, but for the amazing "grace" (as it would have been in that case) which was extended to those who are spared that horrid doom.

But where is the professing Christian who will admit that he believes the God who made us is capable of enjoying such fiendish pleasure? If you are not willing to confess that you entertain that sort of opinion of your Maker, my predestinarian friend, let me beg you, for God's sake, to pause and review the evidence upon which your faith is based, and reflect, as for eternity, upon the legitimate tendencies of your teaching; for that such is the logical sequence of your doctrine of unconditional Election and Reprobation is palpable to every unprejudiced mind.

If you are right in saying that "some men and angels are predestinated unto everlasting life, and others foreordained to everlasting death," without regard to any foresight of faith, " or any other thing in the creature as conditions or *causes* moving him [God] thereunto" (as it is affirmed in the third chapter of that confession); and if God has unlimited power over his creatures, and foreknew what would be the final destiny of each and every one when he made us (as he certainly has and did), — then the conclusion is irresistible that he made each one for the purpose, and with the desire and intention, that we should each fill the place here that we do fill, and occupy the eternal home that we will occupy. Is not this true? And hence, if God made us at all, — as it is agreed that he did, — he made all who will ultimately find their home in hell for the express purpose of sending them adrift, with "the Devil and his angels," down to the depths of that burning abyss! — did he not?

If that be the case, is there not some mistake in regard to the unfriendly relations which are supposed to exist between God and the Devil? Nothing is more clear than that, if but comparatively few of our race are to be saved, as all who trust in the Bible (Universalists only excepted) believe is and will be the case; and if all but the elect few of the innumerable hosts of eternal spirits which have lived here, died and gone to that bad world, from the creation up to the present time — all who are now here, and all who may come after us — were made expressly for the Devil (and he appears anxious to get all he can of us), — the indications are strong that God is aiding and assisting Satan in his efforts to people his dominions, as none but a friend will aid and assist another.

My Christian friend, if you will examine your favorite doctrine of Election and Reprobation carefully, you will find that it is far more complimentary to the Devil than it is to our Creator. Because it represents our merciful God as having unconditionally appointed and unalterably confirmed the eternal destiny of all men (and of angels too!) "before the foundation of the world," and the Devil as merely, and as with lamb-like innocence, accepting those whom God sees fit to give him! And in that way all the responsibility of causing the damnation of all who will finally be lost is adroitly made to rest upon our Maker; and the Devil, and all wicked and ungodly angels and men, are in that way fully relieved from all just cause of complaint in the matter! Is there any way of escape from this conclusion? I think there is not. And therefore we are bound to believe that dogma to have been an ingenious device of the Devil; and that his purpose therein was to dishonor God, and thereby to alienate the affections of his intelligent creatures from him; and so to deceive men, put them off their guard, and cheat them out of all the benefit which they could and otherwise would have realized from the atonement of Jesus Christ.

Abundant and conclusive reasons could be given for believing that the predestinarian creed of faith, as hitherto held and taught, is an invention of Satan; but it cannot be necessary to notice here but a few of them, each of which however will be found hard to answer, should any advocate of that theory assume such task. The first is, because "that form of doctrine" was not derived from the Word of God, and cannot be sustained by that Word, as has already been shown. Second, because, if the Devil is entitled to the credit for shrewdness which the Bible gives him, he is capable of perpetrating just such tricks upon the more confiding class of people. And, lastly, because that belief can do the cause of Jesus Christ no possible good, while it is of incalculable service to Satan. Each party, being fully competent to produce his own creed of faith, the logical conclusion is that every creed is the production of that party whose purpose it best serves.

And with the hope that the indulgent reader will pardon the further digression, and while the subject of creed-making is before us, I will further remark, that if God has never made but one creed of faith for his people (and we have no knowledge of any other), and if all the others have proved more valuable to the enemy than to him (as it is insisted that they have), then the same course of reasoning will bring us to the conclusion that the Devil is the author of all our creeds of religion *but one*,— will it not? In this view of the matter, would it not be better for each one of us to compare all our creeds with one another (the one found in the Bible included), and then select from the mass the one that looks most like God's work, and adopt *that one* for our guide through this wilderness of sin, and then reject all the others?

There remains but one other passage of Scripture to which it is thought worth while to call attention in this connection; and it is this: "At that time Jesus answered and said, I thank thee, O Father, Lord of heaven and earth, because thou hast hid these things from the wise and prudent, and hast revealed them unto babes. Even so Father, for so it seemed good in thy sight" (Matt. xi. 25, 26). To one of the uninitiated, it might and doubtless would prove a puzzle to determine what bearing this text has on the doctrine of Election, or why it is given as one favoring the predestinarian belief; but having been educated in that faith, and long held with that party, as before stated, the writer well understands the reason why it was put there, and the use which is made of it.

For it is the prevailing opinion with predestinarians that there is a Divine mystery concealed in that faith, — a sort of family secret; that none can fully comprehend the mystery, nor will any accept that belief, but those to whom it is specially revealed by the Holy Spirit. Hence the stubborn persistence with which those who embrace that faith cling to it. That text was therefore adduced to remind the "elect" of the high and peculiarly favorable estimation in which *they* are held by the Saviour; and they are taught to believe that they are the "babes" unto whom God was pleased to reveal "these things," and to rejoice that they are "hid" from the "wise and prudent," and reserved alone for their own dear selves! Here we see the imprint of the cloven foot, as distinctly as it was made in Eden. There as here the pride, vanity, and selfishness of our nature were successfully invoked to the deceiver's aid; and, which is still worse in this instance, the prejudices which the poor and ignorant so generally entertain against the rich, educated, or otherwise more successful in the race of life are likewise brought to the deceiver's help. That is done simply by treating the words "wise and prudent" as equivalent to *wise and learned, or great.*

On reading the context from which that text was taken, it will be found that the Saviour intended, by the use made of the term "babes," to remind his disciples of the all important fact that child-like faith and humility are necessary to salvation, and of which and on other occasions he frequently informed them; as, for instance, when he said, "Suffer little children to come unto me, and forbid them not, for of such is the kingdom of God;" again, "Except ye be converted and become as a little child, ye shall not enter into the kingdom of heaven." Little children are earnest, simple, and confiding, ready to hear and believe just what their parents tell them, and to rely upon what they say. And so must our relations become toward our Father and his Christ, or we cannot "enter the kingdom of heaven." There is neither mystery nor election concealed in or taught by that text, except that sort of election which the Bible everywhere teaches; namely, that all who will become and continue as little children *before God* will be saved, and that those who will not so become and continue must be lost. That is all of it.

With those who become fully imbued with the doctrine of absolute, unconditional, and certain election and reprobation, that is cherished as beyond comparison the dearest item of their faith. And they not unfrequently get offended with those who attempt to reason with them against it. This is particularly true of the bigoted and ignorant, whether they profess to be Christians or not. That is a natural result from the quiet of mind and ease of conscience which it affords them. And it may be the case that many who are far gone in the slough of infidelity, but whose minds are not fully at rest on that fearful subject, find some sweet relief from disquieting fears that there may be a God and a future life, in the fact that many learned and good people who believe the Bible hold and teach that nothing we can do in this life will in the least affect our future condition. And relying upon that delusion as an additional chance for future safety, they live the life that pleases them most.

In many instances, Christians of that faith bring themselves fully to believe that any other view of the atonement is dishonoring to God. They insist that God's law is immutable, and therefore the salvation or reprobation of every one must have been unconditionally fixed and settled from the beginning. And, moreover, they hold that if the scheme of redemption requires us to do any of the work necessary to secure our salvation, God is thereby deprived of his glory to that extent. And in this instance, so far as the immutability of God's law is concerned, they are as usual about half right. For God's law is unchangeable; but the question is, what is that law? Is it that A shall be saved, and that B shall be lost? Or is it that all who believe, repent, and keep the commandments shall be saved, and that all who refuse so to do shall be damned? It is most assuredly true that God's law is an unchangeable rule of action, and in all cases; but it is that rule (or system of rules rather) by which he has determined fairly and sufficiently to try, prove, judge, and reward or punish every one of us by and according to our works. Is there any thing wrong in that?

It may have been and doubtless was necessary that God should "try them that dwell upon the earth" in some such way, with a view to our fitness or unfitness for pardon; and for the twofold purpose of justifying himself before his steadfast and holy angels, in restoring any of us to the Divine favor and sacred presence, and to their society; and at the same time to satisfy those who will finally be lost that no partiality had been shown, nor favoritism practised, for the redeemed or against them; but that all had a fair trial, and equally liberal offer of pardon, and that their horrid doom is attributable *alone* to their own persistence in evil doing. Was it not this desire on the part of our indulgent Father to justify himself before his holy angels ("that he might be [considered] just, and the justifier of him which believeth in Jesus"), which St. Paul had on his mind when he wrote the third chapter of Romans? Read that whole chapter.

But to return. As long as the ultra predestinarian stands firmly on his faith, he feels entirely safe as to the future; for it is a part (and the worst part) of that system of belief, that the grace is given to none but the elect fully to comprehend the mystery therein contained, nor to embrace that which many insist is " *the faith* which was once delivered unto the saints"! And, in that way, the mere fact that one so believes affords sufficient evidence for him or her that he or she is one of the elect, the highly favored few; and that God will, at his own good time and in his own way, call and qualify him or her for a happy home in heaven. The warning to all is, "Be not wise in your own conceits;" yet many an ungodly sinner there finds a ready and effectual panacea for all the wounds which the Holy Spirit may inflict upon his torpid soul. And, as there need be no doubt, many on that account are ultimately given up to "believe a lie" (what lie?), that they all may be damned who loved not the truth, "but had pleasure in unrighteousness." Oh, wretched delusion! bane of the Devil! feeder of hell!

It is not pretended, however, that all who hold the Calvinistic faith are on their way to Satan's home. Far from it! For, as already remarked, good men are deceived in such matters as well as bad ones. None of us are entirely free from the insinuating and deceptive approaches of the enemy, while here as men. And it is furthermore true, as I confidently believe, that many of all classes of people, even ministers of the gospel, and who are not only pious and faithful Christians, but some who are considered by themselves and others too as being able and learned divines, so hold and teach.

The difficulty with such teachers is that they have given too much time and labor to the study of their sectarian text-books, and have devoted too little of either to the earnest, unbiassed, and prayerful search of the sacred oracles for divine truth. And should these pages pass under the eye of such an one, he is affectionately requested and respectfully urged by a friend to read 1 Cor. iii. 8–15 inclusive; and then to go back, and in all seriousness do that which should have been his first and chief not to say his sole work, when preparing for the solemn duties incident to his "high calling."

CHAPTER XIV.

Perseverance of the Saints. — Apostasy. — A free Fight. — The unpardonable Sin. — Of Heathen. — Infants, how saved.

THE doctrines of the "perseverance of the saints," and of the possibility of one who has been regenerated apostatizing, — falling away and being ultimately lost, — are inseparably connected with those of "election" and the freedom of the will. And these questions are as much affected by the preliminary one, "What is man?" as are any others. And when the several texts of Scripture on which disputants, who favor election, &c., are considered as having been applied by the sacred writers to pre-existent spirits (as was evidently intended by them), all doubt in regard to these questions will likewise vanish from the candid mind, as the darkness of night recedes before the golden rays of the rising sun.

It is not thought best, therefore, to treat of these points at any considerable length, in a merely suggestive work like this. For if we are fallen angels, and are brought here for the purpose of trying and proving us, with a view to restoring all who may prove worthy of that grace to the Divine favor, and of sending all others on to that place which was "prepared for the devil and his angels," — the term of probation must last with this life, if no unpardonable sin be committed earlier. "And if the tree fall toward the south, or toward the north, in the place where the tree falleth, there it shall be."

In that view of our nature and of the cause of our being here, we must believe that this life is a warfare; that there are but two contending armies; that we are all necessarily and continually engaged in the war, on one side or the other; and that it is *a free fight*, one in which every one is at liberty to take choice of sides, and to fight under the banner of Jesus Christ, or of Satan, whichever each may like the best.

We bring our depraved nature with us into this life, however, and therefore we grow up and mature in the service of Satan, unless we repent and go over to the other side before our majority. That any one may do, with the Divine aid, after reaching the age of discretion. But all who join the army of the Lord must do so under the terms prescribed; namely, that they agree to continue with him during life, and strictly to obey the rules and regulations provided for the government of his soldiers. That service being purely voluntary, however, no one is required to remain in the army of Jesus Christ any longer than he is satisfied and may desire to stay with him; but each has the privilege to leave his service at any time, and return to his old comrades at pleasure.

But all who have been accepted into the army of Jesus Christ are warned (Gal. vi. 7–9) that they " Be not deceived; *God is not mocked;* for whatsoever a man soweth, that shall he also reap. For he that soweth to the flesh, shall of the flesh reap corruption; but he that soweth to the Spirit, shall of the Spirit reap life everlasting. And let us not be weary in well doing; for in due season we shall reap, if we faint not." (But *if we faint*, how will it be with us then?) So we see that, although God is very kind and indulgent toward our sinful race, there is a point beyond which if we go we cannot return. " God is not mocked," as he would be if we were indulged in a whimsical desire to change sides as often as the moon changes her phases.

" And the Lord said, My Spirit shall not always strive with man." How can that be true, if we are allowed to abandon the cause of Christ at will, go over to the army of the enemy at pleasure, and yet the Holy Spirit should pursue, entreat, and bring us back? We are subject to the temptations of the Devil as long as we continue in this life. But St. Paul assures us (1 Cor. x. 13) that God will not suffer us to be tempted above that *we are able to bear*. And hence we must " watch and be sober." St. Peter exhorted his hearers: " Save yourselves from this untoward generation" (Acts ii. 40). Then we have something to do. For we have no promise of more than one probation, one regeneration, one redemption.

We will now notice the leading texts upon which the belief is founded that there is no danger of one who has been truly converted to God, — "*born again,*" — apostatizing and being finally lost. Inasmuch as nothing like an argument of this question will be attempted here, and no more will be offered than a few suggestive thoughts as we pass over the several passages of Scripture, the suggestions intended will be made in most cases by adding such words — as each text is copied below — as may be deemed necessary to indicate the true meaning of each when read by itself; and such words will be included in brackets and printed in italic letters, so as to designate them clearly from the words used by the translators to give the meaning of the original writings. This the translators frequently did themselves, but sometimes omitted, as is well known to all well-informed readers.

And here are the authorities: 1 Phil. i. 6, " Being confident of this very thing, that he which hath begun a good work in you, will perform it until the day of Jesus Christ [*if you prove 'faithful unto death'*]." John x. 28, 29, " And I give unto them [*unto whom?*] eternal life; and they [*who?*] shall never perish, neither shall any *man* pluck them out of my hand [*of course not*]. My Father, which gave them me, is greater than all [*is he?*]; and no man is able to pluck them out of my Father's hand." No Christian will doubt that; and both of these passages are not only very encouraging, but easy to understand. Next we find this, from Rom. viii. 38, 39 : " For I am persuaded, that neither death, nor life, nor angels [*evil spirits*], nor principalities [*of Satan*], nor powers [*of men nor devils*], nor things present, nor things to come, nor height, nor depth, nor any other [*evil*] creature, shall be able to separate us from the love of God [*or God's love*], which is [*given us*] in Christ Jesus our Lord." In that the apostle intended to comfort his readers, by giving them the most positive assurance that God will prove faithful to all who love and obey him; and that no adverse power would *be able* to separate them from his loving kindness as long as they continued steadfast in their devotions to him. And to get his true meaning, it is only necessary to add to the last verse above quoted the three little words, *against our will.* In his immediately preceding remarks, the apostle had asked these questions: "If God be for us, who can be [*prevail*] against us?" and "Who shall separate us from the love of Christ?" In these questions, the idea of some intervening power between us and our God is clearly intimated, is it not? It is not said that we cannot separate ourselves from the love of God; nor did he say that " *an evil heart of unbelief* " would not " *be able* to separate [any one] from the love of God," did he?

That such is the proper construction of that Scripture is too clear to admit of doubt. For to construe it as do the advocates of unconditional perseverance of all who are called, or who enter the service of God, would render absolutely nugatory all such remarks of the same inspired writer as the following: "But Christ as a Son over his own house; whose house are we, if we hold fast the confidence and the rejoicing of the hope firm unto the end." Why is the "if" there? "Take heed, brethren, lest there be in any of you an evil heart of unbelief, in departing from the living God." Did not the apostle think there was danger of such "departing"? "But exhort one another daily, while it is called to-day; lest any of you be hardened through the deceitfulness of sin. For we are made partakers of Christ [or with him] if we hold the beginning of our confidence steadfast unto the end" (Heb. iii. 6, 12-14). Remember that all this counsel and warning was given to and for the benefit of Christians. Where is the necessity of any thing of that sort, if Christians may not apostatize?

But again, the apostle says: "I keep under my body [control my evil nature], and bring it into subjection; lest that by any means, when I have preached to others, I myself should be a cast-away" (1 Cor. ix. 27). Did St. Paul think it impossible that he might fall away, and be lost? "Wherefore, let him that thinketh he standeth take heed lest he fall" (1 Cor. x. 12). Did he not only believe that there is danger of apostasy, but that some deceive themselves upon that subject? "Let us labor, therefore, to enter into that rest, *lest any man fall* after the same example of unbelief" (Heb. iv.

11). "Therefore, my beloved brethren, be ye steadfast, immovable, always abounding in the *work* of the Lord" (1 Cor. xv. 58). "And let us not be weary in *well-doing*, for in due season we shall reap, *if we faint not*" (Gal. vi. 9). "Whatsoever good thing *any man doeth*, the same shall he receive of the Lord" (Eph. vi. 8). Did the apostle intend to deceive us? Who will say that he did?

The above are comparatively but a few of the evidences which St. Paul has left us of his belief in regard to the danger of Christians falling away from the love and service of God, and going back to the service of the Devil; but they are considered sufficient for present purposes. On that question, as well as on the kindred one of absolute election of certain persons and reprobation of others, there can be no necessity for doing more than to present his (St. Paul's) position correctly before the Christian world; for when we look into the teaching of the Saviour as recorded, and of every other sacred writer who has touched the subject, we find him and all of them too clear to admit of doubt. And they all concur fully with St. Paul on these points, as well as upon every thing else that is revealed in the Bible.

As elsewhere remarked, the apostle to the gentiles wrote with a full knowledge of our origin and nature. He also duly appreciated the wisdom, power, and goodness of God "to usward." And in his efforts to impress upon his readers a true sense of that wisdom, power, and goodness, and the success of all the Divine plans and dealings with all his rational creatures, and to do that without using "words which it is not [was not] lawful for a man to utter,"—he, in the language of St. Peter, said "some things hard to be understood, which they that are unlearned and *unstable* wrest, as they do also the other Scriptures, unto their own destruction."

It appears that Peter was well aware of the fact that Paul was more fully informed in relation to "the mystery which was kept secret since the world began," than were any other of the apostles at that time. See 2 Pet. iii. 15, 16; Rom. xvi. 25, and 2 Cor. xii. 1-7.

For the purpose of removing any lingering doubt which

may afflict the reader's mind as to whether a Christian may apostatize, we will now look into what is said by the Saviour (and by others) about the unpardonable sin. He has said that "All manner of sin and blasphemy shall be forgiven unto men; but the blasphemy against the Holy Ghost shall not be forgiven unto men" (Matt. xii. 31; Mark iii. 28, 29; Luke xii. 10). What is that unpardonable sin? St. John says: "If any man see his brother sin a sin which is not unto death, he shall ask, and he shall give him life for them that sin not unto death. There is a sin unto death; I do not say that he shall pray for it [or for one who commits that sin]." Again, what is that "sin unto death"? Let us first see what St. Paul has said in regard to it. He says: "It is impossible for those who were once enlightened, and have tasted of the heavenly gift, and were made partakers of the Holy Ghost, and have tasted the good word of God, and the powers of the world to come, if they shall fall away, to renew them again unto repentance; seeing they crucify to themselves the Son of God afresh, and put him to an open shame." "For if we sin wilfully, after that we have received the knowledge of the truth, there remaineth no more sacrifice for sins, but a certain fearful looking for of judgment and fiery indignation, which shall devour the adversaries" (Heb. vi. 4–6, and x. 26, 27). We will next hear St. Peter on this fearful subject. He says of those "cursed children, which *have forsaken* the right way," &c., "If, after they have escaped the pollutions of the world through the knowledge of the Lord and Saviour Jesus Christ, they are again entangled therein, and overcome, the latter end is worse with them than the beginning. For it had been better for them not to have known the way of righteousness, than, after they have known it, to turn from the holy commandment delivered unto them. But it is happened unto them according to the true proverb, The dog is turned to his own vomit again; and the sow that was washed, to her wallowing in the mire" (2 Pet. ii. 14, 15, 20–22).

The Saviour calls *the sin*, which shall not be forgiven, "blasphemy against the Holy Ghost." But what is that "blasphemy"? From what is said of it in the gospel, as I understand it, the unpardonable sin consists of such words or acts as manifest a disregard for, contempt of, contumely, and, hence, "blasphemy against the Holy Ghost." And that blasphemous contumacy is evinced by disrespect for, trifling with, resistance of, and persistent refusal to obey the timely warnings and affectionate invitations which the Holy Spirit of Almighty God freely gives to fallen man. "My spirit shall not always *strive* with man," saith Jehovah!

It is the office of the Holy Ghost to teach, woo, and warn probationers in this life; to teach them the way that leads to heaven; to woo and entreat them to walk in that way, and to warn them of death, the judgment, and of an eternal hell. "How shall we escape if we neglect so great salvation?" To say nothing of the blasphemy which is involved in a stubborn, contumacious refusal to accept the kind invitations of the Holy Spirit, we cannot escape the doom of the damned, if we so much as *neglect* the proffered salvation!

"The Holy Ghost saith, To-day, if ye will hear his voice, harden not your hearts." If when the sinner hears the voice of the Holy Ghost saying, "return unto the Lord, and he will have mercy upon you," &c., he hardens his heart and refuses to obey the Divine call, does he not sin? And should he persistently neglect or refuse to obey his invitations, and to heed his warnings until the Holy Spirit shall cease longer to *strive with him*, will that sin (of rejecting all such invitations) ever be forgiven him? Certainly it will not. Here, then, we find one sin that will not be forgiven. And we have the assurance of the Saviour that every sin of man may be forgiven but one. Then we must conclude that we have found the unpardonable sin.

Stephen, the martyr, in his defence, chided his murderers thus: "Ye stiff-necked and uncircumcised in heart and ears, ye do always resist the Holy Ghost; as your fathers did, so do ye." For their resistance of the Holy Ghost many of their fathers fell in the wilderness. Many of them, as it is most likely, had grown up, lived on, and died resisting the friendly admonitions of the Holy Ghost. Is not the sin of resisting the saving influence of the Holy Spirit the most common as well as the most damning sin known to this life? And would it not be safe to say that all men will be saved who have not persisted in that one sin? I think that the only sin that kills the soul; but "he that being often reproved hardeneth his neck, shall be suddenly destroyed, and that without remedy!"

The main question now before us is, however, Can one who has been converted — become a Christian — commit that or any other sin: fall away and finally be lost? And the proper answer to that question depends largely (but not entirely) upon another; namely, Are those who have been so "born again" included in the above quotations from the apostles Paul and Peter? The remarks of the former are applied by him to those who have been "enlightened," "have tasted the heavenly gift," "were made partakers of the Holy Ghost," "have tasted the good word of God," &c. And St. Peter calls those intended by him "cursed children, which have forsaken the right way, and are gone astray," &c.; and says that if "after they have escaped the pollutions of the world through the knowledge of our Lord and Saviour Jesus Christ, they are again entangled therein, and overcome, the latter end is worse with them than the beginning," &c.

Do not each of these apostles describe those whom we now call Christians with unerring certainty? All people are divided into two classes, — servants of God and servants of the Devil. Now ask yourself, reader, do the descriptive words used by them apply better to Christians, or to unwashed sinners? But it may be asked, If they intended their remarks to apply to Christians, why did they not make short work of it, and call them "Christians" at once? To that question the answer is easy and satisfactory: the term "Christian" was not in common use in their time. It appears to have been used but *three times* in the whole Bible: but once by St. Peter; and never, in all his writings, did St. Paul (as it is believed) use it at all. If they had called those of whom they were writing "Christians," but few readers of their age would have known what they meant by that term. They had no name nor word by which to identify such persons as are now called Christians. And therefore when they had occasion to speak or write about Christians, the best they could do was to describe them.

And did they not describe them well, in the language employed by each of them, in the above quotations? Or do the words of description there found apply better to hard-hearted, impenitent sinners? Every reader is left to answer these questions in his own way.

The testimony of the apostles Paul and Peter, which has already been offered, is thought sufficient to satisfy all (who really want to know the truth of this matter, and who believe the witnesses) that a Christian may go back to the service of Satan, *provided* they think their remarks as quoted above were intended to apply to such persons, — of which but little if any room for doubt is left. We will therefore pursue this branch of our subject no further than to call attention to a few other passages of Scripture, to show that they did intend to be understood as speaking of such persons as are now called Christians.

In warning his disciples of the hardships, besetments, and temptations which awaited them, the Saviour also encouraged them by saying, "But he that endureth to the end shall be saved" (Matt. x. 22; see also ibid. xxiv. 12, 13, and xxv. 31–46, as to conditional salvation). Of course his disciples understood him as saying that their eternal future depended upon their perseverance in well-doing while here (see further, Luke xii. 41–48). Jesus likewise said to them: "If thou wilt enter into life, keep the commandments" (Matt. xix. 17). Would the Redeemer have given his disciples such warnings if their salvation had already been fixed and settled beyond all doubt or contingency?

When speaking of the mission of Jesus Christ, and of the opposition which he met, St. John says: "But as many as received him, to them gave he power to become the sons of God" (John i. 12). "*Power to become the sons of God*" is that which, as St. John says, the Saviour gives to those who come to him; but it is nowhere said in the Bible that Christ will drag any one back to heaven *nolens volens!* Nothing like that, there, is there? Nor is it said or taught in that holy Book that our Saviour will retain any man in his service longer than he wants to continue with him. Those who would become or continue his people must be "a willing people."

In the case of Jezebel, we have an instance in which a sinner had passed the day of grace while yet in life and a wretched evil doer (Rev. ii. 20-22). And, a little further on, Christians have one of the sweetest promises which is anywhere given them; but it is coupled with sufficient and better warning, that they are not out of danger as long as they remain within the tempter's reach. There the Son says: "He that overcometh, the same shall be clothed in white raiment; and I will not blot his name out of the book of life, but I will confess his name before my Father, and before his angels. He that hath an ear, let him hear," &c. (Rev. iii. 5, 6).

Moses on an alarming occasion besought the Lord to pardon the sin of "his chosen people." "And the Lord said unto Moses, Whosoever has sinned against me [meaning in that matter], him will I *blot out* of my book" (Exod. xxxii. 30-33). So we see that some names have been or will be blotted out of God's book. Are they not names that were written in "the book of life"? Such must be the case; for there is but one other set of books to be used at the Judgment as far as we are informed, and the dead are to be "judged out of those things which are written in *the books*, according to their works" (Rev. xx. 12). And who would object to having his name "blotted out of" those books?

With one other quotation from St. Paul we will pass on; which is this: "Finally, my brethren [Christians, were they not?], be strong in the Lord, and in the power of his might. Put on the whole armor of God, *that ye may be able to stand* against the wiles of the Devil. For we wrestle not against flesh and blood, but against principalities, against powers, against the rulers of the darkness of this world, against spiritual wickedness in high [or heavenly] places. Wherefore, take unto you the whole armor of God, *that ye may be able* to withstand in the evil day; and, having done all, to stand."

(Eph. vi. 10–13.) "Little children, let no man deceive you" (St. John)!

But all such evidence and authorities are deftly answered by the advocates of unconditional election and reprobation (and satisfactorily to themselves "*no doubt*"), by reference to the following text: "They went out from us, but they were not of us; for if they had been of us, they would *no doubt* have continued with us: but *they went out* that they might be made manifest that they were not all of us" (1 John ii. 19). Observe, first, the words italicized are not in the original, but were supplied by the translators to give the meaning *as they understood it*. The first two, "*no doubt*," add nothing to the sense, and might as well be omitted in reading it; the last three words supplied — namely, "*they went out*" — may have been introduced under a misapprehension of the facts; for they may have been *sent* out, "that they might be *made* manifest," &c. Would not that be the better rendering of the two?

But be all that as it may, it is certain that a more unjustifiable, bald-headed perversion of Scripture would be hard to find, in all the unhappy and unholy disputations among Christians which Satan has fomented, than we have in the stereotyped use which is made of that text. Hard run for proof must partisans be, when they resort to such misrepresentations of the plainest sacred writings. All the reply which need be made to the argument which is sought to be educed from that verse, is to call the reader's attention to the preceding one, which is this: "Little children, it is the last time; and as ye have heard that antichrist shall come, even now are there many antichrists; whereby we know that it is the last time." In this the apostle informs us that those who *went out* (or rather *were sent out*) from the society, companionship, of the disciples were *antichrists*, — the enemies of Christ and of his people. And from the two verses together we learn who they were that left the following of the disciples, and why they did so.

And observe, in the next place, that our question is whether one who is now a Christian, may apostatize, and finally be lost? And the passage before us does not touch that question. We learn from it that about that time evil men, who having been with, "went out from" the disciples; but whether they were mere pretenders from the first, or whether after having once been honest, good Christians they apostatized and left them, he does not say. And, moreover, St. John was not then treating of apostasy, but of a very different matter. He was writing of false prophets, teachers, &c., and trying to satisfy his brethren that theirs was "the last time" (that is, the beginning of the last age of the world). And he was striving at the same time to impress on the mind of his readers the fact that "the world passeth away," and the other and most important practical truth that "he that doeth the will of God, abideth for ever" (verse 17).

It cannot be necessary to dwell longer on that passage; but all who entertain doubts whether a Christian may fall away and go back to the service of his old chieftain, the Devil, can be put right upon that question by a careful study of that one chapter from which that little extract is so often taken and so shamefully abused. For the doctrine of conditional salvation, and hence the necessity of faithful and watchful care on the part of Christians to persevere in well-doing, are directly or indirectly, but plainly and repeatedly, inculcated there as well as everywhere else in the gospel. Of some people it is well and truly said, "Eyes have they, but they see not."

In a work of this nature it would be expected that something would be said about the salvation of heathen; but inasmuch as the writer has expressed his views upon that subject in a previous work, it is not thought best to say a great deal of it here.

We are informed by St. John that Jesus Christ "was the true light, which lighteth every man that cometh into the world" (John i. 9). This includes heathen with everybody else. All "that cometh into the world" are enlightened by means of the Holy Spirit sufficiently to enable them to know what "the Great Spirit" would have them to do. And the

Saviour says, "Not every one that saith unto me Lord, Lord, shall enter into the kingdom of heaven; but he that doeth the will of my Father which is in heaven" (Matt. vii. 21). God will not require an impossibility of any one; therefore a heathen, being enlightened by the Holy Ghost as to his duty, can do that which is required of him as easily and certainly as the most enlightened and highly educated Christian can do the will of the Father which is in heaven concerning him: "For unto whomsoever much is given, of him shall be much required," &c.

St. Paul expresses himself in regard to the salvation of heathen in this way: God "will render to every man according to his deeds: to them who by patient continuance in well-doing seek for glory and honor and immortality, eternal life; but unto them that are contentious, and do not obey the truth, but obey unrighteousness, indignation and wrath, tribulation and anguish, upon every soul of man that doeth evil; of the Jew first, and also of the gentile: but glory, honor, and peace to every man that *worketh good;* to the Jew first and also to the gentile; for there is no respect of persons with God. For as many as have sinned without law shall also perish without law; and as many as have sinned in the law shall be judged by the law; (for not the *hearers* of the law are justified before God, but the *doers* of the law shall be justified. For when the gentiles, which have not the law, do by nature the things contained in the law, these, having not the law, are a law unto themselves; which show the work of the law written in their hearts, their conscience also bearing witness, and their thoughts the meanwhile accusing or else excusing one another;) in the day when God shall judge the secrets of men by Jesus Christ according to my gospel" (Rom. ii. 6–16; see Rom. iii. 19, 22, 23). These Scriptures are too plain to require other explanation.

In the case of Justus, we have an instance of a devout heathen who worshipped God, and who was on his way to heaven when the gospel overtook him (Acts xviii. 7). The same may be said of Cornelius (Acts x). And other such cases are to be met with in the gospel writings.

We will now call attention to the following revelations, and close as to that question: "After this I beheld, and lo, a great multitude which no man could number, of all nations and kindreds and people and tongues, stood before the throne, and before the Lamb, clothed in white robes, and palms in their hands; and cried with a loud voice, saying, Salvation to God which sitteth upon the throne, and unto the Lamb" (Rev. vii. 9, 10). From this Scripture alone, all who believe it must see that some people of all nations, kindreds, and tongues which have, do, or may live upon this earth as men, are or are to be saved. But very few, except the Jews only, of any nation which lived before or during the time of St. John had any knowledge of the Old Testament Scriptures; and comparatively few of the many nations, kindred, people, or tongues who have lived since his time have ever read or so much as heard of the gospel. Then, if none can be saved who have not enjoyed the blessed privilege either to read or hear the gospel of Jesus Christ, how can the vision in Patmos be realized? To ask this question is to answer it.

The Bible is so full of authority in regard to this matter, that all who can and will read it may become satisfied as to the truth in this respect.[1]

It is the belief of all Christians, or nearly so, that every one who dies before reaching the age of discretion is saved. And having already shown[2] why and how they are saved, I do not think it necessary to say more on that subject here.

That infant heathen die, all must know; and it is believed that few, if any, well-informed Christians doubt the salvation of "little children," though of heathen parentage. Hence we see that some heathen must be saved, or an innumerable host of infants must burn for ever in hell! Jesus said, "Suffer little children, and forbid them not, to come unto me; for of such is the kingdom of heaven."

---

[1] See War in Heaven, p. 235.   [2] Ibid., p. 297.

CHAPTER XV.

Christian Union and Co-operation. — "A new commandment I give unto you, That ye love one another; as I have loved you, that ye also love one another" (John xiii. 34). — Introduction.

IN submitting to the Christian world a proposition so novel as that which is hereinafter made must be considered by many, it is deemed best to preface it with a few explanatory remarks.

It is made the duty of all Christians to "follow after the things which make for peace, and things wherewith one may edify another." To do that, we must cultivate fraternal relations with each other. But, in so doing, we should ever remember that it is our first and chief duty to love and obey our Creator and Redeemer; and, therefore, we should not expect nor desire that any Christian should violate his own sense of duty to God for any purpose whatever. In urging Catholic and Protestant Christians to cultivate better feeling toward one another, — with a view to that ultimate sympathy, harmony, and co-operation which is necessary to a speedy overthrow of the common adversary of both, — I do not ask either party to dissolve their present Church organizations, nor to abandon their existing forms of public worship; nor would I willingly have any one of either party deny the faith which he honestly entertains at the time for that or for any other consideration. But it is desired that all professing Christians exercise that charity toward all other *Christians*, which the gospel enjoins that we extend to *every man;* and the faithful observance of that one duty by each Christian would bring every family of Christ's children together so fast that it would astonish the friends of Christian union, and terrify the hosts of Satan.

It is, moreover, due to candor that I here admit my own imperfections and possible lack of charity for some Christian families, although I love that God-like virtue wherever I find it. Yet, what poor erring man will say that he is altogether free from the jaundiced influence of prejudice? And it is true that I have long felt in my own bosom a strong and growing distaste for every thing like human creeds of religion, and for every form and act, as of public worship, which the ingenious fancy of man has invented, and which was unknown in the apostolic age. In that I may err; but I freely confess that my best affections are all fixed upon and entwined about that plain and simple system of *faith*, and *practice*, and manner of *worship*, which is taught in the gospel of Jesus Christ.

And now, my Catholic brother, with the frank admission that my opinion in regard to your Church may not be correct in every particular, I hope you will accept it as coming from a friend who loves you, and as one which has been honestly formed, and upon the best attainable evidence, when I say to you in all kindness and candor, as I here do, that I honestly believe a majority of the articles which constitute your confession of faith, as printed and published, have no foundation whatever in the Bible, as revealed from heaven, nor in natural reason, but that they are inconsistent with both. And, further, I consider the whole paraphernalia of signs, images, and mystic ceremonies which are displayed or employed in connection with her public worship, as having originated more in an ambitious desire on the part of her founders and rulers to gratify their ambitious and selfish purposes — by securing the mastery of the mind and will, and the control of the means and conduct of her membership — than in a pious wish to promote the glory of God, or to secure the salvation of men. And, again, it is believed, and not without reason, that some articles of her faith, as well as her imposing but unintelligible ceremonies, were devised and adopted, not for any such godly purpose, but with an eye single to the superstitious fears and idolatrous proclivities of human nature; and that all such bewildering displays, being idolatrous in their nature and tendencies, are therefore displeasing to God, and injurious to the cause of his Christ.

These conclusions have been reached with great care, and

they are recorded here in obedience to that which is a painful, but it is nevertheless considered a sacred, duty to the cause of Christ, and especially to that which heads this article. They are written in love, and, although expressed plainly, yet it is done in the mildest form deemed admissible, and by one who is but a lay-member himself, and, therefore, can have no secular interest in the prosperity of any branch of the Christian Church at the cost of another. See 2 Thess. ii. 3, 4; and compare Exodus xx. 1–6, as in King James's translation, with the same as found in the Douay editions of the Bible,—simply remembering that God will hold us to answer according to the capacity which he has given each of us.

And while addressing my thoughts especially to you, my Catholic friend and brother, permit me to say to you, and through you to a large number of our Protestant brethren, that their views, as well as yours, in reference to the vastly important questions which relate to the trinity of persons in the Godhead, and to some other matters also, have precisely the same origin, and can find no better support, either in revelation or reason. They came by them honestly, however, as they acquired them while in the mother Church, and brought them along with them when they left her.

Notwithstanding that the plan of *Christian union* which is hereinafter advocated looks mainly and ultimately to a hearty co-operation of the several Church organizations, as such, " in every good word and work," it is well known that the Roman Catholic, and some other Churches, will not affiliate with any other body of Christians in any common enterprise whatever at present; yet there is hope of a brighter future. And, therefore, the only hope we have of present help from your Church, my brother, is based upon a confidence in the individual love which many of you doubtless have and cherish for Jesus Christ and his cause, and in your sincerity of purpose to serve him as best you may. For it is confidently believed that there are many among you who have sufficient love of truth, self-respect, and firmness of purpose to induce you to " *search the Scriptures*," and to examine the subject in all its bearings, each for himself; and that, should your judgment approve our efforts in this respect, and your sense of duty to God and to the holy cause in which our Saviour spent his life and met his death prompt you to sustain us therein, you will then rise above any mere prejudice of education which may have hitherto affected you, and that you will mount up to the full stature of that manhood with which the God of Nature has blessed you, and come "to the help of the Lord, — to the help of the Lord against the mighty!"

Of course, we can rely upon individual aid only in this good work from the Catholic and other Churches which are similarly situated for present help. It is insisted that the faith of the Roman Church cannot be changed, and, of course, that cannot be done except in Ecumenical Council. And the creeds and rules of discipline in some other Churches are but little less stringent upon the lay membership. But it is no less true that in this country, and most others of our age, all such objectionable articles of faith, forms of worship, rules of government, &c., can be abandoned; and in that way, should it be found necessary, all such restraining influence and servile control can be avoided.

In his gospel the Master has given all his disciples a plain and simple, yet all-sufficient, form of faith, with all needful instructions in regard to public worship, and other duties of Christian life, — which is brief enough. What more do we need? In that we have a common creed of faith and practice, — one in which we all believe: one that no man, nor body of men, in any subsequent age, has, or had, the right to alter. And it is *the only one* upon which all who love Jesus can meet, agree, and live, love, and serve as one happy family, and at the same time fight our common foe as one army. But all of that, and much more, could be realized without any sacrifice of principle, liberty of conscience, or freedom of thought and expression of opinion, on the part of any one who believes with St. Peter that Jesus is "*the Christ, the Son of the living God.*"

And as the blessed Jesus was raised from the dead, so has his Church been resurrected; and she is again at work in her old nomenclature, as "Disciple," "Christian," &c., under her same old confession of faith,— *the Gospel*,— and with the same offices, forms of government, &c. Here all who want to read the Word of God, and think and talk and act for themselves, and so prepare for that awful day when each and all will be judged, and rewarded or punished according to their works, may come and find a sure and safe retreat, a happy home, where the vile persecutor, whether Catholic, Baptist, or of other name, cannot molest nor reach them. And surely here all Christians may come and worship God, "under his vine, and under his fig-tree, and none shall make them afraid." " And the Spirit and the bride say, Come ; and let him that heareth say, Come; and let him that is athirst come: and whosoever will, let him take the water of *life freely*."

CHAPTER XVI.

Of Christian Love. — All Christians should co-operate against the common Foe. — Cause of alienation between Catholic and Protestant Christians. — How it can be removed. — Is such Union desirable? — Good people deceived. — Should not be more than two Christian Churches. — Heavenly Treasures, &c.

THE Master's command is that his disciples love one another. And he has explained the nature of the love we should entertain for each other in these words: "*As I have loved you.*" He has also prescribed the terms of admission into his holy family, by saying to his disciples and the assembled multitude that, "Whosoever will come after me, let him deny himself, and take up his cross and follow me." And he has moreover, through the beloved disciple, given us an easy and safe test by which we may examine ourselves (but no other) and learn our own relations to him, or to his and our enemy, as the case may be, as plainly as this: "We know that we have passed from death unto life, because *we love the brethren.* He that loveth not his brother, abideth in death."

Now, my Christian friend, are you living up to this standard? Do you love all Christians, — Protestant, Greek, Catholic, and all others, — as Christ loved his disciples? If you do not, what assurance have you that you "have passed from death unto life"? We should observe every precaution that we do not build our hopes of a home in heaven on a sandy foundation; for many who live in delusive hopes of a better fate are to be driven away from the Saviour, on that final and terrible day of account, under the awful curse, "Depart from me, ye cursed, into everlasting fire prepared for the Devil and his angels."

"God is love." Love is the ruling impulse of his nature. Christ is like the Father in that respect as in every other;

and to become Christians we must be like Christ in this redeeming quality. Oh! how careful then ought we to be, that we love the Father who created us, love the Son who redeemed us, and love the Holy Spirit which leads us along the narrow way to life! and that we love every Christian too, who tries to walk with us along that straight and happy way, and by whatsoever name he or she may be called or known.

When we retrospect the history of the Church which was established by the meek and lowly Jesus, whose whole being lives in love, and reflect upon the Inquisition, Crusades, persecutions, cruelties, and death, which men professing to be Christians have inflicted upon others of that faith, and for no other fault alleged than mere opinion's sake, we cannot wonder that few — comparatively but few — of all who claim his sons to be, will Jesus deign to own!

As it has been announced already, the chief good which it is hoped will accrue to the cause of Christianity from this little work, is such as may accrue from calling the attention of Christians generally — and especially of those who mould the faith of the Church — to the effect which the acceptance of the theory of our being which is taught in the Bible must inevitably have upon some of the most vital questions in regard to which the Church now stands divided in opinion. And in this chapter it is designed to show the happy effect which its general approval must have upon the unnatural relations which hitherto have and do now exist between Catholic and Protestant Christians, as between themselves; for in that view, they would all see at once that they have mutually misunderstood each other, and therefore that each has done the other family great injustice. And they would likewise learn that the *sole efficient cause* of the unhappy alienation of feeling which has kept them so long quite as far from the confidence and affections of each other as either should feel opposed to the most ungodly sinner who ever disgraced the cause of the Devil, *has no foundation in fact whatever.*

It is not only true that the cause of all the bitterness of feeling which obtained, and has prevailed so long, on the part of each of these two families of Christians toward the other is utterly unfounded, but to one who is a stranger to any such prejudice it is a matter of wonderment, and it must so strike all such, that the Church should have permitted an enemy of such enormous proportions to have grown up in her own bosom, and which had no other sustenance than such as was drawn from a misapprehension of the nature and intendment of one passage of Scripture, and in regard to which both parties have and do alike agree and err!

Several strange features connected with the interpretation of the Scripture here alluded to should be noticed, and which are the following: (1) It is singular that it ever should have been considered a prophecy, and not a revelation, as it purports on its face to be. (2) After it had been interpreted by common consent as but another prophecy, and foretelling an event which was then believed to lie in the near future, and which did occur very much as anticipated according to previous prophecies, — it is strange that it should thereafter have been construed (and with the same agreement) as prophetic of another and a different matter, and as relating to another and altogether a different people. (3) And after the Christian world had so fully agreed twice (as to the fulfilment of a prophecy which was supposed to be contained therein), and subsequently admitted that they had as often erred in that respect; and not only so, but after they had quarrelled between themselves, and parted company completely, — it is wonderful that both parties should have agreed *the third time* as to its prophetic nature, and that it predicted still another and entirely different dispensation of Providence; and it is more wonderful still that each party should then and since have construed it (and in all seriousness, as charity requires us to hope) as foretelling the certain and total destruction of *the other party!* All of which is not less true than curious, as has been shown already in a previous chapter.

Let the preceding thoughts by way of inducement suffice for that purpose, and we will proceed without further delay to the remarks designed in furtherance of the sacred cause of *Christian union*. And in abundant caution, to prevent if possible all misapprehension in that respect, I now and here reaffirm that the plan which I propose and wish to be adopted, by which to effect a more perfect union of all Christians, is not to form another sect, nor in any way to interfere with present church organizations, either of which would only make the matter worse; but it is simply to show that all Christians could and should learn to love one another, live in peace and camp together, and as one solid phalanx meet and fight the common foe. And it is purposed now to point out the way by which that sort of union can be brought to a happy consummation, for the calm and prayerful consideration of all who love Christ Jesus our Lord and his kingdom here below.

And with that design, the thoughts which follow are affectionately submitted : (1) It is assumed that there is but one insurmountable obstacle in the way to a speedy and happy union of all Christians, of whatever name (who love God more than Mammon), into one body, as far at least as necessary for practical purposes; and that difficulty could readily be removed out of the way. (2) That the obstacle referred to originated in an erroneous interpretation of the account given in the twelfth chapter of Revelation (7–11) of a "war in heaven" (which is the Scripture already alluded to), and in construing it as a *prophecy* and not as a *revelation;* and that the hindering cause lies in *a false impression*, which rests alike on the Catholic and Protestant mind, in regard to the devotional intentions of the other, and to the relations supposed by each to exist between the opposite party and the Redeemer. (3) And that a correct understanding of that one Scripture by all Christians would remove the successfully hindering cause, and open a way to such union and co-operation on our part as would make glad the city of God, and overwhelm the hosts of the enemy with terror and dismay.

This matter demands the most serious consideration on the part of every teacher of religion, and of all others who dare think and act for themselves in search for the way which leads from earth to heaven. And to enable readers of this article to examine for themselves, and with the least conceivable trouble, the passage of Scripture which, as it is alleged, has been so variously and erroneously construed, and from a false interpretation of which an evil of such magnitude has accrued to the Church of Jesus Christ, — it is reproduced here, and submitted with but a few explanatory or rather suggestive remarks thereon, and which are mainly designed to awaken a wish on the part of the reader to know its true nature and value. Here is that remarkable Scripture: —

"And there was war in heaven; Michael and his angels fought against the dragon, and the dragon fought and his angels, and prevailed not; neither was their place found any more in heaven. And the great dragon was cast out, that old serpent called the Devil and Satan, which deceiveth the whole world: he was cast out into the earth, and his angels were cast out with him. (And I heard a loud voice saying in heaven, Now is come salvation, and strength, and the kingdom of our God, and the power of his Christ, for the accuser of our brethren is cast down, which accused them before our God day and night.) And they overcame him by the blood of the Lamb, and by the word of their testimony; and they loved not their lives unto the death."

Now, honest reader, what does this Scripture mean? Read it first, omitting the parenthesis (the tenth verse) thus: "He was cast out into the earth, and his angels were cast out with him; and they overcame him by the blood of the Lamb," &c. The most natural, literal, and logical meaning is simply this: Satan was cast out of heaven and down to this earth, and his angels (those who fought under him) were cast out and down with him; and that they (Satan's angels) overcame him (Satan) by virtue of the blood of Jesus Christ. Is not this the fair, true, and in fact the only reasonable interpretation of it?

If this is the correct view of the passage quoted (and who will say that it is not?), the question as to the origin of our race is settled, — is it not? And with that must go her twin sister — the other question, which like that has sorely vexed, harassed, and perplexed the Christian world for lo these many ages, — as to whether the Pope and his adherents, or

Luther and his followers, are the parties intended by the terms "dragon," "serpent," "Devil," "Satan and his angels," as used there!

Now go back and read the whole five verses, including the tenth, which is here (and properly) given in parenthesis, and you will find that after having the true meaning first suggested by reading the ninth and eleventh verses in close connection, the construction here given is strengthened by reading the entire passage as St. John wrote it; for any other rendering would involve the absurdity of holding that "our brethren," who were "accused before our God day and night," were intended as those who overcame (and were to overcome) Satan "by the blood of the Lamb;" and they obviously are and were the steadfast and holy angels of heaven. And it is confidently believed that no sane man will seriously insist that they are the "lost" whom Christ came "to seek and to save."

Should any doubt whether this is a prophecy of things yet to come, or a revelation of things that are past, still linger in the mind, just read it as relating to the future, changing the tense thus: "7. And there was [will be] war in heaven; Michael and his angels fought [will fight] against the dragon, and the dragon fought [will fight] and his angels. 8. And prevailed not [will not prevail]; neither was [will be] their place found any more in heaven. 9. And the great dragon was [will be] cast out, that old serpent called the Devil and Satan which deceiveth [will deceive] the whole world: he was [will be] cast out into the earth, and his angels were [will be] cast out with him. 10. And I heard [will hear] a loud voice saying in heaven, Now is [will come] salvation, and strength, and the kingdom of our God, and the power of his Christ; for the accuser of our brethren is [to be] cast down which accused [will accuse] them before our God day and night. 11. And they overcame [will overcome] him by the blood of the Lamb, and by the word of their testimony; and they loved not [will not love] their lives unto the death." How will this rendering do?

If the above is a prophecy of future events, to get the

meaning we must read it as if written in the future tense. Is not this true? Now, study it carefully, as so written above, and it will be found that it prophesies of but two events: first, that God will overcome all his enemies; and, second, that Satan and his angels will live unlovely lives. That is all. And what Bible reader did not know that much before? If, therefore, it was intended as a prophecy, and foretells nothing that was not known before, it is of no value whatever. And, which is still worse, if it is a prophecy relating to the warfare which is progressing *here on earth* between Michael and Satan and their respective angels, it is calculated to deceive and not to instruct; for this war was about two-thirds over at that time, as all Christians, or nearly all, agree.

In that view, it seems that Satan is to be cast out into the earth. When is he to come? Some people think he is here now! Is this world to be afflicted with another " Devil and his angels"? It appears that there was (or is to be) great rejoicing in heaven; for the accuser of the brethren, " which accused them before our God day and night," was (or is to be) "*cast down*." Did the infidel Jews or heathen Romans ever accuse Christians before "*our God*" day or night? Or do Catholic and Protestant Christians now accuse one another "*before* our God"? It is true that some of each do accuse the other party of a great many bad things before their congregations and readers, of which evil practices, in many instances, the accused are not guilty, — *for that pays!* But all who " do such things " (and who are not infidels) know that God has no need of their *accusations* to enlighten him as to what men are doing in this world; " for his eyes are upon the ways of man, and he seeth all his goings."

That " Revelation " was first construed as a *prophecy* relating to the Jewish war and the destruction of the city of Jerusalem. The second construction of it was, that "It contains predictions of the persecutions of the Christians under the heathen emperors of Rome, and of the happy days of the Church under Christian emperors, from Constantine downward." This opinion obtained after the destruction of Jerusalem, and upon the cruel persecutions of Christians by heathen emperors; and it prevailed down to the Reformation of Luther and others, as the settled opinion of the Church.

But from that Reformation down to the present time the Catholic Church has construed it as "a prophetic declaration of the schisms and heresies of Martin Luther, those called Reformers, and their successors, and the final destruction of the Protestant religion;" while, on the other hand, the Protestants as a body *protest* that it contains "prophecies concerning the tyrannical and oppressive conduct of the Roman pontiffs, — the true Anti-Christ, — and foretells the final destruction of Popery."

And so stands the controversy between these two great Christian families at the present time, each fully (hopefully?) expecting the final destruction of the other![1]

As long as Catholic and Protestant Christians continue each to esteem the other as identical with the parties who were called by the messenger of God "the Devil and his angels," it is not likely that either will covet such *union* with the other party as death could not dissolve, — is it?

But further comment here on the construction of a Scripture which, in and of itself, is the equivalent of a "thus saith the Lord," cannot be necessary. Were it desired to pursue this branch of our subject further (but it is not), it would be more profitable to look into the causes which have led to such perversions of that which is plain as written with the inspired pen; and therefore, with but one remark in that direction, we will pass on.

The Christian Church may, and unquestionably has, suffered to some extent from the ignorance of her teachers; but that she has suffered incomparably more from their selfish wickedness is equally true. This remark does not apply to any *well-intending* Christian, of whatsoever denomination he may be, or may have been, a member; but it applies to those only whom St. John calls "antichrists." They know themselves, and God knows them. And it applies just the same to the political troubles of this world.

[1] See the Preface to Dr. A. Clarke's "Notes on Revelation."

It is true, as is well known, that some good people (as we consider them, and as they want to be) have a sort of notion that it is best for the Church that she should be divided, as at present. But to that objection either of the answers which follow ought to be sufficient to satisfy every Christian man and woman who so thinks, that they are wrong in that respect, if in no other. The first is, that the Saviour thought differently; and those who profess to be his disciples should respect his opinions, whether they obey his commands or not.

Jesus says: "If a kingdom be divided against itself, that kingdom cannot stand. And if a house be divided against itself, that house cannot stand" (Mark iii. 24, 25). The Church of Christ is elsewhere called a *kingdom*, and it is likewise called a *house;* and we must believe that he desired his Church to *stand;* and it was for that reason that he admonished his disciples of the absolute necessity of avoiding divisions among themselves. With politicians it is a maxim that "In union there is strength." "For the children of this world are in their generation [vocation] wiser than the children of light."

We are commanded to "love one another;" and if we will all do that, the holy cause of Christian union will take care of itself. St. Paul exhorted his Corinthian brethren to "be of one mind," and "live in peace;" and that counsel well kept would soon restore the unity of the Church. And, as we have seen, we cannot have the evidence of our own acceptance with Christ, which is promised to the faithful, unless "we love the brethren;" but, on the contrary, we are fully assured that "He that loveth not his brother abideth in death." Therefore we should examine ourselves carefully in this respect.

It is easy to love a brother who is our neighbor and personal friend, as well as a member of the same society with which we meet for, or to witness, divine worship, as the case may be. But that is not enough, my Christian friend. To bring yourself within the rule prescribed by the Master, you must love all who profess to love and hope for redemption by Jesus Christ, and whose conduct proves their sincerity in that profession, and notwithstanding you or he may be a Catholic and the other a Protestant. That is the sort of love which is required of us, and which alone will result in Christian union. We have the most conclusive proof that the unity of his disciples was a desideratum most earnestly desired by him who gave himself a ransom for us, in his fervent prayer for his disciples, "That they all may be one," even as he and the Father "are one." (See John xvii.)

The second answer to that objection which was alluded to above is that there is an evil genius, a deceiver, in the world, — the same of whom we have just read, that "he was cast out into the earth, and his angels were cast out with him," and who "deceiveth the whole world." (See also Zech. iii. 1, 2.) Observe, he deceives "the whole world;" this includes all men, the good as well as the bad; therefore we must know that good men are deceived by that evil fiend as well as bad men. And although he may not be able to satisfy an experienced Christian at the first interview that there is no God, no after-life, nor of any other damning heresy, — yet he may, by persistent efforts, succeed in deceiving such an one into erroneous views of Christian faith and duty in some particulars. This he constantly does, as we are compelled to believe from the widely differing opinions which good men entertain on some important subjects in relation to which all revealed evidence is on one side. For God will not deceive any one who goes to learn of him; and, therefore, when we meet with one who professes faith in Christ, and whose holy walk and godly conversation demand our confidence in his sincerity (and there are many such), and yet who believes that it is best for the cause of Christ that his Church remain divided, as at present, we may safely certify that Satan is responsible for that error. But whether he or his dupe will be held to answer for it at the great day, God only knows. The safer way, however, is to form our opinions on this as well as on all other such matters, from what Christ has said of such things.

We are informed by the Saviour that, "Not every one that saith unto me, Lord, Lord, shall enter into the kingdom of heaven; but he that doeth the will of my Father which is in heaven. Many will say unto me in that day, Lord, Lord, have we not prophesied (taught) in thy name? and in thy name have cast out devils? and in thy name done many wonderful works? And then will I profess unto them, I never knew you [as my disciples]; depart from me, ye that work iniquity" (Matt. vii. 21-23). That priests and ministers of the gospel are intended in these fearful words of our Lord is too manifest to justify any argument to prove it.

Then, my Christian friends, let us all heed the warning. Somebody — nay, "*many*" are to be sorely disappointed on that dread day, for which all other days were made. For none but those who will be truly and sorely disappointed, at the position assigned them during the eternal future, would make such appeal to him who now is our most affectionate, devoted, and merciful friend, but who will then return as the stern, unyielding Judge of both quick and dead, and avenger of the violated law and contemned mercies of the Father, — would they? Therefore, all who lie under the sacred responsibilities which devolve upon every one who undertakes to teach in matters of religion in any way (and notwithstanding we may have done so in obedience to what we felt it our duty to do) should often revert to that divine and timely warning, and in the dust of humility inquire at the mercy-seat, "Lord, Lord! is it I?"

This word of counsel comes from an older and far more reliable "James" than is his erring and unworthy namesake, the writer of this. He says: "If any of you lack wisdom, let him ask of God, that giveth to all men liberally, and upbraideth not, and it shall be given him." And, again: "The wisdom that is from above is first pure, then peaceable, gentle, easy to be entreated," &c.; and further: "Ye ask and receive not, because ye ask amiss, that ye may consume it upon your lusts [or pleasures]" (James i. 5, iii. 17, iv. 3).

If we would not be of those who "ask and receive not, because [we] ask amiss," we must not harbor within us, before the throne of God, any unholy desire to teach that which is more popular or profitable than the naked truth as found in the gospel, for the purpose of gratifying our "lusts" for fame, gold, or any thing of that sort; but to secure the Divine favor we must go there with clean hands and pure hearts, denying all "ungodliness and worldly lusts," — "For if ye live after the flesh ye shall die; but if ye through the Spirit do mortify the deeds of the body, ye shall live. For as many as are led by the Spirit of God, they are the sons of God" (Rom. viii. 13, 14).

The same enemy of God and man who so often deceives the best of Christians in regard to matters of faith and duty, not unfrequently deceives those who are over-fond of the pleasures, wealth, or honors of this world into downright infidelity. Such men, being unconsciously deceived themselves, in some instances become fond of deception, and take pleasure in deceiving others. The Church affords a ready ambuscade for such men. There they lie concealed from the unsuspecting eye of those who frequent her sacred portals, and there they ply their skill unknown of men. And some such fiends "steal the livery of heaven to serve the Devil in;" and when so clad, they ascend the consecrated desk. And perhaps such an one may ere long be esteemed "a burning and a shining light" in the Church of Jesus Christ, and many become "willing for a season to rejoice in his light."

In writing of such men, I prefer to copy from the pen of inspiration rather than risk my own to photograph them. That pen counsels all humble and sincere Christians in the words which follow: "Now I beseech you, brethren, *mark them* which cause divisions and offences contrary to the doctrine which ye have heard; *and avoid them.* For they that are such serve not our Lord Jesus Christ, but their own belly; and by good words and fair speeches deceive the hearts of the simple" (St. Paul). Again: "I know this, that after my departing shall grievous *wolves enter in among you,* not sparing the flock. Also of your own selves shall men arise, speaking perverse things, *to draw disciples after them*" (ibid.).

It may be well enough to say of the last quotation, that the apostle had reference to two classes of dangerous leaders. By the "grievous wolves" who would "enter in" the Church, he evidently intended such as have not faith in Christ nor regard for the well-being of his Church, but who were mere pretenders, hypocrites from the first; and by those "of your own selves," well-intending but deluded and ambitious men are referred to. But the motives of those who seek to disturb the peace or unity of the Church are not proper subjects of inquiry: first, because none but God can in all cases read the thoughts and scan the motives of men; and, secondly, because their motives are not material, for the consequences are the same whatsoever their intentions may be; and therefore it is made the imperative duty of all good men alike to mark and avoid all who so act.

The Saviour has given us the following warning and direction concerning that class of men: "Beware of false prophets [teachers or preachers] which come to you in sheep's clothing, but inwardly they are ravening wolves. Ye shall know them by their fruits. Do men gather grapes of thorns, or figs of thistles?" (Matt. vii. 15, 16.) In the light of this admonition, and of what the blessed Jesus elsewhere says about it, should we consider one who is trying "to draw away disciples after him," or to perpetuate existing schisms of the Church (by nourishing the prejudices of her members against each other), as bearing good or bad fruit? This question admits of but one answer; and therefore all Christians should "beware of" such men "and avoid them." For of all such one of two things is true: they are "wolves in sheep's clothing;" or, if they believe in Christ at all (as some such doubtless do), they have permitted the Devil, by flattering their vanity, feeding the fires of their ambition, &c., to deceive them, and to lead them away far from the peaceful path of Christian duty; and, in either case, the evil effects of their doing are the same.

To render justice to the memory of good and true men who have gone before us, and who have served the cause of Christianity well; and to avoid forestalling others who may come after us, and labor earnestly and faithfully to restore the Church to her native purity, — it is here repeated, that those who are properly called "reformers" are not obnoxious to the charge of selfishness nor of being disorganizers: we should rather esteem them as peacemakers and restorers of the Church. Of the latter class were Martin Luther and his coadjutors, — although unfortunately they did organize new churches, — and more recently the Messrs. Campbell, father and son. The latter, however, did not deem it necessary to constitute another sect upon another creed; all they attempted was to recall their brethren to the apostolic faith and practice. The first sought to reform that branch of the Church which, as it is believed, first introduced infant baptism, and still observes it; and the latter brethren also labored (and doubtless in like good faith) to reform in other respects the church which adheres to and practices the administration of that baptism which was first introduced by the forerunner, St. John.

And I pause here to remark (with the hope that the digression will be pardoned), that there is not now, never was, and never can be, any real necessity for more than two church organizations. All Christians who love Jesus as they should, and who are willing to deny themselves, take up the cross and follow him (as all must do to be recognized as his disciples), could find kindred spirits and happy homes either in a church constituted on the basis of infant baptism, or in one which follows that of John, the harbinger; for none should expect to be considered Christians, and treated as such even in this life, who will not deny themselves so far as to exercise the charity toward others which is necessary to prepare them to love and live in peace with brethren who may not agree with them in opinion on other and the minor points of faith, respecting which Christians differ among themselves, and upon which non-essential questions the Church is now divided into so many great parties, and little factions more.

Until Christians agree in relation to baptism and kindred questions which grow out of that, there may be some excuse for perpetuating two (not more than two!) church organizations; but there is no good reason why the members of these two divisions of the Church (or of all that we are now afflicted with) should not "live in peace," "love one another," and, as two wings of one great army under the same victorious chief, all scheme and work and fight as one, and against his and our common foe (the Devil) and those who are *his angels* still.

In these remarks, as it must have been perceived already, Mohammedans are not included; but, as regards all other professing Christians, it is confidently believed that a careful examination of the whole matter (in the light of revelation and in the absence of the Deceiver) will satisfy every one that the position above assumed is well sustained by gospel authority.

Why should Christians war against each other? Have we not a common foe, — one worthy of our steel, — and who is now drawn up in battle array against us? This life is a warfare, and the world is but a battle-field; and but two parties are engaged in the fight. Each and every one, all who have descended from Adam, and who now live on earth, stand enrolled to-day on one or the other of the two army lists. Michael and his hosts, and Satan and his angels, are the opposing parties now as in the beginning.

> There is no neutral ground, no bomb-proof place,
> Where one may skulk and hide, his God disgrace;
> But all must war with Christ, while here we may,
> Or camp with Satan now, hence with him stay!

Will any well-informed Protestant say that all Catholics are against Christ? that they are all serving the Devil and going to hell? Or will any intelligent member of the Catholic Church say that all Protestants are so engaged, and drifting to that bad world? The twin sisters, *Truth* and *Charity*, answer both these questions simultaneously and emphatically with the monosyllable, No!

It is true that *tares* are allowed to grow with the *wheat*, and will be till the harvest. We should therefore expect that bad men ("wolves in sheep's clothing") are to be found in every branch of the Christian Church; but to believe that all Catholic officials and people on one side, or that all Protestant teachers and church members on the other side, are either fools or knaves, would require a degree of ignorance or bigotry which it is believed but few possess.

We all profess to believe that Jesus is "the Christ, the Son of the living God," and to hope for salvation in virtue of the atonement he has made for us. We all expect to meet at the same judgment, and all base our faith on the same Bible; do we not? Nor is this all; for every pious Catholic and

Protestant, of ordinary capacity and information, fully agree in every thing that it is necessary any should believe that they may be saved by and through our glorious Redeemer.

All that is refreshing, but it is a painful truth that at the same time a large majority of both agree also in a false construction of that important Scripture. And out of that one common error all the present alienations of feeling and mutual distrust — not to say hate — which each entertains toward the other has grown.

The following evidence is offered to prove that the passage under consideration is a revelation and not a prophecy: (1) It purports to reveal (make known) to us an occurrence *of the past*, and does not appear to prophesy of *things to come*. Will any one deny this? (2) The Christian world has *twice* agreed as to its application as a prophecy, and each time, and with the same unanimity afterwards, abandoned the first and likewise the second construction of it; and while both of the two leading families of Christians now agree that it is a prophecy, they disagree *hugely* (as we have seen) relative to its application. (3) That when construed as a revelation, its meaning is clear, natural, and reasonable; its application is certain, and its value is manifest to all. For it is capable of reconciling every alleged conflict in the Bible, and thereby disarming infidelity. And it also shows that Satan is the Anti-Christ mentioned by the apostles, and that neither the Pope nor Luther is the dreadful enemy of Christ and his Church; and thereby a way is opened to a perfect reunion of all the disciples of Christ into one happy family.

And inasmuch as the opinions of the Church in this particular have and do counterbalance, and thereby destroy each the other as all must see, we should not regard either one of them as of any value whatever. But the interpretation of that Scripture should be held and treated as an open field, rich in heavenly treasures; and therefore as one which offers the most hopeful and sacred inducements to every thoughtful, learned, and real friend of the Christian religion, and in fact to all who can read their Bible.

But the prevailing opinion with the Orthodox (?) teachers

in matters of religion, in this degenerate age, seems to be that there is really no such thing as laying up treasures in heaven, more than merely to gain admission to that good world. That will do very well for those who wish to hold the full mastery of the thoughts and conduct of their flocks. A very different view of the matter, however, is everywhere taught in God's Word. We are there informed that every man will be rewarded or punished (as the case may be), in the future state, according to his works here. Christ promised his disciples that he would reward them in heaven for all their sufferings in this world; he denounced against certain wicked scribes " greater damnation ; " and he counselled his disciples, and all who heard him, in these words: " Lay up for yourselves treasures in heaven." How can all this be, if all are equal in heaven, and if one is to suffer no more than another in hell ? But I do not propose to argue that question here.

The value of a proper understanding of that revelation cannot be over-estimated, if all the good which it is alleged will result from it can be had at a cost so cheap; for in that case a sure panacea is found for all the ailments that affect so hurtfully the Christian world. A proposed construction of any passage of Scripture (which appears to be both natural and reasonable in itself) which if found to be the true one will have the happy effect of removing out of the way every apparent discrepancy which, as the enemy affirms, does exist in the Bible as at present construed, and of reconciling every inconsistency which has been or may be alleged against our system of religion, and which if approved by all will at the same time overcome and crush out the only cause that has or can split in twain and keep asunder those who are and should feel as one in Christ (Catholic and Protestant Christians), — certainly deserves a careful investigation, does it not ? How sad it is to those who love the Lord Jesus Christ, and all who love and serve him, to see Christians stand aloof — affections cold — even opposing one another, as Jews and Samaritans! The present alienated condition of the Church is unnatural; it is wrong, sinful, damning! and alike so as regards those who caused it, and others who now approve and perpetuate it.

That is a work of the Devil; and Christ will destroy it, as he will all the other works of his enemy. Mark that!

But ours is said to be a practical age. In secular matters it is eminently so, I admit. And some may ask, Is a union of all Christians into one family practical in this late period of the world? To that question the revealed Word answers in advance, that it is not only practical, but it is necessary and certain. When or how such union will come I know not; but God knows. We may continue to be called by different names, as were the immediate disciples of Christ: but they all loved one another; they lived together in peace; and all worked in concert, and with one mind. Of the twelve disciples one was a devil; and there are doubtless devils among us now. It cannot reasonably be expected that a less proportion of bad men are connected with the Church now than were then. And Judas carried the bag then, and the same love of gain may now invite such as he was to high position among the brethren. He was put out of the way, and another was chosen in his stead. A similar elimination may become necessary again; if so, it will be made.

As we have seen, Christ prayed for the unity of his disciples, and for all who should believe on him "through their word;" that they "all may be one," as he and the Father "are one." But that is not all, for he prophesied that his sheep should all be brought into " one fold," and fed by " one shepherd " (see John x. 1–16). In these remarks, the Saviour evidently had in view, and intended to indorse, such prophecies as those found in Isaiah xi. 1–9, and in Ezekiel xxxvii. 22–27. Many similar predictions have been put on record, and must be fulfilled. When the hindering cause is satisfactorily agreed upon and well understood by all better informed Christians, then will the work of unification begin in good earnest; and from that glorious epoch the time will be short until all will constitute but *one fold*, "and they shall have [but] one shepherd." And, as suggested already, the deep chasm which lies between Catholic and Protestant Christians (which has been washed out, and made wider and deeper continually, by the floods of error which have flowed so freely during these murky centuries from a false construction of that one Scripture) will then be speedily bridged over and completely filled up.

And it is no less true that all the deep and dark prejudices of our nature, with other available means at hand, have been employed by the Devil to aid him in dividing and sub-dividing the Protestant Church into the numerous families and sects of which she now consists. They too have been deceived. In some instances they have been led into error as to the views entertained, and in other cases as to the motives which actuate other Protestant people and families.

"My brethren, these things ought not so to be!" And they would not so have been, but for the unholy desire on the part of ambitious and misguided men to direct the thoughts and control the actions of their fellow-men. This desire at an early day culminated in the evil practice of making creeds of religion, and of forcing their acceptance and approval by others, and at whatever cost that became necessary.

The shallow pretext which was offered as an excuse for so doing was that the Scriptures are too mysterious to be rightly understood by the laity of the Church, and that it was necessary that the substance of the divine teachings should be put in such plain and brief forms that all could readily comprehend their meaning, and observe and keep the whole law. And to forward such purposes the plainest oracles of God, as written by the inspired penmen, were skilfully represented as being enigmatical. And in some cases truths which are plain and simple, as taught in the Bible, are so rendered in our popular creeds and confessions of faith as to make them appear mysterious or wholly unintelligible. That which is called the "holy doctrine of the Trinity" is an illustrious specimen of priestly mystification. That is artfully put in such shape that no one can understand it. And yet intelligent people have been required to profess that they believe it, although it appears to be impossible. In former ages (as we have seen), and where the laws of State permitted it, the penalty of death was inflicted upon those who dared deny what was called the Holy Trinity; and now the same "heresy" is punished by excommunication from our so-called Orthodox churches, whether Catholic or Protestant! The people were taught to believe that it is dangerous for them to read the Bible, and attempt to form their own opinions there as to Christian faith and practice; and that the sacred duty of interpreting that mystic Book should be discharged alone by those who, to that holy work, were —

> The called of God, as it was said;
> And by whom all our creeds were made.
> But how called, when, for purpose what,
> And whether called by God or not,
> What boots it? for, by craft or lot,
> The work they did the Devil got.

To the several and conflicting creeds of religion and confessions of faith which conceited bigotry or moral obliquity, or both combined (under the leadership of Satan), have imposed upon those whom Christ came to emancipate, the Church is indebted for all the persecutions, wars, and bloodletting for opinion's sake by which she has been afflicted down to this present writing. If the Redeemer's counsel and that of his apostles had been followed, and the gospel recognized as the only standard by which questions of Christian faith and duty should be settled; and if disturbers of her peace had been detected and disposed of as instructed and directed by him and them, — the Church would have enjoyed uninterrupted peace within down to this time, and none but wars from without would she have known.

But in that case the delightful sport of hunting, chasing, catching, trying, hanging, and burning of heretics vile would never have been invented; and all that "innocent amusement" for priests, preachers, and all the good people would never have been known; and the Devil would have lost all the fun of that sort which he (or his, rather) has relished so well! All such losses would have been sustained, it is true, but for the timely intervention of human creeds; but would nothing have been saved which was lost on that account? Have the conquests of the gospel been less, or greater, than they would have been if the peace, harmony, and unity of the Church had been uninterrupted? Or, to be brief, will a house stand longer, or a kingdom protect her subjects better, or extend her conquests further, united or divided?

It cannot be necessary to waste time in writing, printing, or reading answers to the preceding questions, nor in argument of the subject; for all capable and candid minds must come to the same conclusion in regard to it. And, moreover, the good cause of Christian union, as between Protestants themselves, has an able corps of advocates already enlisted; and she has her Evangelical Alliance, Young Men's Christian Associations, and other valuable instrumentalities already well organized and in successful operation. It is only necessary, therefore, to caution them not to mistake the Pope for the Devil in their warfare against evil, and to aid and assist them in their good work, and invoke the Divine blessing upon them as far as they propose to go; and at the same time encourage them to explore the territory which lies beyond that for the conquest of which they have enlisted, and see whether even brighter laurels are not to be achieved there than any which can be won within the field to which their operations have hitherto been limited.

The highest ambition which prompts this writing is to excite such hope, if possible, on the part of learned, great, and good Christians who are now so engaged, — and of all such men and women too, — of finding a way which will lead to a perfect union of all Christians (whether known as Catholics, Greeks, Protestants, or by any other name) into one harmonious and happy family, as will induce them to look searchingly into the matter for themselves, and find that way; and, having found it, that they may walk therein with gladness. What sacrifice would not the meek and humble follower of the blessed Jesus gladly make, to bring his whole family into one holy union and happy communion! And, my Christian friend, that — all of that — can be done! It must be done! it will be done! When, or how, such radical change will be effected, God only knows. And whether, or how closely, the Church will have to be pruned, and the large numbers of which she now consists cut down, to purify and prepare her for such perfection of glory, He alone can tell.

The law is written, and it is proclaimed to the Church: "Every tree that bringeth not forth good fruit, is hewn down and cast into the fire." And further: "By their fruits ye shall know them." And it is made the duty of every intelligent Christian of every name, to observe the fruits of those who minister to them; and, if they bring "evil fruit" to "mark" and "avoid them." And furthermore, we are not left without instruction as to how we may distinguish evil fruit from that which is good; but we are fully informed on that subject also. Among "the works of the flesh" (the evil fruits) are enumerated the following: "emulations," "variance," "strife," "wrath," "envyings," "and such like." And St. Paul says that "they which do such things shall not inherit the kingdom of God." On the other side, he says: "But the fruit of the Spirit is love, joy, peace, long-suffering, gentleness, goodness, faith, meekness, temperance; against such there is no law."

We must not however, I repeat, undertake to judge of the correctness of all the opinions entertained by others, nor of their motives, before extending to them our Christian fellowship. That is strictly forbidden; and for the sufficient reason that we are utterly incompetent to the task. For we are all imperfect, and may labor under error in some particulars ourselves; and we cannot look into the hearts of others, and there read and scrutinize their motives. But with the help of the light which is revealed to us (and for that important purpose), we can observe their works, and judge truly of them. And, as before remarked, it is perfectly immaterial *to us* what the opinions or purposes of others may be; for, if they "do such things" as tend to produce *variance* or *strife* among the brethren, we are commanded to *mark* them and to *avoid them.*

If all Christians of the three great families — Roman, Grecian, and Protestant — would work together as friends and brothers should in their missionary operations alone, until every benighted heathen on earth should have the gospel preached to them, and the Bible printed in their native tongues, the chief good sought to be achieved by the advocates of Christian union would at once be realized. How much more *Christlike* would such conduct appear to those who view from the glory-world above the "wars within" which now afflict, distract, and so sadly paralyze the arm of God's Church below! Would not such service, my brethren, be far more acceptable to our indulgent Father and gracious Redeemer, as well as more successful in spreading abroad through all nations and to all people the "glad tidings" that *the Christ has come* "to seek and to save that which was lost"?

Should such catholic spirit once pervade the Christian Church as a whole, the world will no more behold such ungodly strifes between sectarian chiefs as culminate in hostile missions in heathen lands. But wherever one family of Christians may be found peaceably and successfully at work, on any missionary ground, all others will invoke Heaven's choicest blessings on their heads, and turn away to find some other ground where Christian feet have never trod, and there unfurl the gloriously victorious BANNER OF THE CROSS!

CHAPTER XVII.

The same Subject continued. — Judge not, lest ye be judged. — Duties of the educated Laity. — Appeal to Lawyers. — Their advantages over the Ministry in construing the Scriptures. — Gold is King. — Small Errors lead to great Evils. — Nature of the Union advocated. — Conclusion.

THE proposition which was laid down in the last chapter, — namely, that it is immaterial to us what the faith or motives of others may be, and particularly as applied to pastors and other officers of the Church, — may strike some as novel, if not as being nonsensical. It is nevertheless true, with this one qualification: *provided* we have used due care in forming our opinions, from his and their conduct and conversation (*their fruits*), of the sincerity and fitness of those who are called to, and retained in, such sacred trusts, and believe that they are all right.

This subject being one of the first value with regard to a proper discharge of our Christian duties, it is deemed best to pause here, and offer some evidence that I am correct in the position assumed. It is believed that no one will insist that one church member is responsible for the acts of another any further than we may be considered, to some extent, ancillary to the wrong done. The law is, that "The soul that sinneth, it shall die." Or, as elsewhere given, in this form: "So then, every one of us shall give account *of himself* to God. Let us not, therefore, judge [as to the motives of] one another any more." The words contained in the foregoing parenthesis are thrown in to show the application of the word "judge," as it is clear from Matt. vii.

But to illustrate: Christians generally esteem the ordinances of the Lord's supper and of baptism as most sacred. None such would consent knowingly to receive either from the hands of an arrant hypocrite. Suppose, my brother or sister, that the man who baptized you, and who has often presided at the Lord's table at which you ate and drank, has proved, or should yet prove, to be but another Judas, — would you be held to answer for his sins? Certainly you would not, if you were ignorant of them, or from any cause could not prevent them. Would it be *right* for you to be so held answerable for another? If not, you are safe that far; for "the Judge of all the earth will do right." Or, in such case, would your obedience to the requirements of the gospel be any the less acceptable to our Lawgiver, Saviour, and Judge?

Pursuant to the divine law just referred to, the acceptance of all our offerings depends alone upon the motives and devotedness to the cause of Christianity which induce us to make them; and it cannot be affected in any way by the fitness or unfitness of the officers who administer them, *provided*, as before, that we have been sufficiently careful in selecting the necessary ministerial officers, and have employed and retained such only as we honestly believed had been approved by the Master; and that the offerings themselves are such as He has promised to own and bless.

Some well-intending church members are afraid to partake of the eucharist with others whose fitness they doubt. With regard to our duty as to that ordinance, the command is this: "Let a man *examine himself*, and so let him eat," &c.; and, immediately following that injunction, the best of reasons is given for that sort of examination, to wit: "For he that eateth and drinketh unworthily, eateth and drinketh damnation [*condemnation*] to himself," &c. But not a word is said about our inquiring into the spiritual condition of others before eating with them, for with that we have nothing to do.

One of the greatest difficulties with us in this life arises from the fact that we do not appreciate our individuality as we ought. We should learn that there is a personal matter of variance between each one of us, as individuals, and our common Father, — that "all have sinned" against Him; and that He has brought us here for the *sole purpose* of trying us and proving us, each one for himself or herself, and with a view to our restoration to the divine favor, should we prove worthy of such grace; and if not so found worthy, then preparatory for our final banishment to the place and condition "prepared for the Devil and his angels." And, above all things else, we should remember that "God is no respecter of persons," and that, when the end comes, we will all be judged, every one for himself or herself; and that each will be severally rewarded according to what we have done and left undone, while here in the body, whether our works have been good or evil.

We are too much disposed to learn from other people, and to lean upon the opinions of others; to imitate them rather than to look into the inspired Word, and learn our duties there for ourselves. There appears to be a sort of vague notion pervading the mind of Christian communities (and with those who do not as well as those who do profess to be followers of Christ) that men will be disposed of at the judgment in classes; and that we will be classed more with regard to our belief in Jesus Christ as the Saviour of the world than to what any one of us, as individuals, may have done in this life. And, by such reasoning, many seem to quiet their fears as to any close scrutiny of their individual conduct. It is true that we will all be disposed of at the judgment in classes; but we must first be judged by our works individually, and then each one will be assigned to one or the other of the two classes, according to whether he has served Jesus Christ or Satan while here on probation.

And such reasoning to the contrary, kind reader, comes from the enemy; and it is offered as a lethe to your disquieting apprehensions as to the future. "Be not deceived; God is not mocked; for whatsoever a man soweth, that shall he also reap." That sort of soothing cordial is freely applied to the consciences of the lay-members of our churches; in many cases where a selfish, disappointed, or ambitious *priest* or *preacher*, or a combination of such men, is or are trying to damn the reputation, or otherwise destroy the influence of a greater or better man than themselves; and in cases where a vain bigot is laboring to divide a church and to lead off a part of her members, for the purpose of getting up a new sect of religionists, that he may make a name among men.

In such cases, laymen are prone to stand aloof, and, as a general rule, they are disinclined to interpose for the protection of the deserving innocent or the preservation of the peace and unity of their churches, as, in all such emergencies, they should at least try to do, and which, with proper effort, they usually could succeed in doing, if they would use the capacity and energy which God has given them for his glory and their own good. There is a grave responsibility resting upon intelligent and educated lay-members of the Church of Jesus Christ, with regard to her peace and unity, of which, as a general thing, they appear to be and to have been wholly unconscious. God has made it the special duty of that class of Christians to observe the deportment of those who minister in sacred things, and to protect the flock from the depredations of " wolves " who come to them " in sheep's clothing."

To whom, but to the wise and learned laity, did the Saviour address this remark: " By their fruits ye shall know them "? And was it not for them that the cautions and the injunctions (to "mark" and "avoid them") which are found in Rom. xvi. and Phil. iii. were intended? The unlettered and the ignorant are not capable of making the requisite discriminations which must be made if that duty is discharged properly. And it is not to be expected that the " wolves " will detect and expose one another. Nor could the sincere minister of the gospel of peace expose such intruders with any due regard for his own usefulness. The best they can do is carefully and silently to *avoid them* as far as practicable; and therefore on the learned laity that delicate, yet sacred, duty rests.

And I beg leave right here to make an appeal to my professional brethren who love the cause of Jesus Christ, in behalf of the holy cause of *Christian union*. Upon your shoulders, my dear brethren, more than upon any other class of Christians, the Saviour has laid the imperative though unwelcome duty to guard with zealous care the portals of the sacred desk. Who is better qualified than you, my brother, to detect the " wolf," should one essay to enter there? You who frequent the courts of justice and participate in the trials of all such cases, both civil and criminal, as come before them, — as none but you can do, — have facilities for learning the art of *reading men* which others cannot have.

In the discharge of your professional duties, you are necessarily brought in contact with every class of people. More than any others you study human nature. You often scan the conduct and conversation of an opposite party litigant to learn his motives and intentions respecting your client, should he fall under the power of his adversary. You note with still more care all the surroundings which would be likely to bias the mind of every juror for or against your client, and have a watchful eye to all such circumstances during the whole progress of the cause. And should opposing counsel, or even the presiding judge, unfortunately have weak points, you study them likewise, and with the utmost care, and uniformly invoke the benefit of such weakness to the help of your client. But a few years' practice is sufficient, as you well know, to enable a competent lawyer to read any ordinary witness with about the same ease with which he can read Blackstone. And if the witness is a false one, and opposed to him, he can and will "spot him" with unerring certainty. And in professional circles it is (as you will bear me witness) a pleasurable source of conversation and congratulation, that, as judges of human nature, lawyers have no equals.

That claim to pre-eminence is well founded. And now, brethren, ever bear it in mind that God gave you all the ability you have. And in view of his abundant goodness to us, let us humble ourselves at his feet, and invoke the Good Spirit to dissolve our hearts in thanksgiving and praise to Him for this special gift to our profession.

Moreover, brethren, let us not forget that Christ has put us on notice, that, " Unto whomsoever much is given, of him shall be much required." Inasmuch, therefore, as God has given us a quality which fits us pre-eminently for the discharge of a particular duty, and which is a work for which but few are competent (yet it is one which must be done, if the Church is to find protection at all against the aggressions and devastations of bad men, who enter the sanctuary of God for the most selfish and ungodly purposes),—we should expect to be held to answer for the manner in which we may have discharged or neglected this special duty.

And while particularly addressing you, my brethren, as a class who have acquired special qualifications for the discharge of certain duties, I beg leave of the general reader to depart from our present line of thought far enough to make you this one other suggestion. The peculiar training which was necessary to prepare you for the practice of your profession, qualified you at the same time to construe the sacred writings more perfectly than any other class of uninspired men can do it. Have you not thought of that before? You have been made acquainted with certain rules for the construction of wills and other writings, which come before the courts for a correct interpretation of certain matters of doubt which arise as to the true meaning and intention of testators, or contracting parties. These rules are properly said to contain the result of the combined wisdom and experience of the bygone ages, in the difficult task of learning how to find the true meaning of some writings which appear ambiguous. And the same rules apply as well in the construction of the sacred as of other writings. And that power you have; and if you are a Christian (as many of you doubtless are), it is an imperative duty which you owe alike to yourself, your fellow-men, and to your God that you faithfully exercise this extraordinary skill for your own and their eternal good, and for His glory.

In advising Christian lawyers to "search the Scriptures," and to construe them as they do other writings, it may not be amiss to caution them at the same time that, should they undertake that sort of interpretation, they must lay aside their former method of reaching conclusions, and adopt the aim and pursue the mode of the chancellor, whose duty it is to ascertain and pronounce the result of a fair and thorough investigation of each important question brought before him. For otherwise your opinions on such matters would be worth no more than are those of learned divines,—some of whom have hitherto claimed (and still insist upon) the exclusive prerogative to examine and expound what they represent as being the mysterious writings which constitute the Christian's Bible.

One of the chief advantages that lawyers have over ministers of the gospel of equal capacity, in that sacred work, arises from the circumstance that the former have no present or secular interest involved in the solution of such questions; and therefore, when they go out of the field in which they earn their food and raiment, they can afford to lay aside all pre-conceived opinions and mental bias, and search in all sincerity and disinterestedness for the simple, naked truth of God just as it is revealed to man. And having found that precious jewel, he can fairly present it to those for whom it was sent. In so doing he has nothing to lose by it in this world, whether the result of his labors are received with applause, or with scorn and contempt, by the sectarian and psuedo-Christian ministry of his time. But on the contrary, even if he is reviled for having done his duty, he has the precious promise of the Saviour to cheer him on his way: "Blessed are ye, when men shall revile you, and persecute you, and say all manner of evil against you falsely, for my saké. Rejoice, and be exceeding glad; for great is your reward in heaven."

On the other hand, it is impossible for the educated minister to investigate any controverted question free from bias; and, of course, one who is uneducated is incompetent to that task. All learned ministers are educated (in theology if nothing more) in some one of the sectarian schools, colleges, or seminaries; and this is not complained of, for it is the best they can do. Each denomination of Christians has its own peculiar views of revealed truth, and most of them have a written creed, or confession of faith, — one manufactured by each for themselves. The creed of the Church, whose institution it is, gives form, size, and proportions to the faith which is taught therein. The professors all believe the creed of the Church for which they teach, of course; and if pious, good men (as in most instances they no doubt are), they will impress upon the young, confiding mind of every student under their care that which they devoutly believe to be revealed truth, and with all the energy and power they have, — will they not? Of course they will.

Now, remember, that the greatest and best men of our age differ in opinion, as far as the east is from the west, in regard to many points of Christian faith, which they mutually believe to be of sufficient importance to justify God's children (who are commanded to " love one another " and "live in peace,") in withholding their church fellowship from all who do not believe with themselves touching these questions; and notwithstanding the rejected appear to love Jesus as well, and to serve him as zealously, as do those of their own communion. Is it not the most natural thing in the world, that young men who are educated in each one of these theological schools should leave them perfectly satisfied with the venerated professors whose disciples they have been, and with the main tenor of the instructions they have received? That such would be the result they fondly hoped on entering them; and it should be expected as a matter of course. And as another matter of course, they bring out of their far-famed institutions precisely the same opinions which they took into them when boys! Is not this also true? As the general rule it certainly is; and if there be exceptions, they are few and far between.

Then whence do our distinguished doctors of divinity get their various and conflicting opinions, with which they have so long and so sadly harassed, crippled, and disgraced the Church of Jesus Christ? Are they all found in the Bible? To the credit of these doctors be it said that, notwithstanding they differ so much about other questions, they unanimously agree that the only admissible answer to this one is, No! The question therefore recurs, and with increased interest, If not from the Bible, where and how do they get them? In conversation with a very intelligent and candid Jew upon one occasion, I took the liberty to ask him where and how his people get their opinions of Jesus Christ? "We draw them from our mother's breasts," was the prompt and emphatic reply.

Leaving here the inquiry as to how the learned, the wise, and the good, as well as the untutored, the simple, and the vile, get such variant, conflicting, and erroneous opinions relative to divine truth and Christian duty into their minds, we will pass on, and deal with things as we find them. For it is sufficient for present purposes to know that the fault does not lie in the Bible; and that, nevertheless, the dogmas affirmed in the creed of his church (if she has one, as nearly all have) are as firmly fixed in the head of the young minister the day he leaves the seminary to look out for an empty pulpit, as the handle of a jug is fastened on the outside of that (in some cases) less harmful little vessel.

Now follow the young divine a little further, just to see what his fitness is likely to be for a fair and impartial interpretation of the controverted passages of Scripture. He is pleased to hear of a congregation which wants a pastor, and goes at once to see the official or more influential members of the church to seek employment. If pleased with the first impression made by him, they invite him to preach for them on a day appointed. He knows, as well as they know, that they are anxious to hear him before either making him an offer or refusing to make one. They want to see him in the pulpit, and hear him expound some of the so-called mysterious texts of Scripture, that they may learn something of his ability; but more particularly to satisfy *themselves* in regard to his *Orthodoxy!* — all of which he knows well. The candidate for place prepares himself to satisfy his newly-made acquaintances and brethren in that important particular (if he had not done so before he went to see them), by the selection of a text which leads to a discussion of *the article* of faith to which his branch of the Church attaches the most importance. He collects all the leading texts and stereotyped arguments relied upon to sustain his and their views on "that vital question," whatever it may chance to be; and he does his work in the most approved style of the art. Of course he does.

Our young aspirant to the favor of his denomination (as we will suppose) is engaged to serve the church on terms satisfactory to all parties. He enters upon his ministerial duties, realizing the fact that his relative position with his people, during his natural life, depends more upon his ability and assiduity in the advocacy and defence of the creed of his church than on any other consideration. And consequently he devotes his time, talents, and energies to the tread-mill work of pleasing his hearers by the discussion (?) of the same questions (but always on the same side of each) week after week, it may be, during a long life. How many errors in the church creed, which he labors so faithfully to sustain, is it likely that he will detect and expose? Or how many new ideas will he dig up, and present to his church and congregation? Should he by some mishap unearth either the one or the other, he would hide it as carefully as a thief would a bundle of stolen goods on seeing a constable with his *posse* coming to search his house! Certainly he would. For if it should leak out that he has any thing of that kind in his possession, even though he may have come by it honestly, the bare fact that he has it and keeps it would, if known, cost him the loss of the means by which he gets his bread and butter!

The case selected to illustrate the condition of the sectarian minister, is that of one whose church employs her own pastor; but the condition of those who get their appointments from some ecclesiastical body is certainly no better in that respect, as but little reflection will convince any one.

Such, in brief, are the influences which enslave the mind of sectarian teachers, and which absolutely disqualify them for the high vocation whereunto (as it is hoped) the Master has called them. That there are exceptions to this, as well as to all other general rules, it is true; and they stand out in bold relief, to the credit of poor human nature. But unfortunately they are very rare indeed. How many exceptions to it do we find recorded in Church history? Has there been exceeding one exception in a thousand cases, on an average, since the first so-called human creed of religion saw the light of day?

But I must desist. For inasmuch as this work is intended

as merely suggestive of the several facts and thoughts alluded to, seldom argumentative, and when so, to some extent, never exhaustive, — all that broad field, which is better adapted than any other in our age to the production of rich harvests for heaven, must necessarily be left for the cultivation and reaping of others.

Christian lawyers have, indeed, many advantages over all others in the proper construction of the Scriptures, in protecting the Church from the domination of, and the devastations caused by, bad men who sit in high places, and in restoring her to that peace, love, and unity which prevailed in the apostolic age, as already remarked.

But the Church has many other wise and good men in other respects, who could, if they would, render efficient aid in this all-important work. Of such may be mentioned physicians, educated farmers, merchants, mechanics, and especially Christian gentlemen of leisure, who, to natural endowments of a high order, have the additional advantages afforded them both by liberal education and ample fortune. And there are others who could be added to the list with propriety, — especially a host of Christian ladies, who could render the cause valuable service, in divers ways, without any impropriety. All truly pious and capable Christians, of every walk in life where such are found, could find ample employment, and make the best possible investment of time, labor, and skill in the field above commended.

Human creeds have been allowed to displace, if not to supersede, the gospel of Jesus Christ. His Church has thereby been divided, and her power for good sadly paralyzed. Christian leaders have departed from the Word of God, and have "hewed them out cisterns, broken cisterns, that can hold no water." Their "cisterns" should be exposed as cunning devices of the enemy, and those who trust in them should be encouraged to return — come back — to the simple faith and obedience that are taught in the gospel, "that they may recover themselves out of the snare of the Devil, who are taken captive by him at his will."

If Christians of every denomination — Catholics, Protestants, and all others — are ever to be harmonized and brought into one communion this side of the Judgment, it must be done through the instrumentality of the laity operating on the clergy. The former have hitherto been and now are ruled by the latter, as with a rod of iron. This is at once unnatural, unscriptural, and wrong. It is nothing less than the servant governing the master (see Matt. xxiii. 11, 12; Mark. x. 42–45). That has ever been the case in the political world, but the reverse is the rule prescribed by the Master for his Church. The old rule for the government of the Church — the democratic rule — must be restored, if the evil consequences of the opposite one (which has so long ruled and ruined the Church) is to be overcome, and the peace and unity of the people of God again restored. To use a homely but appropriate form of expression, "The boot must be put on the other leg." Learned, pious, and competent lay-members of the Church, in all her branches, should promptly and boldly come to the front. They should at once assert the rights and exercise the powers for good which God has given them; and, like men, meet the responsibilities that devolve upon them in virtue of the advantages they have, and in humble gratitude to the Giver of all good discharge a solemn obligation they are under to him, and the most sacred duty they owe their fellow-men.

"Money is power." This axiomatic truth applies as well in matters affecting the interests of the Church as of the State. The laity hold the purse-strings; and therein lies all the power necessary, not only to a speedy and complete liberation of themselves from the state of vassalage in which they have blindly lived and meekly served for long ages past, but by a prudent use of the same lever, — a wise manipulation of the purse-strings, — they can also restore the Church to her primitive purity, peace, and *union!*

A few years ago we had a political party here in the South, whose motto, rallying cry, and watchword was, "*Cotton is King!*" Their leading spirits honestly thought so; and a number sufficient to put their opinion to the only true test rallied around their standard. But about four years of close dieting, hard fighting, and blood-letting proved sufficient to satisfy them that they had made a sad mistake as to the identity of the royal personage who presides over the temporal destinies of this world, and that they should have lettered their banner in this way, " GOLD IS KING."

Slight, incipient errors often lead to disastrous results, as in that instance. And all the intestine divisions, strifes, wars, and consequent cruelties from which Christians have suffered so long and so severely, were no more than the natural consequences of one mistake which the priesthood made at an early period in our Church history. Having been called to the *service* of the Church, they (most innocently, as we should hope) thought it necessary that they should take upon themselves all the responsibilities which devolve upon lawgivers and judges, over their fellow sinners, — thereby assuming the authority of *masters*, instead of the more humble and peaceful place assigned them. And, as it would seem, they entirely overlooked the fact that Christ had reserved precisely that position for himself, and had directed that we all, priests and people alike, should obey him. And that little mistake on the part of the priests unfortunately brought the lay membership under the necessity of *trying* to " serve two masters." But that is just the thing which the Saviour says no man can do. Hence the trouble.

All men are liable, more or less, to be led aside from the narrow path of Christian duty. Ministers, priests, and all other ecclesiastic officials are but men, fallen sinners, as we come into this life, and fallible creatures while here. And conceding them all to be good men, as compared with others, yet they are imperfect, and subject to be influenced to some extent by the evil insinuations of Satan; and especially so, whenever he finds a chance to bring the fearful weight of sectarian bias, personal ambition, or pecuniary interest to bear in his favor.

If that be not true, how can the painful fact that wise, good, and great ministers of the gospel differ in opinion so far, in reference to a number of questions of faith and practice? Is it the fault of the Bible? None of them will say that it is. Then are all teachers of religion, who entertain erroneous views with regard to what is taught in the Word of God, hypocritical pretenders, "wolves in sheep's clothing"? Some of them are false teachers, of course; for it is impossible that all can be right, and at the same time hold views which are diametrically opposed to one another. The observation of every intelligent Christian must satisfy him that learned and well-meaning ministers stand opposed to each other on many questions, which they mutually agree are of sufficient importance to justify divisions of the Church of Christ into sects and parties, based upon them as at present; and therefore the only feasible solution of this enigma is to be found in the admission that some of the best men are deceived and betrayed into error by the Devil. This is indubitably the most charitable and the only admissible solution of the matter.

If, then, our greatest men and most distinguished divines are liable to be deceived and betrayed into error by the enemy of all that is right, good, and true (as we have the best authority for saying that they are), we of the laity should feel ourselves at liberty to comment freely, but affectionately, upon the views entertained and forms of worship observed by one another, and no one should complain, or feel in the least offended, at being criticised with respect to either, provided always that it is done in a kind, Christian-like way. Nor should any priest or preacher complain of the most strict observation of his conduct and conversation, not for the purpose of judging his *motives*, but his *fruits*, — the tendency of his manner of life, his influence, his teaching for good or for evil; but all humble, pious ministers of the gospel should, on the other hand, court just that kind of protection from the slanderous whisperings of the Devil.

The importance of a correct understanding of God's Word, of an acceptable observance of all his requirements of us, and of a pure and holy priesthood towers above all other considerations. With these inestimable blessings all Christians would of course be of one mind and live in peace. And with that sort of a ministry, the glorious work of *Christian union* would require but a few months, or brief and happy years at most.

Are all such imaginings Utopian? Are they not, on the contrary, based and well founded upon God's Word? I think so; and am therefore willing to work to that happy end. But the question arises, How can that happy end be reached?

The best, if not the only, way by which Christians of all denominations can be brought together, is in the first place to bring about a correct understanding and due appreciation of the views and purposes of one another. That can be done by their associating freely with each other; by friendly, frank, and full interchange of ideas with each other; and by joint inquiry for themselves into the proper interpretation of such texts of Scripture as are made the bases of the different opinions which prevail, and which have given some plausible excuse for the divisions of the Church that have been made. And we must keep a strict watch, at the same time, over the several pastors who minister to us, and sustain none but those who fully sympathize and cheerfully co-operate with us in our labor of love.

As it has already been remarked, this sacred duty devolves mainly on the educated and influential lay-members of the Church. They can bring all Christians together, if they will try to do it. The whole thing with them is a mere question of will. They can and should purge the Church of all time-serving, money-loving, church-dividing priests and preachers, — "wolves," who scatter that they may devour the flock! The whole weight of the fearful responsibility of permitting the Church to continue divided, and at war as clansmen against one another, rests upon that class of the laity.

It is true that the clergy were chiefly responsible for bringing the Church into her present lamentable condition. But it is now too late to do any good by pausing to inquire why they did so. The evil is upon us, and we should dispose of the matter as we find it. It is, however, but a just tribute to the memory of some whom we have good reason to believe are now saints in heaven, and yet who took active parts in some of the movements which have resulted so disastrously to the peace and prosperity of the Church, that they doubtless acted in good faith, but were really deceived as to the propriety and effects of the policy which they in all honesty of purpose then pursued. But with the motives of others, I repeat, we have nothing to do. We are not to sit in judgment of the thoughts and intentions of others, because we are not competent to that task. But it is not only our privilege, but a sacred duty resting upon us, carefully to observe the conduct of those who minister to us in holy things, and to judge of the fruits of their doings; and if their example or teaching be such as tends to foment, or longer to perpetuate, divisions and strifes in the family of Jesus Christ, we should promptly and fearlessly "mark and avoid them."

All priests and preachers ought to be good men; and many of them unquestionably are as good as men in this life get to be: but we have the authority of the Saviour, and of his immediate disciples and apostles, for saying that they are not all as they should be. It is said that extremes often meet; and it is believed safe to say, that the best men who are passing through this world on their way to heaven, and the worst men who are travelling the broad road that leads from earth to hell, often meet *in the pulpit!* And inasmuch as the judgment of those who want to be good men is liable to be perverted by a sense of personal interest; and knowing as we do that such considerations absolutely control those who are so appropriately called "wolves in sheep's clothing,"— one of the most successful plans that could be devised, by which to influence the ministry as a whole, and bring them into our union movement, would be to convince them that "honesty is the best policy" for this life, whether all of them believe there is a future state awaiting us or not. For should they all become satisfied that there is more money in the service of the cause of Christian union than in sowing seeds of discord among the brethren, they will all "with one accord" fall into line, — some purely because it is right, and others because it is more prudent to do so. In that way, the Devil may be cheated out of the value of his best servants. But be that as it may, with the help of all the ministry the disciples of Christ would very soon become one, as he so fervently prayed the Father that they may be.

In that case, it is true, "tares" would still be mixed with the "wheat;" but that is no objection to the proposed plan, for that will be the case until the harvest any way, and the damage to the wheat would be much less under such circumstances than it now is.

Politicians watch the signs of the times, as it is well known; and when they observe a general tendency on the part of leading men of all parties in favor of any important measure, as a general rule they set their sails so as to fall in line a little ahead of the moving masses if possible, so as to rank as leaders in the movement. That is sensible! And all men are by nature very much alike in their habits, tastes, and proclivities, are they not? It is therefore reasonable to expect that, if the prominent lay-members of the Church of every denomination should manifest an anxious desire for, and a settled determination of purpose on their part to superinduce, a cordial union and practical co-operation by all Christians against the common foe, the ministry of no one family would still be found marching the other way, and that but few if any would wait to bring up the rear, — would they?

Then, my Christian brethren, go to work in good earnest, and with full confidence that success awaits your efforts in that direction, as certainly as you try to earn it. The only serious opposition with which you will have to contend in that godlike enterprise will arise from the deep-seated prejudices which the Devil (by means of the erroneous construction of the important revelation already alluded to) has excited and settled upon the minds of Catholic and Protestant Christians against one another. That he only succeeded in doing with the assistance of certain vain, bigoted, and ultra-sectarian priests and preachers of his own deceiving.

And the first thing to be done, with a view to peace between these two great families, is for the members of each to look into that Scripture individually for himself and for herself, with what help can be found, and with the care which the importance of the subject demands, so as to become perfectly satisfied that such prejudices are wholly unfounded, and that God-fearing men and women — pious, good Christians — are to be met with alike in Catholic and Protestant churches. And in that search it will also be found that neither the one branch of the Church nor the other is the "great dragon," "serpent," "Devil," and "Satan" of Revelation.

When satisfied on that point, Protestant and Catholic brethren — and sisters too — who are personal friends, residing in the same city, town, or neighborhood, and who desire to go into that ever to be blessed work, should confer freely and frequently together, and enlist others with them as opportunity may offer; and at the proper time adopt such measures as may be thought best, in view of surrounding circumstances in every case, to effect the common purpose. And it should be carefully impressed upon the public mind, everywhere, that this movement is not to affect existing church organizations nor relations in any way; but it is simply designed to bring all Christians of every name closer together, so that they will mix and mingle together as but one family of "little children," and become *one in love* as they are now one in purpose and destiny; — to the end, first, that the individual members of each denomination may visit all the others, when convenient, and unite with one another in public worship, when mutually agreeable, or sit as visiting friends and brethren to witness and profit by the exercises of the hour, as each may think best upon every visit; and lastly, so that all may be brought to co-operate as one body and one army and in every practical way against our common enemy, and so that all may ultimately become one in love, purpose, and destiny, as the Father and Son "are one."

It is gratifying to witness a better feeling growing up between the masses of Catholic and Protestant Christians within the last few years than existed previously. They appear to attend the public worship of each other more frequently than formerly; and more liberality is manifested toward one another in the way of contributions to aid in the building of churches, founding colleges, &c., than heretofore. The most pleasing instance of the latter, which has come under the observation of the writer, occurred when the Catholic authorities were soliciting contributions for their now flourishing young college at Macon, Georgia. On that occasion, Protestant editors of the secular press generally urged their brethren to help them freely; and which, it is said, was done by many. That was a move in the right direction.

Thus, while the leading clergymen and partisan press of each, as a general rule, are denouncing the other branch of the Church as the great Anti-Christ, and, in some cases, even going so far as to misrepresent the views and practices of the other party,—thinking and liberty-loving members of both are breaking loose from the hold of those who have held them at a distance from one another for many ages, and are beginning to think and act for themselves. This, too, is as it should be.

Of a sinful race, put here on probation, every one of whom is to be judged and rewarded, or punished, during an eternal future "according to his works," it is both reasonable and right that all should be allowed the privilege to read, think, and act for themselves. And would it not be more prudent and wise for every one who is capable of doing so to go back to the Bible, and read and construe the Word of inspiration for themselves? Doctors differ; somebody is in error.

The plea of ignorance sometimes avails in our temporal courts; but with what favor will that plea be considered by the august Judge of all the earth, when filed by the learned, the wise, and the great rulers, teachers, doctors, lawyers, and judges of the Christian world? Would you not, my professional brother, about as lief stand mute, or even plead guilty, as to file a plea of *ignorance* before that or any other tribunal? Remember, we are all under notice that, "Unto whomsoever much is given, of him shall much be required." And forget not the rebuke of our Judge: "Yea, and why *even of yourselves* judge ye not what is right?"

The preceding remarks have been mainly directed to the propriety, practicability, and necessity of trying to induce better relations between Catholic and Protestant Christians, as the reader must have observed. That was done for two reasons: first, because the leading purpose of this writing required it; and in the next place, as before stated, for the reason that the cause of "Christian Union," as between Protestants themselves, already has many and more able advocates earnestly and successfully laboring in her interest, and who work both as individuals and as associations. And, my brethren, these things " ought ye to have done, and not to leave the other undone."

In the holy cause of Christian union, all who wish to lay up for themselves treasures in heaven can find ample employment with the most liberal wages. Here a field is opened in which the peacemaker's blessing can be secured by all who love peace and will labor for it. Do you ask, What is that blessing? The Saviour says: " Blessed are the peacemakers, for they shall be called the children of God." And as his children, all who so labor will be rewarded according to what each shall have done in the interest of "peace on earth," even though it be for peace between the sons of Belial. Then man cannot imagine how glorious the blessing will be which Christ at his coming will award to those who have labored for the restoration of peace between and among his own beloved disciples, whom Satan has artfully set at war with one another! We may safely say, however, " Blessed is that servant, whom his Lord when he cometh shall find so doing."

INDEX.

	PAGE
ADAM, his creation — soul — body	48
Alienation between Catholics and Protestants grows mainly out of one error of both	199
American Bible Union, Matt. iii. 11 as rendered by	112
Amusements, priestly	203
Angels, all men are to become	123, 125
Angels and men, all made as best for themselves, — free and happy	62
Angels fallen, their claims to divine favor and ours contrasted	30
Antinomianism, a delusion	126
Apostasy, possibility of	166
Armies, but two, all men belong to one or the other	198
Atonement, nature and extent of	126
Babes, predestinarians the "babes" in Christ	160
Banishment, final, of the impenitent	208
Baptism, purpose of, and why administered in the name of the Father, Son, and Holy Ghost	89
Belief of Christians, the same on all essential points	198
Blindness, temporary, sometimes providential	154
"By their fruits ye shall know them"	210
Catholic and Protestant Christians getting nearer together	224
Central gospel truth	143
Christians, Catholic and Protestant, mutually in error as to each other	185
Christian love	184
Christian, this term not in general use in the apostolic age	172
Christian Union	179

INDEX.

	PAGE
Christian Union, how it may be effected	221
Christ, prophecies of	25
Christ, the object of his mission	26
Churches, Christian, but two at most necessary	197
Clark, Dr. A., on the different constructions of Rev. xii.	20
Comforter, the same as the Holy Ghost	116
Cotton is king	218
Covenant, for our redemption, what and when made	16
Creation of this world, by whom and in whose presence	70
Creator, a, and not chance	41
Creeds of religion, all but one contrived by the Devil	159
Creeds, human, the cause of divisions, persecutions, &c.	203
Deceived, all men are	193
Devils, will be called angels	123, 125
Discrepancies, apparent in the Scriptures, how reconciled	73
Divisions of the Church, policy of	192
Eden, why was Satan permitted to enter there?	34
Educated laity, duties of	217, 221, 222
Election, absolute and unconditional, a scheme of the enemy	127, 159
Election, a class elected and another class rejected	132, 141, 150, 161
Eternal, the term construed	70
Eternal punishment, if we are new creatures	32
Eternal punishment, if we are of the fallen angels	33, 37
Extremes meet, in the pulpit as elsewhere	222
Faith, all men mould their own	94
Faith, the gospel creed of	14
Fall in Eden, how induced	128
Father and Son, seen together	82
Foreknowledge of God	143
Foreknowledge of God, not prejudicial to man	150
Fruits, "By their fruits ye shall know them"	210
Gill, Dr., as to identity of Michael and Christ	23
God, personality of	41
God, locality of	44

INDEX.

	PAGE
God is a spirit	54
God derives his pleasure, his glory, from the happiness of his creatures	61
God is love	184
Godhead, the term noticed	102
Gods many, and lords many	121
Gold is king	219
Hardened, who are, and why	151
Heathen, salvation of	176
Heaven, a place, the home of God	58
Heavenly treasures	200
Hell, is there such place or condition	32–37
Heresy, a modern charge of, alluded to	96
Holy Ghost, impersonality of	89
Holy Ghost, the voice of God, &c.	106
Holy Ghost, office of	171
Honesty the best policy	222
Human creeds supersede the gospel	217
Ignorance, plea of, at the judgment	225
Individuality of Jesus Christ	70, 80
Individuality, our own not duly realized	208
Imitative, Christians too much so	209
Infants, salvation of	178
Inquisition, cause of	185
Jacob and Esau, one loved, the other hated	144, 147
Jehovah, a personal being, Creator of all else	41
Jesus Christ, a distinct individual	67
Jesus Christ, an eternal Spirit	70
John i. 1, 2 construed	70
"Judge not, lest ye be judged"	207
Judges called gods	122
King James's edition of the Bible	112
Laity, the, and not the clergy, should govern the Church	217
Lawyers, Christian, an appeal to	210
Lay members of the Church, responsibility of	209

	PAGE
Likeness, the body of Adam made in the likeness of God	49
Locality of God	65
Mark and avoid them that cause strife, &c.	205
Michael the Archangel and Christ the same	23, 25
Ministers disqualified for construing the Scriptures	213
Money is power	218
Moses talked with God about his body	47
Omnipresence of God	65
Origin and nature of man well known to St. Paul	169
Origin of the human soul, different views in regard to	15
Paul the apostle more fully inspired than others	137
Paul, his style of writing	136
Perseverance, doctrine of, reviewed	167
Personality of Jehovah God	47
Politicians and ministers, alike to some extent	223
Predestination, doctrine of, stated, &c.	129–132
Pre-existence of the soul, believed by the disciples of Christ	138
Presbyterian confession of faith cited	129
Priestcraft	93
Questions, why was Satan permitted to enter Eden, — and others	84
Religion, natural, as revealed, in twelve propositions	39
Rev. xii., how construed by Catholics; by Protestants	20
Rev. xii. examined	188, 199
Salvation offered to all, on terms	137
Saved, who will be	193
Scriptures, consistent when properly construed	145
Sectarian education of ministers, effect of	213
Sin, unpardonable, what	170
Size, the body of Jehovah larger than those of men or angels	52
Sons of God, holy angels and redeemed men are and will be	123
Soul, different views as to nature and origin of	15
Soul, pre-existence of, the old belief	17
Soul of Adam not created when his body was made	48

	PAGE
Spiritualists, their opinion of the Christian religion	34
Start right, importance of so doing	13
Theologians all agree, how far	13
Trinity, popular doctrine of, a priestly mystification	202
Triune, trinity, &c., not Scriptural terms	102
Union of Christians favored, not to interfere with existing Church organizations, &c.	187
Unpardonable sin, what	170
War begun in heaven, progressing here	18, 24, 29
Wickedness, more injurious to the Church than ignorance	191
Will, freedom of the	130
Wolves in sheep's clothing	196

Cambridge: Press of John Wilson & Son.

www.ingramcontent.com/pod-product-compliance
Lightning Source LLC
Chambersburg PA
CBHW021824230426
43669CB00008B/859